QUALITY
IS
FREE

QUALITY
IS
FREE

The Art of Making Quality Certain

Philip B. Crosby

McGraw-Hill Book Company

New York St. Louis San Francisco Auckland Bogotá
Düsseldorf Johannesburg London Madrid Mexico
Montreal New Delhi Panama Paris
São Paulo Singapore Sydney Tokyo Toronto

To
Harold S. Geneen

Bringing Quality Management to the head table was not exactly the same as introducing black baseball players to the major leagues; but there were enough similarities to make me feel toward Harold Geneen what Jackie Robinson felt toward Branch Rickey.

In both cases the motives were the same: to increase the probability of having a winning team.

To quote HSG: "Quality is not only right, it is free. And it is not only free, it is the most profitable product line we have."

Library of Congress Cataloging in Publication Data

Crosby, Philip B
Quality is free.

Includes index.
1.   Quality assurance.   I.   Title.
TS156.6.C76   658.5′6   78-6804
ISBN O-07-014512-1

3 4 5 6 7 8 9 0   M U B P   7 6 5 4 3 2 1 0 9

The editors for this book were W. Hodson Mogan and Carolyn Nagy, the designer was Elliot Epstein, and the production supervisor was Thomas G. Kowalczyk. It was set in Times Roman by The Fuller Organization.

Printed by The Murray Printing Company and bound by The Book Press

CONTENTS

PART TWO

THE DOING
The HPA Corporation Quality Improvement
Program
161

PART THREE

THE TOOLS
261

Preface

I have learned to carry my typewriter with me as I travel. Renting is iffy, and unreliable at best. Checking the machine with the airlines is not wise. Portable typewriters are just not packaged for "luggage" treatment. Machines that can survive this system cannot be lifted.

Naturally, your traveling companions ask if you are a writer. Now if you really are a writer, all you have to do is say yes and an interesting conversation is established during the trip. However, I have never considered myself a writer. I consider myself a professional manager who communicates through many means; one of these is writing.

That may seem like a small difference in terms, but it is really more than that. Trying to explain your ideas so others can understand them is what this sort of thing is all about. Trying to offer concepts in attractive packages so the communicatee has to at least consider them has been the struggle of my life. Some of these concepts have been accepted, but usually only several years after I began developing them. That is only fair since it takes a lot of years to conceive them.

I wasn't born a manager; my family always envisioned me as a medical person. My father was a chiropodist, my uncle, a physician, and the whole outfit was involved one way or another in the medical field. I grew up assuming I would enter it too.

It is not my intention to relate the story of my life; you would doze off before reaching the end of the page. No life story, but there is a point to all this. I started at the bottom of the business and have had each and every job on the way up. Inspector, tester, assistant foreman, junior engineer, reliability engineer, group engineer, section chief, manager, director, corporate vice president — all of them. This has produced a "dirt under the fingernails" education I would not have received if fate had dealt me relatives who believed in the God of engineering or accounting.

Because of these experiences, I tend to see things in terms of those who must finally wind up doing the job. I see concepts and their implementation as people-oriented. Once in a while I get a glimpse of the future, enough to know what will be accepted and what will be ignored. In preparing this book I have tried to emphasize the practical actions of communicating programs and concepts in a way that will bring results.

This book took an awfully long time to write. Much of the material I put together over several years has been discarded. The Grid is a new development as is Make Certain. Both programs are unique, cheap, and remarkably effective. If you can't communicate with management using the Grid, and with people using Make Certain, well, then you are in trouble too deep to be helped by this little book. Not company trouble, comprehension trouble.

My staff has been very patient with me during the preparation of this material. Virginia Brauneck, my secretary, has struggled through translating my clumsy typing into English. Alternately scowling and breaking into giggles, she put a great deal of herself into this work. I appreciate it.

My leaders encouraged me through their comments and interest. Not all corporations would understand when one of their senior executives sits alone in a hotel room at night making clickity-click noises. My corporation recognizes communication as the engine that makes our society operate or strangle.

More people have helped me through these twenty-five years than I can name here. Three of these individuals have passed on. They were special to me and I would like to publicly remember Tom Willey, Jim Halpin, and Murray Hack.

And, of course, the Crosby family: Shirley, Phylis, Philip, and Kathy. They always understand; they love me anyway.

I hope you will read the first three chapters in order. It will all make more sense to you that way. After that you can hop around any way you please. After all, it's your book.

Philip B. Crosby
JOHN'S ISLAND, FLORIDA

PART ONE
The Understanding

Quality is free. It's not a gift, but it is free. What costs money are the unquality things—all the actions that involve not doing jobs right the first time.

Quality is not only free, it is an honest-to-everything profit maker. Every penny you don't spend on doing things wrong, over, or instead becomes half a penny right on the bottom line. In these days of "who knows what is going to happen to our business tomorrow" there aren't many ways left to make a profit improvement. If you concentrate on making quality certain, you can probably increase your profit by an amount equal to 5 to 10 percent of your sales. That is a lot of money for free.

This book is about the art of making quality certain. Managers of any operation or function can take practical, nontechnical steps to improve their quality. They can prevent those computer programming errors; those burred screws; those cold steaks; those lost parcels; those miscalculated bills. All the ways, means, and concepts of making quality certain are laid out in this book.

1

Making Quality Certain

What does "making quality certain" mean? "Getting people to do better all the worthwhile things they ought to be doing anyway" is not a bad definition. "People" includes top management as well as the lower levels of the organization. After all, part of the top job is making certain that all management functions have the opportunity to perform their responsibilities. The problem is, of course, that everyone who arrives at a top management job gets there by moving up through one division, like finance or engineering, that has a limited, specific function, and may or may not have any ideas about overall quality. Top managers may or may not realize what has to be done to achieve quality. Or worse, they may feel, mistakenly, that they do understand what has to be done. Those types can cause the most harm.

It is up to the professional quality manager to assume the responsibility for instructing top management about this portion of their job. It is not necessary to be extremely clever or brave to accomplish this; it is only necessary to be able to explain it all in terms that cannot be misunderstood. Professionals in any role who obscure explanations by using mysterious terminology do themselves, and their roles, a disservice. They get some satisfaction from seeing obvious confusion on the face of their superiors, but that confusion just makes everybody's job harder.

I started in the quality business as a junior technician testing fire control systems for B-47s. Completely untrained and uninformed, I learned the simple tasks of adjustment and measurement without ever really wondering why it was all being done at all.

In fact, during my first four or five years in jobs like that, it never occurred to me to wonder. But then I had the opportunity to be exposed to reliability concepts and practices. Most of them were rather mushy and mathematical, but they revealed an element I hadn't thought about before: prevention.

That thought brought out a possibility I had never dreamed existed: "Why spend all this time finding and fixing and fighting when you could prevent the incident in the first place?"

The entire world, it seemed, was convinced that prevention — at least on a grand scale — was highly desirable but completely unattainable and impractical. It was always referred to as a sort of dream along the line of King Solomon's lost diamond mines. I had a great many long and earnest talks with sincere people who were clear that there was no way to attain true quality through prevention: "The engineers won't cooperate." "The salesmen are untrainable as well as a little shifty." "Top management cannot be reached with such concepts." "The quality professionals themselves do not believe it."

I knew immediately that I had found the opportunity I was looking for. Here was a problem that everyone wanted to solve but felt was not their responsibility. All I had to do was find a way to get them committed to improvement without having to reveal that they had been wrong all along.

For the next several years, as I learned more about managing quality, I realized that the conventional approach was not effective. Quality managers proudly stood up and announced that they personally were responsible for qual ity in a particular operation. Just as regularly, and not so proudly, they were sent down in flames when they were unable to resolve all the "quality problems" of the company.

As a project quality manager, I was berated each week by the program director in his staff meeting for not meeting desired goals while the real culprits from engineering, manufacturing, and sales hid their yawns and wished the whole thing would go away so they could return to their important work.

It was all too clear that some beliefs are so basically ingrained that they cannot be changed just by suggesting they are wrong. (I should note that my knowledge of this fact is part of the reason I have been very supportive of the activities of minorities and women in trying to throw off the roles assigned and attributed to them.) However, my active revolution as quality manager didn't really begin until the day one of the company lawyers told me, in all sincerity, that he couldn't really understand "what a bright guy like you is doing in a little cul-de-sac like quality." If I had ever thought of leaving the quality business, that killed it. Some changes had to be made.

So I began to concentrate on the real problems. First, it was necessary to get top management, and therefore lower management, to consider quality a leading part of the operation, a part equal in importance to every other part. Second, I had to find a way to explain what quality was all about so that anyone could understand it and enthusiastically support it. And third, I had to get myself in a position where I had a platform to take on the world in behalf of quality.

I think all these goals have been attained. As a member of senior management of one of the largest industrial companies in the world, I make as much money, and have just as many rights, as other senior managers. We have installed effective and routine ways of understanding quality, and communicating from the top of the organization to the bottom, as well as the other way around. I have not been accused, in the past five years anyway, of having some "quality problem" that I should do something about.

You can do it too. All you have to do is take the time to understand the concepts, teach them to others, and keep the pressure on for prevention. It helps if you train yourself to be articulate, and it helps if you can keep from becoming emotionally involved in the problems of others. But the whole of it is attainable and highly practical.

This book is structured to lead you directly through all the actions required for a proper quality management program. Case histories, all based on my personal experience, explain practically everything so you can see how others reacted in real situations. One of the most interesting of those case histories involved installing a quality management program in the ITT Corporation. I include it here without listing any names of those involved because there were just too many. ITT, at this writing, employs 350,000 people and has yearly sales of over $15 billion. There are 2500 or so executives and over 200 senior executives. You will have to take my word for it that everyone participated. If I listed all their names, it would look like the San Francisco telephone book.

I will tell the story primarily to give background evidence supporting the basic premise of this book. Quality is an achievable, measurable, profitable entity that can be installed once you have commitment and understanding, and are prepared for hard work. The case history is a record of strategy and effort, not a personal job résumé.

In 1965, the top management of ITT decided that they wanted to do something about quality on a corporate basis. It was apparent that quality was a missing ingredient in the corporate sense of things that were important. It wasn't that quality was deliberately considered unimportant; no one was against it. But as an ingredient of industry, like labor, manufacturing, engineering and so forth, it didn't exist. To me, however, quality is the all-important catalyst that makes the difference between success and failure, and my first goal was to create a corporate-wide concern for quality. This meant that absolutely correct requirements would be established and would be absolutely conformed to, and that everyone would want to do things right the first time. This concern had to become a part of daily life.

Four objectives were established for the ITT quality program. These objectives have served well through the years, and I commend them to other objective makers:

1. Establish a competent quality management program in every operation, both manufacturing and service.

2. Eliminate surprise nonconformance problems.

3. Reduce the cost of quality.

4. Make ITT the standard for quality — worldwide.

These objectives could not be accomplished by assembling a huge staff at headquarters for the purpose of strangling every potential problem in its crib. There was only me and the secretary I shared with two other guys. It was sort of like assembling a raft from the material you obtained while being swept down the rapids.

So I embarked on a deliberate strategy of establishing a cultural revolution — a cultural revolution that would last forever and become part of the corporate woodwork. Fire-fighting would have to be replaced with defect prevention; quality would have to be recognized as a genuine "first among equals;" the habit of doing things right the first time had to become routine; and, most important of all, the whole thing had to happen within the units (ITT's word for subsidiary or other companies) because they wanted it to happen.

To me, a complete corporate quality program has always been a "table" containing all the "integrity" systems. Quality control, reliability, quality engineering, supplier quality, inspection, product qualification, training, testing, consumer affairs, quality improvement, and metrology; and all the other systems and concepts of quality rest on this table. Management selects what it needs from each and applies these tools to their total problem. It isn't necessary or wise for each and every operation to have exactly the same quality program. At ITT, for example, the personality and needs of one unit may bear little actual work relationship to those of another, yet they all need programs both appropriate to them and effective in terms of the total corporation.

To establish such a program requires much more knowledge and participation than just a listing of the tools available in our workchest. It requires that this *integrity systems* table be supported by four pillars, or legs, and that they all be constructed to complement each other. Although these were actually built as part of the same operation, we will discuss them one at a time. The four legs are:

- Management participation and attitude

- Professional quality management

- Original programs

- Recognition

Management participation. "Participation," rather than "support," is the right word for this leg. Management has to get right in there and be active when it comes to quality. Those of us who work for others are liable to monitor and measure them constantly. We examine them continually to determine which attitudes and beliefs are the stronger. We want to know what pleases them, or, perhaps more accurately, what displeases them. And we get very good at finding and calibrating this information. Therefore causing management at all levels to have the right attitude about quality, and the right understanding, is not just vital — it is everything.

The first struggle, and it is never over, is to overcome the "conventional wisdom" regarding quality. In some mysterious way each new manager becomes imbued with this conventional wisdom. It says that quality means goodness; that it is unmeasurable; that error is inevitable; and that people just don't give a damn about doing good work. No matter what company they work for, or where they went to school, or where they were raised — they all believe something erroneous like this. But in real life, quality is something quite different. Quality is conformance to requirements; it is precisely measurable; error is not required to fulfill the laws of nature; and people work just as hard now as they ever did. These concepts are covered in detail in the following chapters. What should be obvious from the outset is that people perform to the standards of their leaders. If management thinks people don't care, then people won't care.

At ITT, most of our actions during the formative years were directed toward dispelling the erroneous beliefs and replacing them with those capable of supporting the integrity systems table. We conducted seminars throughout the ITT world on a regular basis. Those managing directors and general managers who had participated in programs and who had learned to understand quality properly testified to the others. They became involved in this evangelic crusade and the word spread: "The programs actually do work and you can trust the quality guy." In 1967, one other quality executive joined the staff and in 1968, quality was set up as a corporate department of its own. At that time, three senior quality managers were brought in from the units to become part of the operation.

Working on a group-by-group, unit-by-unit basis, we worked our way through the corporation. Orienting, helping, talking, guiding, badgering, and whatever, we kept the pressure on. New managers joining the corporation were made to feel that participation in the quality program was routine and expected. Therefore, they just sailed right along. Today you would have difficulty finding anyone at the executive level anywhere who hasn't been exposed to the true belief.

Professional quality management. In the early days, it was not possible to find many of the quality people in ITT units, since they were buried inside the technical and manufacturing operations, if they indeed existed at all. When found, most of them were not permitted to travel. And so we formed quality councils on an area basis. Both in the United States and in Europe, quality professionals joined together to help each other and to determine the types of programs required from the corporate staff. Today there are twenty-seven councils set up by product line or service, and some councils grouped by country also still operate. In addition, there is an executive council on each continent consisting of the chairpersons from all the quality councils. Communication among all branches is comfortable and positive.

To support the councils, and the programs, we instituted the Quality College. Teaching such courses as Quality Management and Product Qualification, the college has issued certificates to over 24,000 people in its lifetime. It is the backbone of the total effort. Every time we think there is no one left to instruct, we find the enrollment full again. The program has been very effective. All the quality professionals of ITT understand the programs the same way. They have been freed organizationally, and report at least on the same level as those they are measuring. This increases the possibility that the programs will be implemented properly.

Original programs. Traditional quality control programs are negative and narrow, and it was no different at ITT. Primarily oriented toward product performance, they often turned off the management they were supposed to entice. To overcome this, we constructed numerous programs involving practical activities which could be implemented at the unit level.

Quality improvement through defect prevention, a fourteen-step program for improvement, is the foundation of all ITT quality programs. Described in detail later in the book, this program has been implemented in every industry or business of the corporation. Some have been very successful; some have not done as well. But none ever got worse.

It takes four or five years to get people to understand the need for, and learn to have confidence in, such an improvement program. I originally sent a sixteen-page brochure accompanied by a tape explaining the Zero Defects concept to every unit. The results were amazing. No one paid the slightest bit of attention. None of them was even sent back. It was apparent that the conversion and instruction had to be done on a unit-by-unit basis until we could get some success stories to use in the seminars.

Other original programs developed were Buck a Day (BAD), a cost-reduction idea program; Zero Defects-30 (a thirty-day program contained in one box with enough material for a supervisor and eight to ten of the supervisor's people); Consumer Affairs; Environmental Quality Self-Audit; Quality Management Maturity Grid; Model Quality (a system for printed circuit board manufacturing); Service Company Quality Improvement; Make Certain; and many others.

Recognition. This vitally necessary component of any quality program is often overlooked or conducted improperly. Done correctly, it becomes the shining star of the entire integrity system. We established the Ring of Quality program in 1971. The initial thought was to give recognition to those people who had offered outstanding support to the quality program for a period of five years, or had accomplished one sensational, specific, and unique act. However, it quickly became a program where the winners were nominated by their peers. On that basis, we have processed thousands of nominations and have awarded 182 gold rings to winners. We have also presented several hundred silver pins and citations to other nominees. In every case, we tossed out those who were nominated by their subordinates. Peer nominations make it all come out right.

The Ring of Quality program is taken very seriously. The awards are presented at a formal dinner by the corporate president or chairman. For many of the recipients, it is literally the biggest moment of their life. Like the rest of the program, the presentations are treated with dignity and respect. Reaction to the rings and pins has made one thing very clear: Cash or financial awards are not personal enough to provide effective recognition.

Developing and implementing the four legs of the table involved traveling millions of miles, talking thousands of hours, and eating tons of food. It was well worth the trouble, as the following comparison of results obtained with the initial objectives should demonstrate.

Establish a Competent Quality Management Program in every Operation, both Manufacturing and Service

When we began, about 5 percent of our companies had quality programs that could be considered acceptable. In 1977, better than 85 percent were in that category. Pioneeer programs were established for the first time in hotels, insurance, car rental, and other service industries. The number of competent quality management and professional people has grown to where their availability is no longer a problem.

Eliminate Surprise Nonconformance Problems

Surprise nonconformance problems have disappeared. We still have problems, and some of them are pips. But never is one all grown up before we find it.

Reduce the Cost of Quality

The cost of quality (described in detail in Chapter 7) is the expense of doing things wrong. It is the scrap, rework, service after service, warranty, inspection, tests, and similar activities made necessary by nonconformance problems. Between 1967 and 1977, the manufacturing cost of quality at ITT has been reduced by an amount equivalent to 5 percent of sales. That is a great deal of money. The savings projected by the comptroller were $30 million in 1968; $157 million in 1971; $328 million in 1973; and in 1976—$530 million! We had eliminated—through defect prevention—costs amounting to those dollar figures.

Now obviously not all of this was accomplished just by the quality people in the units. Rework people disappeared when there was no more rework. Warranty costs stopped when the properly qualified products didn't fail in the field. There were and continue to be many contributions.

But the facts of life today are that each year your cost of sales rises faster than your prices. That means you have to eliminate or reduce costs in order to make a profit. The best single way to do that is by defect prevention.

Results like these are why I say that quality is free. And not only free but a substantial contributor to profit.

Make ITT the Standard for Quality – Worldwide

The last original objective was to make ITT the standard for quality – worldwide. In trying to determine how to show how we stand, it is fair to ask: "Who says so?" Obviously, we are far from completely achieving this goal, but there has been a lot of progress.

In Europe, all customers for telecommunication are government administrations. In 1965, they were inspecting everything we did. They had resident quality people in every plant we had in Europe, in every country. Today, they let us do the final inspection and testing everywhere. In many countries, they have actually issued us the inspection stamps, and just audit once in a while. These administrations tell our competitors that their operations should be as good as ITT's.

- The Russian Ministry of Electronics surveyed Western quality management systems, and then came to ITT to ask that we come show them how to do it.

- When McGraw-Hill was producing a new encyclopedia of professional management, they asked ITT to write the chapter on quality management.

- American Express said five years ago that Sheraton was the worst hotel chain when it came to quality. This year they rate Sheraton as the best.

- Other companies continually ask for information.
  During a typical year we receive over 400 requests
  in the corporate office.

All these achievements represent the result of a great
deal of planning and plain, old-fashioned hard work. But it
wasn't just planning and hard work that made it happen.
One of the most vital components was our success in con-
structing the first leg of the integrity table—top management commitment.

One of the reasons I cheerfully share these programs
with other companies is that I know that many will probably not be able to use them. Not because they are not capable, but because they do not have a top management willing
to be patient while the program is ground out four yards at a
time. It took five to seven years of unrelenting effort to
achieve the cultural revolution at ITT—and I seriously
doubt if it will ever be eliminated there.

We recognize that our top management is special because once they understood the realities of quality, they
supported the projects, participated in them, and encouraged us all the way along.

The details of how, why, and what are contained in the
following chapters. This very brief overview of the strategy
behind the ITT program was put in only to show a little bit
about how the program all fits together. I know that if I had
had the Quality Management Maturity Grid several years
ago, the job would have been finished earlier. I know if I had
had the ITT experience to play "show and tell" with, it
would have been less of a problem to obtain attention.

You have them. Take advantage of what has gone before. Why not learn from the past?

2

"Quality May Not Be What You Think It Is"

There is no doubt in my mind that those who pick up this book are hoping it will contain some single piece of information that will permit immediate clarification and ultimate resolution of all their problems with quality. Perhaps some wise and perceptive sentence, like: "Quality is ballet, not hockey."

I wish it could be so. Unfortunately, the business of quality management is not all that easy. It isn't all that hard either, but it does encompass more than a single gulp of philosophy. It also requires unblinking dedication, patience, and time. The problem of quality management is not what people don't know about it. The problem is what they think they *do* know. It is made difficult by the conventional assumptions about quality that people develop over years of successfully making a living in some line of work other than quality management.

In this regard, quality has much in common with sex. Everyone is for it. (Under certain conditions, of course.) Everyone feels they understand it. (Even though they wouldn't want to explain it.) Everyone thinks execution is only a matter of following natural inclinations. (After all, we do get along somehow.) And, of course, most people feel that all problems in these areas are caused by other people. (If only *they* would take time to do things right.) In a world where half the marriages end in divorce or separation, such assumptions are open to question.

It is difficult to have a meaningful, real-life, factual discussion on sex, quality, or other complicated subjects until some basic erroneous assumptions are examined and altered. The only ones who are usually willing to take that step are those who are ready to admit they are in trouble, or have an intellectual interest in improvement. I have had hundreds of discussions with operating managers over the years and can state absolutely that their interest in quality is proportional to the amount of profit-deteriorating situations they are experiencing at that exact moment. I can't speak for their attitudes toward sex.

Given the chance to explain quality management to people who will listen, regardless of their motives, it is possible to make a case for becoming deeply involved. No other action a manager can take will generate improved operations, increased profits, and reduced costs so quickly with so little effort. But before all that can occur, we have to examine the thinking processes that lead some to believe that quality is merely goodness that always costs more.

In discussing quality, we are dealing with a people situation. The entire concept of quality management in this book is oriented toward that thought. People conduct the business of every company, whether it is a foundry or a hotel. Each individual performs an individual service. This service has been identified, described, and assigned by the management. If the service is constructed and performed correctly, it follows that the operations of the company should be successful. That applies to any industry or technology. I am not differentiating between manufacturing quality and service quality. All the quality actions we are talking about apply, regardless of the business of the company. There are technological differences, but they really involve only the last few percentage points of involvement. The programs defined in the following chapters permit you to deal with those exceptions in a planned fashion.

To understand those programs, and quality itself, in the

most practical terms, it is necessary that we deal with five erroneous assumptions that are held by most management individuals. These assumptions cause most of the communication problems between those who want quality and those who are supposed to effect it.

The first erroneous assumption is that quality means goodness, or luxury, or shininess, or weight. The word "quality" is used to signify the relative worth of things in such phrases as "good quality," "bad quality," and that brave new statement "quality of life." "Quality of life" is a cliché because each listener assumes that the speaker means exactly what he or she, the listener, means by the phrase. It is a situation in which individuals talk dreamily about something without ever bothering to define it.

That is precisely the reason we must define quality as "conformance to requirements" if we are to manage it. Thus, those who want to talk about quality of life must define that life in specific terms, such as desirable income, health, pollution control, political programs, and other items that can each be measured. When all criteria are defined and explained, then the measurement of quality of life is possible and practical.

In business the same is true. Requirements must be clearly stated so that they cannot be misunderstood. Measurements are then taken continually to determine conformance to those requirements. The nonconformance detected is the absence of quality. Quality problems become nonconformance problems, and quality becomes definable. All through this book, whenever you see the word "quality," read "conformance to requirements."

If a Cadillac conforms to all the requirements of a Cadillac, then it is a quality car. If a Pinto conforms to all the requirements of a Pinto, then it is a quality car. Luxury or its absence is spelled out in specific requirements, such as carpeting or rubber mats. The next time someone says someone or something has "lousy quality," interrogate that person until you can determine just exactly what he or she means.

The second erroneous assumption is that quality is an

intangible and therefore not measurable. In fact, quality is precisely measurable by the oldest and most respected of measurements—cold hard cash. Ignorance of this fact has led many managements to dismiss quality with a wave of the hand as something beyond handling. They are thinking of quality as goodness and spend their time having emotional discussions which make it impossible for management to take specific, logical actions to attain quality.

Quality is measured by the cost of quality which, as we have said, is the expense of nonconformance—the cost of doing things wrong. These costs are divided into prevention, appraisal, and failure categories. But they all are a result of not doing things right the first time. You can spend 15 to 20 percent of your sales dollar on such expenses without even trying hard. A company with a well-run quality management program can get by with less than 2.5 percent of sales, which is spent on the prevention and appraisal activities necessary to make certain the company is maintaining its standards of excellence. Measurements should be established both for measuring the overall cost of quality and for determining the current status of specific product or procedure compliance. These measurements should be displayed for all to see, for they provide visible proof of improvement and recognition of achievement. Measurement is very important. People like to *see* results.

There are those who will assume that some tasks are just plain unmeasurable. To them, you must raise the question of just how they know which people are the best at what jobs, whom to fire, and whom to reward. Anything can be measured if you have to do it.

The third erroneous assumption is that there is an "economics" of quality. The most-offered excuse managers have for not doing anything is that "our business is different." The second is that the economics of quality won't allow them to do anything. What they mean is that they can't afford to make it that good. This of course, is an indication that they don't understand quality and that they are just wishing you would go away. Pressed, they will relate some case of "goldplating," where a designer made a product unsalable by insisting on adding some luxury component. At that time, it is proper to explain the real meaning of the word "quality" and point out that it is always cheaper to do things right the first time. If they want to make certain that they are using the least expensive process that will still do the job, they should get deep into process certification and product qualification. These are part of a mature quality program. We musn't get faked out by words that have no meaning, and "economics of quality" certainly has no meaning.

The fourth assumption that causes problems is the one that says that all the problems of quality are originated by the workers, particularly those in the manufacturing area. It is hardly possible to find a business magazine that doesn't have some sort of article about the falling standards of workers and how lousy the quality is on the assembly line. Few quality professionals can discuss product conformance for very long without emphasizing how people don't perform the way they used to. In reality, the people in the shops work as well as they ever did and much more productively than in the past. They contribute a lot less problems than their white collar brethren.

It is a matter of record that just as much crime is committed per person by middle and upper-class individuals as by people from the lower economic classes. In fact, the most expensive rip-offs, such as computer crimes, are committed exclusively by the well educated. Yet it is accepted without question by most people that ghettos produce criminals as routinely as tomato patches produce tomatoes. People "prove" this by pointing to prisons, where primary occupancy is by people from low-income backgrounds.

The real reason for this is not that most crimes are committed by the poor, but that the police tend to look for crime in areas where people are less mobile, more easily identifiable, and less liable to offer a significant defense. (Of course, there are a lot of people around ghetto areas who do wrong things. But almost every successful executive I have ever met claims to have originated in some "tomato patch" or other — so the tomato patch can't be all that bad.) The quality control people have much the same conditioning as the police. They march blindly past the defects of accounting, engineering, computer programming, and marketing on their way to the manufacturing ghetto to look for errors. And, by golly, they find a lot of them out there. It is an important place to look for ways to lower unnecessary costs. But the people in the manufacturing ghetto can contribute only a little to the prevention of problems because all planning and creation is done elsewhere. And it is the "elsewheres" that need attention when it comes to reducing the cost of quality. You will find the causes of most of our expensive problems at the other ends of pencils and telephones.

The fifth erroneous assumption is that quality originates in the quality department. Unfortunately, most quality professionals feel that they are responsible for quality in their company, so this assumption is really entrenched. However, the high attrition rate of quality management people who insist on being responsible for quality problems should make us think a little. People who insist that "quality problem" means that the quality department made a mistake of some sort are laying a clear, if inaccurate, track back to their teepee. They must learn to call problems by the names of those who cause them: accounting problem, manufacturing problem, design problem, housekeeping problem, front-desk problem, etc. Otherwise they will be held responsible for resolving problems over which they have no control.

Quality department people should measure conformance by the various means at their disposal; they should report results clearly and objectively; they should lead the drive to develop a positive attitude toward quality improvement; they should use whatever educational programs can be helpful (such as Zero Defects, Make Certain, and others described later in this book). But they should not do the job for others, or the others will not change their evil ways.

This is the primary weakness of modern professional quality management. The desire to be actively involved in the creation, production, marketing and managing of a company's product or service is almost irresistible. But it only takes a little involvement to destroy the objectivity that is the quality professional's most precious possession. Once integrity is compromised, it does not return to its original pristine state.

It is not an easy thing to refuse a good friend who tearfully begs for just one more drink. But you must do so if you are to keep that person alive. Similarly, you do no one a favor when you create new "temporary" requirements on the spot. The designated requirements are either met or they are not. If we don't need a criterion, and the customer doesn't need it, then have the requirements officially changed — but go through the system and make certain that no step has been left out.

Now let's get to the business of what quality management *can* do for a company. It may be helpful to begin with an analogy. Each day, thousands of people board hundreds of airplanes and fly to dozens of cities. With few exceptions, these planes arrive and depart as planned and few injuries occur. Meals are served and consumed; movies are projected and viewed; drinks are offered and drunk; storms are spotted and avoided; and many personal services are provided. You are safer riding in a commercial airliner than sitting in your home.

However, suppose that these same activities took place with the pilots and other crew members not on the plane. Suppose the crew were in an office building somewhere, flying and managing the aircraft by remote control. Suppose they first issued each order to subordinates who then transmitted the instructions to the autopilot equipment.

Suddenly, we are faced with a new equation. The concept of flying has changed dramatically. Under the present system, the pilot goes along with you. If you crash, the pilot crashes. When the pilot is subject to the same fate as the passenger, he or she is bound to be personally concerned with every detail. But if the pilot were managing from an office, he or she would not crash when the plane went down. The pilot might be investigated after a crash, but it would never be all that clear whether the pilot, a subordinate, the system, or perhaps one of the in-flight passengers was at fault.

If you were going to travel under those circumstances, you would want to make certain that every plan, every control, every consideration was tested, controlled, and audited. You would want the most competent and professional management of every aspect of the flight. You would want to make certain that everything was done exactly right – the first time.

Quality management is a systematic way of guaranteeing that organized activities happen the way they are planned. It is a management discipline concerned with preventing problems from occurring by creating the attitudes and controls that make prevention possible.

Quality management is needed because nothing is simple anymore, if indeed it ever was. Our sophisticated business world is like those planes flying by remote control with instructions filtered through layers of subordinates. The people who really control activities do so from offices, laboratories, studios, and other remote places. The further the administrator gets from the administered, the less efficient the administration becomes.

Although individuals at lower levels can add to the deterioration of a process, there isn't a great deal they can do to improve a product or service. It makes you wonder why so much attention is given to improvement in those areas and so little to management and administration. If effective quality management is to be practical and achievable, it must start at the top.

This book is set up to provide you with a way of measuring the exact status of your present quality program and to show you what positive steps you can take to evaluate and improve that program. The evaluation system, the Quality Management Maturity Grid, is explained in detail in the next chapter. The grid was used through all the various industries of ITT, and was successful in every case. The beauty of the system is that you don't have to be a professional quality type to apply it. All you have to do is know what is going on in your company. (If you don't know that, then the problem is different.) Each stage of maturity is covered in enough detail so you will be sure to recognize some of your operations. But don't rate yourself too high at first. Once more information is available you may find that you are not quite where you think you are. It is said that the difference between an optimist and a pessimist is that the pessimist has more data.

After the grid chapters, a detailed case history on quality improvement is given. This case is one that can be role-played with other members of management, if you wish, and it works very well as a teaching aid. But its real purpose is to display the logic and philosophy of quality improvement so that it can be understood clearly. I recommend that you give the chapter on management style special attention. After all, quality management really is more like ballet than hockey.

3

The Quality Management
Maturity Grid

Management is the function responsible for establishing the purpose of an operation, determining measurable objectives, and taking the actions necessary to accomplish those objectives. Although management is usually thought of as having to do with chartered corporations or organizations, it operates elsewhere also.

Managing a family, for instance, is probably the most difficult of all jobs. It is clear that very few have been completely successful at that task. The small number of people who actually achieve their hoped-for potential could be explained as a matter of random success, considering the billions of individuals who have lived in the past and the billions who are living now. *Somebody* has to succeed!

The family suffers from three primary obstacles when it comes to management. The first is that the members of the organization are brought aboard without benefit of personal evaluation, psychological testing, or any of the other techniques that formal organizations use to screen employees. Thus, each member is an unknown quantity.

The second is that you are sort of stuck with the family group. If your three-year-old gives you a hard time, you can't fire her or toss her out in the snow. The neighbors will toss the child right back in. The hold that family managers have on their family personnel has an emotional and circumstantial base, and emotions and circumstances are changing all the time.

Third, the family managers, and in fact the family itself, are not trained for the job. They have no methods of measuring performance except in terms of their own limited experience. They are required to provide financial means, security, and educational activities, often without having had the chance to learn by experience or practice. Once they do learn how to do the job, they are classified as obsolete and are forced to sit back, while not interfering, as the children take their turn at family management.

Families and business operations have a great deal in common. Both are people-oriented, and both have difficulty in measuring some important aspects of their progress. Family management measures everything against the manager's personal standards. Thus, approved activity is always several fads behind. The children like one kind of music, the adults like another.

Measurement becomes a matter of defining the "entitlements" and expectations of human existence. What are the members of each generation entitled to receive? What can they expect as their right from the family and what are they expected to contribute? As families grow more affluent through the years, the specifics change. Grandpa may have felt he was entitled to take the plow horse to school, riding with two siblings. Granddaughter may feel that each sixteen-year-old deserves her own car. Mother, who assumes her right to household conveniences, may also feel that she should receive unceasing adoration from each member of the group.

All individuals have developed some idea of the things society ought to provide for their physical and emotional well-being. A very few may have some idea of the things *they* should accomplish to attain those goals, or what they should give to others.

Families have difficulty setting goals, measuring performance, and accomplishing tasks. Like all human beings, they are also faced with difficulties of communication, difficulties that are compounded by emotional involvement.

Quality management has always been looked at as a subjective operation, hard to define and measure. That is because it has been relegated to the role of a results-oriented procedure rather than a planning operation. Just as the folklore of family management states that if you don't spoil children, and are sure to raise them with loving discipline, they will turn out to be good, so the folklore of business management states that if you have good in your heart, you will produce quality.

I have no desire to poke fun at these platitudes; they aren't all wrong. But you know from your own experience that it is a rare parent who doesn't feel that he or she has given a child the best possible upbringing under the circumstances. We kid ourselves into thinking that if our offspring had only listened more intently to us, things would have been better for them. Finally, however, no one knows any way to guarantee the best for their children, so parents take their chances and do the best they can.

However, quality management has just become too important to leave to chance. In this day of crushing taxation, mysterious methods of accounting, rollicking inflation, and unsettled politics, it may be that quality is the last chance we have to make profits controllable. But if quality is to be a "first among equals," then management must have a way of measuring and controlling. You will not be surprised to know that I have developed just such a system.

Using the Quality Management Maturity Grid, even the manager who isn't professionally trained in the quality business can determine where the operation in question stands from a quality standpoint. All that is required is knowing what is going on. If the manager doesn't know that, then we are both in the wrong book.

For years I have been saying, every way I could think of, that quality is too important to leave to the professionals.

Professionals must guide the program, but the execution of quality is the obligation and opportunity of the people who manage the operation.

However, I just didn't have enough objective evidence to convince everyone. Every step of achievement was done the hard way. We had to kill a mouse before they would give us a rat-catching license. Eventually, we worked our way up to a dragon a week. This method requires eight to ten years from the first conversation to a completely implemented quality program. It is never possible to assume that the program will continue to prosper. Every day requires the identification and destruction of new menaces. If you can't produce a dead dragon each week, your license may be revoked.

Robert Burns wished that we could be given the gift of seeing ourselves as others see us. Many of us echo that thought, probably because there is little chance of it happening. After all, our own version of ourselves is usually more flattering than that of others, and most people really don't want to know the truth about themselves.

Not many people really want to know the future, either, especially if it might hold disaster. Those who can predict the future have never been appreciated in their own times. History, mythology, and real life are full of situations where someone warned others of events about to happen—only to be scorned or ignored. Noah and the flood; Cassandra and the Trojan horse; Churchill and World War II; the list goes on and on.

People would rather handle the expected and mundane chores of today, like making a living. Typically, as individuals go through life, they collect a store of clichés and experiences that serve as a memory bank to draw on in handling situations as they arise. New thoughts or unfamiliar ideas must survive their encounter with this memory and experience library. Otherwise, they are cast aside as being unworthy.

It is this test of worthiness, this comparison with the

past, that causes problems in the development and implementation of new thoughts and programs. Changing mind sets is the hardest of management jobs. It is also where the money and opportunity lie.

Take quality management in its truest sense as a "for instance." The purpose of it is to set up a system and a management discipline that prevents defects from happening in the company's performance cycle. To accomplish this you have to act now on situations which may cause problems some time from now. Act now for reward later.

Management has to commit money this year to conduct quality testing so there won't be problems two years from now. A training program that costs a lot of time and money and may produce benefits must be established right away. Inspections and tests and corrective actions have to be accomplished before problems become big enough to become disasters.

Prevention like this is not hard to do—it is just hard to sell. It requires the ability to convince people that bad things will happen to them if they don't take early action. Most of us are unable, or unwilling, to accept such things intellectually, and are convinced only on the basis of experience.

But to wait until a failure is unassailable before learning from experience and only then advancing one more step is too much to expect of anyone. A career could be over before a person had the chance to experience each and every thing that can go wrong.

That is the frustrating part of it all. How can you bring the top operating people in your company, the ones with the money to spend or withhold, the ones who get to decide who does what—how can you bring them around to understanding quality management and all the things it can do for them?

Until the development of the Quality Management Maturity Grid, this conversion process was exclusively a function of the personal charm and convincing attitude of the quality management professional. If people liked and trusted the quality manager, things got done. However, even though good results produced evidence that the system worked, they did not necessarily guarantee the quality manager's right to increase efforts for prevention. It is a strange thing, this business of success not breeding more opportunity, but many management people have been frustrated by it.

In many cases, for instance, a value analysis job produces outstanding cost reductions, design improvement, and true profit growth. However, the next time such a study is proposed, it is met with blank stares. Success in these functional areas does not seem to provide a foundation on which to build further successes. Apparently, it is a matter of what particular effect is needed in the business at a particular time.

The need for long-range programs in quality can be deduced intellectually through the Grid. A manager of any operation can spend a few moments with the Grid, recognize familiar events, and pinpoint where the operation is at that moment. Then all that is necessary is to refer to the following stage of the Grid in order to know what actions need to be taken for improvement. And in the cases where an established program is now deteriorating, the Grid can be read backwards. You can see the last point at which you were successful and figure out how to get back there.

The grid is divided into five stages of maturity. Six management categories serve as the experience relations you must go through to complete the matrix. By reading the experience condensed in each block, it is possible to identify your own situation.

All of this recognizing is done unemotionally and without anyone else knowing about it. Even if pride causes a little clouding of the exact status, it will usually only cloud to the extent of one stage, unless you are completely kidding yourself. That still means improvement is necessary. Said improvement can be recognized when it comes.

To become familiar with the Grid, it is necessary to recognize the content of each stage of maturity. Stories and case histories are utilized in the following chapters to assist you in gaining this understanding. But you can know from just looking down the columns that the stages have a definite recognition pattern. I like to call the behavior at each level by its "stage" name.

Stage 1, *Uncertainty,* is indeed confused and uncommitted. Management has no knowledge of quality as a positive management tool. They speak regularly of their quality function in terms of being the policemen, or "gumshoes," whose job it is to catch the criminals in the act. Problems of nonconformance are considered the fault of not being tough enough on the "bad guys." Uncertainty learned management control from the Clint Eastwood movies.

Uncertainty casually places the quality function deep in the bowels of one of the operating departments: manufacturing, administration, operations, engineering, and so on. Inspection is sometimes a separate operation and is assigned to the production people so they "can have the tools to do the job."

These restrictions create the self-fulfilling prophecy that unsolved problems will always be around. Every problem is considered unique, even if it has been encountered before. Problems breed problems, and the lack of a disciplined method of openly attacking them breeds more problems. The result is emotion on the management level. The question becomes "who," rather than "what," caused the difficulty. Personalities are the predominate factor in problem attacking. This sometimes results in illogical firings and quittings as it becomes impossible to methodically examine a situation and solve whatever problems exist.

The cost of quality is not in the Uncertainty glossary, probably because local quality management doesn't know very much about it. However, anyone bringing up the subject will receive an audience if for no other reason than that it will be something no one has considered before. This is the key to starting some action in this type of company.

But quality improvement will never be part of a company in the age of Uncertainty. These companies are some-what like alcoholics, whose number one symptom is em-phatic denial that the condition exists. Therefore, improvement is not considered as an option. Uncertainty-age companies know they have problems but don't know why, although they do know it isn't because they aren't working hard. Everyone in Uncertainty works hard, and most are frustrated at the amount of brute force it takes to keep the operation moving.

Stage 2, Awakening, is more pleasant, but no less frus-trating. Here management is beginning to recognize that quality management can help, but is unwilling to devote the time and money to make it happen. If pressed into strength-ening the quality operation, they will opt for putting one of the "gang" in that job. Selection is done on that basis be-cause of the mistaken idea that the need for someone who understands the product or service is greater than the need for someone who understands professional quality manage-ment.

Awakening hasn't awakened enough to recognize that quality management takes more than understanding the technical aspects of a product or service. At this stage, how-ever, inspection and testing are performed more often, and problems are identified earlier in the production cycle. This cuts rework costs a little while permitting some attention to resolving problems.

Chronic problems are listed and assigned to teams for action, although prime attention is still paid to keeping the product moving. In service companies the customer is ca-joled more at this stage. Service problems are corrected quicker. But the basic problems are still not solved. Teams set up to attack problems accomplish quite a bit, but their scope is limited to the near future. Long-range solutions are not considered seriously.

An interesting thing happens when the cost of quality is calculated for the first time. The quality manager, having read a paper or attended a course, sits down with the comptroller to calculate this number. They assume the walls are coming down about them and they do a very detailed calculation, only to find that the cost of quality is very small. It may only be 3 percent of sales or less, which is the level that really well-run companies aspire to achieve. This often serves to convince everyone that things aren't as bad as they seem because "we can prove it by the number." However, as they will find out much later, they have been fooling themselves. They just don't include everything they are supposed to include.

Take inspection, for instance. In an Awakening company the inspection is conducted by a lot of different people in a lot of different areas. Because the quality department is so disorganized, when they are calculating inspection costs, they don't include the people who do adjustments and similar measurements on the production line. They don't include the burden on all inspection activities, and they probably don't include the inspectors who are working for manufacturing.

Awakening's warranty costs, for instance, include only the expense of replacing the product with a new unit. That is just the shop cost. How about all the correspondence? How about the repair time, the handling, the everything else? It is enough at this point to say that about one-sixth of what really exists will be calculated. That will be all they can find. But it is a start.

Awakening really comes to life when the magic of *motivation* has been sold. The idea is that if you hang up posters and have a contest, you will get people turned on to quality; then things will get better. The fact is that people do enjoy entertainment and attention, and so they will respond for a few days. Then they tire of it and go back to what they were doing before.

So Awakening will put together a motivation package. They will make a few speeches and have a special lunch and even talk to the people. Immediately the results of this communication show themselves. Every measurement chart shows improvement. But it only lasts a little while—just long enough, in fact, for the employees to recognize that the effects of the effort are really short-term.

Realization of this usually causes Awakening to reevaluate the commitment to improvement, and may drive the company back into the Uncertainty stage. Complete regression is possible when the shock sets in. However, the employees of the company will usually offer encouragement and urge Awakening to continue stumbling along on the path of quality inprovement. The employees have a much more practical view of things. They know instinctively that the company has to offer more constant quality in service and product alike or its very life will be threatened.

Such is the hard life of Awakening.

The stages of quality maturity do not provide individual guided tours like Scrooge's ghosts. They are easily identifiable, but they have no particular schedule. Lack of attention or a management change can quickly send Wisdom crashing to Awakening.

However, there is a moment when you can tell precisely when one stage is entered. *Enlightenment* appears with the decision to go ahead and really conduct a formal, regulation, card-carrying quality improvement program. With the establishment of a regular quality policy, and the admission that we cause our own problems, management enters the stage of Enlightenment.

In making this commitment it is necessary that Enlightenment establish its quality department as a balanced, well-organized, functioning unit. This group is to lead the crusade, and it must have the capabilities and resurces to do so. All inspection and testing, quality engineering, data reporting, and similar activities must be included. And the department must have a quality education budget.

One of the most recognizable changes in the Enlightenment stage involves the approach to problem resolution. Facing problems openly, without searching for individuals to blame, produces a smoothly functioning system for resolving those problems. Systems, of course, are only road maps; it is personal enthusiasm that makes them work or fail. When task teams are responsible for both resolving a current problem and preventing it in the future, they respond enthusiastically. Constant reassurance is necessary if people are expected to work into the future. They need to know you understand about gestation, birth, growth, and death.

The cost of quality will now get its first fair evaluation. Those who do the calculating will still miss a third of the costs, but they will develop a reasonable enough estimate to provide direction for cost eliminations. Nothing is quite so effective as having cost data to show competing areas that one department has more effective methods of reducing costs than others.

And, of course, quality improvement is now headed up by an official quality improvement team, headed by someone other than the quality director. This team takes the time to understand the content and intent of each step before launching it. Their purpose is to establish a system and attitude that will last for a long time—one so well entrenched that it would take a hard-working quality reduction team to deactivate it.

Enlightenment still has problems and will have them for some time. But the quality team now feels confident that there is indeed a light at the end of the tunnel, not another train coming at them.

Wisdom is another matter altogether. Those involved deeply in this stage, and there aren't all that many of them, find themselves wondering why they used to have all those problems and why the quality department always lived in the other room. Things are basically quiet. Cost reductions are in effect; when problems appear, they are handled and they disappear. This is the point that every political administration strives to reach but usually does not because time runs out before it happens. Wisdom is the stage at which the company has the chance to make the changes permanent.

Because of this, it may be the most critical of all the stages.

The quality manager usually receives a promotion, probably being made a vice president of the company. This can lull the manager into thinking about more exotic things than the constant pressure needed to maintain quality improvement. The reduction in management "noise" is in itself a temptation to reduce the efforts that brought the changes about.

Problem handling may be passed down to the lower levels of the organization, and checks on progress may be bypassed. This can cause the return of a "whodunit" type of organization. Incisive, in-depth reviews must continually be conducted on a "no mercy" basis. Relaxation of this practice is a sign of weakness.

Wisdom reports the cost of quality more accurately than any of the previous stages. The absolute number of dollars saved by paying attention to the cost of quality is usually far more than anyone expected. In many cases quality management has been thought of as just another measuring system with a clumsy title and definition. Now the company is finding that quality control is real, and people may expect too much too soon.

Wisdom is a great time to be running a company. Any task you want accomplished can be tackled successfully. The attitude, the systems, and the enthusiasm are all there waiting. As long as these three are not taken for granted, they will continue to produce.

You will know a Certainty company if you ever see one. It is all summed up in one sentence: "We know why we do not have problems with quality." What a delightful Buck-Rogers-in-the-twenty-fifth-century comment! But it can be done; I know a few operations that have accomplished it.

Certainty considers quality management to be an absolutely vital part of company management. In fact the quality honcho is a member of the board of directors. In Certainty companies problem handling may become something of a lost art. Certainty's prevention system is such that very few significant problems ever actually occur. The cost of quality is down to where it consists almost entirely of the compensation for quality department members and the costs of proofing tests.

The quality improvement team is restructuring and recycling for the umpteenth time. Their most important project may be inviting all those who have served on the team at one time or another to come to a picnic during the summer.

It is a long, long way from Uncertainty to Certainty. But traveling that road is what the fun of management is all about.

The Grid As a Comparison Measurement

If you would like to use Grid measurement to compare different operations, keep in mind that the purpose of comparisons is to get those moving who aren't moving. It is not simply to report the results.

The company, division, or whatever should be rated by three individuals: the quality manager of the operation, the general manager of the operation, and a staff member who is not assigned to that location.

Have the individuals mark the Grid in the appropriate blocks. They should check the stage they think their operation is in for each of the six measurement categories. Let them know that you recognize that the evaluation is a subjective one, but that they are paid to be managers, and managers are mostly subjective. Award a point value for each stage according to its number. One point for an Uncertainty mark; two points for each Awakening mark; and so on. The maximum possible score is thirty. If someone comes up with thirty points, have an awards dinner and forget the whole thing.

If you handle the Grid right, you can use the comparison between the three individual raters to provide a motivation for becoming involved in improvement. You may be surprised to find that the general manager usually gives the company a lower rating than the quality manager. General managers have a better view of the herd.

QUALITY MANAGEMENT MATURITY GRID

Rater _____

Measurement Categories	Stage I: Uncertainty	Stage II: Awakening	
Management understanding and attitude	No comprehension of quality as a management tool. Tend to blame quality department for "quality problems."	Recognizing that quality management may be of value but not willing to provide money or time to make it all happen.	
Quality organization status	Quality is hidden in manufacturing or engineering departments. Inspection probably not part of organization. Emphasis on appraisal and sorting.	A stronger quality leader is appointed but main emphasis is still on appraisal and moving the product. Still part of manufacturing or other.	
Problem handling	Problems are fought as they occur; no resolution; inadequate definition; lots of yelling and accusations.	Teams are set up to attack major problems. Long-range solutions are not solicited.	
Cost of quality as % of sales	Reported: unknown Actual: 20%	Reported: 3% Actual: 18%	
Quality improvement actions	No organized activities. No understanding of such activities.	Trying obvious "motivational" short-range efforts.	
Summation of company quality posture	"We don't know why we have problems with quality."	"Is it absolutely necessary to always have problems with quality?"	

Unit _____

Stage III: Enlightenment	Stage IV: Wisdom	Stage V: Certainty
While going through quality improvement program learn more about quality management; becoming supportive and helpful.	Participating. Understand absolutes of quality management. Recognize their personal role in continuing emphasis.	Consider quality management an essential part of company system.
Quality department reports to top management, all appraisal is incorporated and manager has role in management of company.	Quality manager is an officer of company; effective status reporting and preventive action. Involved with consumer affairs and special assignments.	Quality manager on board of directors. Prevention is main concern. Quality is a thought leader.
Corrective action communication established. Problems are faced openly and resolved in an orderly way.	Problems are identified early in their development. All functions are open to suggestion and improvement.	Except in the most unusual cases, problems are prevented.
Reported: 8% Actual: 12%	Reported: 6.5% Actual: 8%	Reported: 2.5% Actual: 2.5%
Implementation of the 14-step program with thorough understanding and establishment of each step.	Continuing the 14-step program and starting Make Certain.	Quality improvement is a normal and continued activity.
"Through management commitment and quality improvement we are identifying and resolving our problems."	"Defect prevention is a routine part of our operation."	"We know why we do not have problems with quality."

The Grid is at its best when used to project a view of the company that all involved can accept. For this reason it is valuable in comparing the status of different companies or divisions. It also provides a continual source of direction concerning what needs to be done next. Managers may come to use the stages of maturity as a sort of verbal shorthand.

"We're just entering Enlightenment."

"We were Enlightened for a couple of years, then we got a new general manager who thinks quality is expensive. We'll have to drop back a stage or two until he gets educated."

4

Management Understanding
and Attitude

A CASE HISTORY

Harold Gooding peered around the corner of the tool crib wall, nervously scanning the machining area before entering. He did not want to meet Austin Welding, the general supervisor. Austin would want him to stay late that evening, on his own time, to dispose of a table full of parts that had been rejected by Inspection. Harold had plans of his own.

Every time a batch of bad products showed up, Austin and the other manufacturing supervisors acted like it was a personal vendetta instigated by Inspection. As the one and only quality engineer, Harold tried hard to get problems identified and corrected, but they were so numerous, and sometimes so complicated, that they would often come around again before they had been entirely resolved the first time.

Harold turned to see Austin bearing down on him. His plans began to evaporate. The old arguments would start anew. Austin would drag him to the table and they would go through each rejection one at a time. Austin would argue that it wasn't all that bad, or that it could be reworked, or that the specification had been unreasonable, or something. He always saved the worst part till last, when resistance was lowest. Harold didn't look forward to another evening of playing referee.

He held up his palm to the advancing foreman.

"Back dark spirit, in the name of Helen of Troy I command that you return to that black and mysterious cave from whence you emanated. Bother me no more. Disappear, I command you."

Austin flung an arm around Harold's shoulder.

"Come on, little buddy, you don't really mean that. I know you want to get out of here to go to a meeting. The items I want to look at won't take but a moment of your time. Then you can be on your way. There are only twenty-five or so of them."

Suddenly a flash of light appeared on Harold's memory screen. He was inspired. Perhaps there was a way out of this mess.

"Austin, I'll make a deal with you. I am on my way to the ASQC meeting."

Austin looked blank.

"American Society for Quality Control. All the quality professionals in the area belong to it. We meet now and then to conspire against guys like you. Tonight we have a guest speaker who is going to talk about taking the opinion out of rejections. Are you interested in taking the opinions out of rejections?"

"Am I? I sure am. If we could resolve all these opinion things my job would be easier. I wouldn't have to chase all over the place looking for quality engineers to sign off on the silly little things the inspectors find. Am I for eliminating opinions? I'm more for that than anything I can think of."

Harold smiled to himself.

"OK, I'll make a deal with you. The cocktail part of the meeting starts in half an hour. Then there is dinner and the speaker. The whole thing will be over by 9 p.m. You go along with me, and if you still want to come back here and process these parts after the meeting, I'll come with you."

"You want me to go with you and spend the evening with a bunch of quality types? I might lose my professional standing. However, if it would get these problems solved, and if you'll pay, I'll go."

During the cocktail hour Harold watched nervously as Austin chatted with various members. Everyone thought it had been a good idea to invite him, and a few resolved to take a similar step for the next meeting. At dinner Austin entertained the table with a few amusing stories about the toe-to-toe battles he and Harold had conducted. Laughing, each of the others agreed that their life was very much like that also.

"I guess we have chosen a line of work that just naturally requires purposeful conflict to make it work," commented one member. "It seems to produce stronger people, and I think the interface is positive."

"I'd like to hear the speaker comment on this," said another. "He is all wound up in definitions as I understand it. In fact the chairman told me that his subject is 'What does quality mean?' "

Austin smiled. "Trouble, that's what quality means. Trouble."

He then held forth for the next fifteen minutes, good-naturedly kidding the table about the well-known impracticality of quality people.

"If you guys would be reasonable, we could double production in this country overnight. Then we could all have more time for fellowship dinners and educational programs."

At that moment the chairman called the meeting to order and, after introducing several committee members who made status reports, he let the program chairman introduce the speaker.

"Mr. Wilson," said the program chairman, "is the vendor quality manager for Albiex Corporation, which as you know manufactures specialty engineering items. I have heard Bill say many times that he runs the world's biggest job shop. Anyway, his present job requires that he deal with hundreds of suppliers and customers. He has been successful in doing this, and as a matter of fact, since I happen to be one of his customers, I can say without polishing him up that he and his people are straightforward about dealing with us. They call a spade a spade. Here is Bill Wilson."

Wilson came to the podium as the group offered polite applause.

"I come to you tonight under false colors. My subject is 'What does quality mean?' and that is what I meant to speak about when I agreed to do this, which was a year ago. At that time it was all very clear to me what quality meant, how you got it, and everything about it. After all, I'd been in the business for fifteen years.

"However, last spring we decided to make up a little booklet for our suppliers that would help them understand our requirements and methods better. Nothing too spectacular, just a booklet on the basics of dealing with our company.

"Well naturally the first thing we wanted to put down was a list of definitions. After all if you can't define something you can hardly discuss it. The first word on the list to be defined was *quality*. That was six months ago and we have just now arrived at the second word."

Al looked questioningly at Harold. His eyebrows arched enough to intimate that the two of them would be smart to ease themselves out the door. Obviously they were in the company of a dummy.

Wilson continued. "The usual definitions just didn't seem to come clear to me. Defining quality as 'desirable characteristics,' 'subjective evaluation,' and other phrases just didn't seem right. After all, I didn't want to be known as the desirable characteristics manager.

"I began to get a little panicky. All those years in the business and I couldn't even tell any one what it was I did.

"We looked at some of the modern definitions. 'Fitness for use' has a nice ring, and in fact has a lot of meaning particularly when you are talking about the design concept of a product. If you think about a toaster, for instance, 'fitness for use' immediately brings a lot to the top. You need handles, and connections that won't break even when they are used incorrectly, and a shine that will stay, and coils that do the job in the correct time period. It is a valuable concept.

"But that isn't what we are doing. We are buying and manufacturing things. The design and concept decisions were made long ago. When our program manager gets an order from us, he only wants to know what we want, how many, and when. He is not too concerned about how we are going to use it or the 'fitness for use' evaluation.

"In short, we had to come up with something we could use in practical terms that everyone could understand and that we could use to do the job. As one of my people put it, 'We need something you can use to make a living.' She was so right.

"So we went back to the basics. We asked ourselves just what the quality function does, and why?"

("I wonder that myself sometimes," muttered Al under his breath.)

"We kicked around ideas about defect prevention and taking measurement and corrective action and all that stuff. Finally we reached a combined conclusion. And this conclusion produced our definition of quality. I promise that once it sinks in, you will never look at things in the same way again.

"We decided we were in the business of causing and measuring conformance to the requirements. Therefore, quality means conformance. Nonquality is nonconformance.

"Suddenly the whole thing becomes clear. Instead of thinking of quality in terms of goodness or desirability we are looking at it as a means of meeting requirements.

"Now you have to accept the fact that this puts us, as quality professionals, out of the design business we all love so dearly. We are no longer accepting or rejecting characteristics based on our judgment of whether or not they are good enough, or even necessary. Many of us were used to telling manufacturing that they could use something not quite to tolerance because we knew that the thing was too tight to begin with. We can't do that any more. It's conformance or nonconformance and that is it."

The group began to fidget a bit at this point, and several little discussions broke out quietly at the various tables. Wilson noted this and smiled.

"I see that some of you are reacting to this thought. I assure you that this is only normal. Suppose we stop right here and go into the question and answer session."

He looked at the chairman, who nodded approval.

"OK, let's have the first question."

"I understand the process you went through to get to this definition of quality Bill, and I think that you and your group are to be congratulated in doing such a fine analysis. However, you don't really expect to implement this definition as policy for your company, do you? After all, you have to be practical."

"We think this is very practical, and it is also easy to understand. Why do you feel it would be a problem?"

"Well, for one thing, it would stop any production line cold. Nothing else would ever be produced anywhere. No design is perfect—you always have to make some allowances."

Bill nodded.

"I agree that designs are far from perfect and that corrections need to be made. But how are you going to get those corrections made until you find the problems and identify them? Once all the corrections have been implemented the product moves right along.

"Just the other day I ran across something that really made me take notice. We were running behind in the machine shop, and so we took some parts we had been making for years and put the raw material plus the paperwork in a box and sent it out to a very good machine shop. You know what. They couldn't make them. If you did it just like the print it didn't compute. No way. All kinds of little variations were involved. And none of them were written down. We found that we have several very proud craftspeople in our shops who know just how to shave a little here and there in order to make a product come out usable in spite of faulty specifications.

"Do you realize how horrible that was? The company management didn't control the place anymore. They were at the mercy of the mister fixits in the shop, who were glorified by the leaders we had selected to direct them. As all this sunk in, I became quite depressed about it.

"I made my presentation at the general manager's staff meeting and it was received with blank looks. Nobody seemed to realize the impact of what I was saying. They could hardly wait for me to finish. Imagine! There I was with the greatest discovery of my career, and they couldn't possibly have cared less. If it's common knowledge it isn't important.

"But you see, if you can't count on producing something in your manufacturing areas that looks like what you designed in engineering, then the whole business is a useless waste. No one knows what is going out the door. So all the marketing, surveying, research, warranty planning, and five-year planning—the whole thing—is just a farce if we don't make it like the drawings, so we can see if it will work."

As Bill leaned forward, his voice dropped and there was mist in his eyes.

"There is no use running life tests and all that other stuff on things that may not even look alike."

Al sat there with his mouth open. He was entranced.

"So I decided that there had to be a way of getting the message across. After much cogitating I decided to attack the staff through the lunchroom. They are all real eaters.

"I went up to the dining room manager's office and talked him into assisting me in my conspiracy. He was just making up the day's menu, and we looked at it together.

"At lunchtime the special was a plate of corned beef and cabbage. One person got a tiny little sliver of sliced corned beef and a huge mess of cabbage. Another got it the other way around.

"Those who ordered a sandwich got it with toast on one side and bread on the other. We fixed up seven or eight of these little tricks. I waited until there was considerable murmuring and my confederate had begun to look a little pale around the gills. Then I went into the room and raised my hand for silence.

"You have just had lunch on the basis that the requirements mean nothing. Each plate has been prepared according to how the cook felt at that particular moment, with no consideration as to what the menu, or even you the customer, specified.

"I arranged all of this and will take all the blame. But I just wanted each of you to see on a personal basis how dumb it is to not insist that the requirements be met every time.

"All of them agreed to rethink the matter except the comptroller."

"The comptroller wasn't convinced?"

"Oh, she was convinced, but she was the one who got three scoops of ice cream instead of the one scoop she had ordered. She liked the system."

"Well, Bill, isn't it kind of chaotic to get so honest all at once? Don't you really have to shut down the whole place and start over?"

"No. You just work your way out of the problems, making changes as you find they are needed. It is hectic for a while, but it all works out. You have to put a team together on some problems.

"One of the most interesting problems was in order writing. We found that they had been very casual for a long time since they knew the shop wouldn't pay much attention to them anyway. Now, all of a sudden we were doing everything exactly like it was written, and they had to get with it. The order-writing people take a great deal of pride in their work these days. We have learned that a correctly written order produces a better chance of conformance from the shop."

After the meeting Harold rode back to the company with Austin to fulfill his promise. Harold had hoped that the experience of the evening would change Austin's mind, and perhaps bring forth a little more interest in defect prevention. But Austin hadn't said much of anything since leaving the meeting.

As they started through the first few pieces of rejected material, Austin put his hand on Harold's wrist.

"I think I'm beginning to get the message. You know, we have been rejecting the break angle on this same part for the last two or three years. Engineering always says it's OK to use it, but they never change the drawing. And look at this subassembly! It always produces too much backlash when the gears are mounted. Always."

He looked at Harold.

"You know, I think it is time that we got honest with ourselves. Let's just leave this pile here. We'll tell engineering and production control that we're not producing one more part until they tell us the exact date the proper changes are going to be made.

"You and I have got better things to do than sitting around doing other people's work. Let's go home."

Harold nodded.

"Perhaps we should start with the lunchroom?"

UNDERSTANDING RESPONSIBILITY

Using the Grid

As a result of the experience described above, Austin Welding stepped from Uncertainty to Awakening — according to the Quality Management Maturity Grid. He had become aware that there was a better way, that it might be open to him, and that he could do something about it. He didn't understand everything that was going on, but he did know that there was a change in his managerial life-style.

His attitude had changed. And attitude is what management understanding is all about.

People are fond of saying that they were poor when they were children, but they didn't know they were poor. Those were the happiest days of their lives, they report. Everyone they knew was in the same situation, and somehow or other it all seemed to work out.

However, I have noticed that absolutely none of them consider taking the simple step necessary to return to those great days. Having sampled a life with more choices available to them, they do not again select a life of zero options. They want something over which they have more control.

That is sort of what the Quality Management Maturity Grid is all about. I am sure you would like to know what is available to you, what benefits you can achieve in return for what labors, and how you can make your own choices. But instead of taking the time to live it all out, to learn only through often bitter experience, use the Grid. It lets you peer into the future, with the reminder that you can fall backward as well as move forward. Those comforts obtained through hard work and virtue can be lost with one roll of the cubes. *Won* doesn't mean *kept.*

Improvement itself is never the real difficulty. Once individuals recognize and agree on their position, it is never difficult to improve. The unfortunate part is that very few of us own up. We don't admit how much time it really takes to commute; we always break 90 on the golf course; we tend to shade references to our age. We are a fragile and vain group, we humans.

I have had discussions with executives in hundreds of different businesses and industries. Regardless of the nation, product, service, or group I am never disappointed. Someone always says: "You have to recognize that our business is different." Because they usually see only their business, they never realize how alike most businesses are. Certainly the technology and the methods of distribution can be very different. But the people involved—their motivations and reactions—are the same. What works in one industry to improve quality will work in others—if you take the time to understand quality and its content.

Faced with a group of management or professional people who are waiting to hear some miraculous disclosure of a no-fault method of quality improvement, I tell them I need information. I ask them to state their biggest single specific problem. They are to just state the problem in one or two sentences. No discussion, no analysis. And they are not allowed to say that their biggest problem is "people," "communication," "peace on earth," or other nonspecific items. I ask them: "If the good fairies came down to earth and told you that you could get rid of one problem, what would that be?" The lists are always alike:

- They never give us accurate data.

- People just don't do good work.

- Our competition can buy cheaper than us.

- They don't meet the commitments they establish themselves.

- These government regulations make you hire un-qualified people.

- Top management just won't understand that we have to change our ways.

- The turnover rate is so high you can't train people.

- Interest rates are eating us up.

- The union is completely unreasonable.

The list could go on. I'm sure you have your own items.

After writing these items on the board, I tell the group that apparently we have invited the wrong people to the meeting. This group has nothing to improve. Everything that is happening to them is caused by others. If I could bring the other 4 billion people in the world into the conference room, there would be a chance of getting the list of problems solved. Otherwise there is no hope.

I have done this exercise several hundred times. Not one person has ever put forth a "biggest problem" that he or she caused. No one ever says:

- I can't buy as cheap as the purchasing guy at the competition.

- I have been unable to convince the boss; I need to learn more about how to do that.

- I am not reaching my people; their turnover rate is too high.

- My planning has not been adequate on this matter.

By making a big deal about it, I finally get everyone to admit that they would do well to look at themselves when they are looking for the cause of problems. They always agree. But it just takes too long for them to put the knowledge to use.

When it comes to the responsibility for managing a company or a function, you have to be prepared to admit that some of the problems might be caused by the individuals responsible for that management. Otherwise corrective action will never happen. That is why the Grid comments on management understanding and attitude are important.

Uncertainty

Uncertainty has no comprehension of quality as a management tool. People in the Uncertainty stage tend to blame the quality department for quality problems. This is because of lack of information on the subject, and the erroneous assumptions discussed in Chapter 2. It is important to recognize the real meanings of words and functions. The baseball umpire who said that what the pitcher throws is "nothing until I call it something" was precisely correct.

Uncertainty lives in the present. Each day dawns on a new world, and each night ends that world. Problem prevention is not a real part of Uncertainty's operation, since to prevent, you must look into the future. Therefore it is easy to identify the quality function in an Uncertainty situation. It consists of inspectors and testers, who probably report to the manufacturing department, and who sort the product as it moves along. Management expects them not to let anything that is "too" bad get out of the place.

Uncertainty's idea is do whatever you have to do to find

and solve today's problem, letting tomorrow take care of itself. Since no reasonable person will ever admit that he or she would think such a thing, you have to look at what a particular operation *does* if you are going to establish its rating.

If the problem is something that can be fixed with a waiver or a paperwork change, then Uncertainty is in business. That is much preferred to the time it would take to identify the cause of the problem. Furthermore, if the real cause of a problem were found, an operation could get involved in redesign, tool rework, training, and all kinds of time-consuming things. That is not attractive. And anyone suggesting that such actions could eliminate problems in the future is taking her life in her hands. There is no future. There is only today.

Awakening

The difference between uncertainty and Awakening is somewhat like President Eisenhower used to say was the difference between a true conservative and a liberal conservative. The conservative didn't want to do it. The liberal conservative definitely wanted to do it, but not at this time.

I often hear executives say that they want to begin the quality improvement program, but they want to wait until some problems are cleared up first. They don't want to start the problem-resolving program until they have resolved some problems. How does that grab you? It is the Catch-22 of the unenlightened.

What Awakening is really afraid of is commitment to the future. Uncertainty doesn't know about the future and so can't be bothered by it. Awakening knows about it, and is bothered. Both do nothing, but for different reasons. The result is the same. Awakening people are more willing to talk about long-range corrective action, and even willing to let it happen now and then. However, they are not ready to spend the money on the quality program yet. They don't relate money spent to money saved. Money spent is real

money; savings in the future are not. It is not enough to
explain that quality is really a self-funding program. Awakening moves only when the true cost of quality is
understood.

In fairness to the line managers, I have to say that the
quality professionals who work for Awakening are usually
not too much help to those of us trying to push improvement. One plant I visited showed me an interesting paradox.
The young general manager was enthusiastic about quality
and recognized that she needed to take action. She called the
quality manager out of the shop and got me started on a
tour. The quality manager told me endless tales of nonconformance, and of horrible situations that needed to be corrected immediately. He pointed out that management just
would not listen, that he had tried and tried, but to no avail.

In my exit interview with the general manager I carefully told her about all the problems her quality manager
had. She immediately called the man to the office, apolo-
gized for not listening, picked up her pencil, and asked for a
complete list of problems that needed attention.

My informant looked her right in the eye and said,
"Nothing I can't handle, chief."

I have never forgotten that lesson. Since then I have
never attempted to recondition management until the quality professionals have it clear. Their ideas and assumptions
are often more deeply ingrained and more definite than
those of top management. Like I said, it takes a little time.

Enlightenment

I hate to keep talking about attitudes, but attitudes are
really what it is all about. The difference between the best
and the worst platoon in the army is not equipment or location. It is attitude. The mysteries of creating both the nega-
tives and positives of this still elude me, as they have others.
But once in a while it all comes together, and that is beauti-
ful to see. Some of it occurs during Enlightenment.

The first thing you notice when a management moves into Enlightenment is the relaxation of tension. Suddenly communication begins and defensiveness reduces. This comes about primarily because they have admitted to themselves — out loud and by action — that they need to improve. It is sort of an industrial "born again" phenomenon.

By formally establishing a quality improvement team representing every department, Enlightenment has clearly stated that everyone is involved. No operation is being singled out, no one is being fingered. "We are all in this together." What magic words. With no need to plot and scheme in order to protect their department, all work together. Naturally the progress is swift and immediate.

One nice thing about the fourteen-step program of quality improvement (described in detail in Chapter 8) is that it brings immediate improvement because problems get immediate attention. This generates enthusiasm on the part of the quality team that is transmitted to others. Of course the company personnel immediately send out their sensors to determine if this is really a sincere endeavor or just some quick "motivation" thing.

Part of Enlightenment is the recognition that you cannot, and should not, fool the people. That sounds about as basic as you can get, but not too many believe it. Many have a stereotyped image of the "worker," and think workers are completely predictable. But workers are individuals, and they know when they are being put on.

Top management must go out of its way to provide support for the quality management at this time. The professional quality team is working hard to educate the rest of operating management at all levels. This is not an easy process. Just because the general manager and the department heads have gotten religion doesn't mean that anyone else has. There is always a clutch of Uncertainty- or Awakening-type behavior right in the middle of the operation. People still in those stages will probe continually to measure the depth of top management commitment. They are not on any team, they don't get to plan the campaign, they don't receive rewards. At least that's what they think. When they reach their personal Enlightenment, that will change.

Wisdom

Wisdom, having reaped the fruits of Enlightenment's labor, concentrates on not losing it. People in the Wisdom stage actively participate in the entire program. They serve as personal examples, and take the time to learn more about the subtleties of the philosophy of quality management. And a subtle thing it is. Wisdom must indeed be wise to recognize that the time it takes for true, long-lasting, never-to-be-overcome improvement to set in is years. And even then you can never be sure. You have to work constantly, ever creating new interests, ever looking for new ways to prevent nonconformance.

Many companies in this stage use the Buck a Day* program to seek out ideas for improvement. BAD is a five-week program that lets you go to the people in an entertaining fashion and ask them to provide ideas for their jobs that will save $1 a day by eliminating some unnecessary expense. That is $250 a year per person. If a company employs 1000 people, it becomes $250,000 a year. The program always succeeds, and the return is usually $100 for each $1 invested. Savings are real, but the major advantage is the improvement in communications and morale.

Those who consider quality improvements a motivation program never reach the age of Wisdom. They are always looking for gimmicks that will take the place of genuine participation and involvement. Wisdom doesn't have this problem. Wisdom runs the program over and over in different ways, never losing sight of the goal of defect prevention.

*BAD is marketed by Industrial Motivation, Inc., 331 Madison Avenue, New York, New York

And that means *complete* defect prevention, so that the writing of a rejection tag is never heard, and all the rework stations are closed, locked, and forgotten.

Certainty

Certainty has reached the stage of complete defect prevention. When a defect does occur, it is examined with the same rapt attention given the ultrarare case of smallpox found now and then by a big-city hospital. Certainty has learned something that couldn't even be explained to Enlightenment. Certainty has learned that if you don't expect errors, and really are astonished when they occur, then errors just do not happen.

You probably don't believe that now, but someday you will. Examine the Grid, examine your goals, and prepare for a long but rewarding trek on the way to Certainty. Why not? Think where your company could be if you completely eliminated failure costs.

CHANGING MANAGEMENT'S ATTITUDES

The most effective way to bring operating and other management people to their senses is to put them in contact with someone they will believe. Obviously, they are not going to accept the unsupported word of the staff professional. It is like believing the automobile salesperson is unbiased.

No potentate who ever existed was subject to more persuasion than the individual who is president of a company, general manager of a plant, or otherwise the head person in an industrial or business organization. Their life is a constant stream of people explaining how if only the chief would implement such and such a plan everything would be hunky-dory.

One general manager told me that he has calculated that every year he is offered the opportunity to save $30 million—in a company which only has $25 million in sales! Each day brings inputs from dedicated, thoughtful, sincere people who want you to do things their way. It is a dreadful obstacle to overcome.

Believing that quality is free, we are going to work to overcome this obstacle by taking a clear look at reality—by examining the facts. But facts presented by peers, not by those devious souls on the staff. In the Jungle Habitat operations, you drive through a zoo in your car while the animals roam around free. There are two signs as you enter, one stating the price of admission and the second making it clear that you must not open your windows or leave the car because the animals are not the least bit tame. However, it is possible to imagine a third sign, placed by people like those who run plants or offices for large corporations, reading "Headquarters staff personnel on bicycles admitted free." This sort of all-too-common attitude means that people who are trying to change things must work with people who trust one another, if only because they feel they have a common enemy.

In every operation there is one area that is more open to new ideas than the others. This operation should be encouraged to conduct a pilot program for your project. With a minimum of personal visibility you can assist them in planning and implementing the program. Once there has been sufficient accomplishment, congratulate those involved and ask them to share it with the world. Schedule a management seminar, and invite all the general managers and other senior executives of the companies who haven't yet participated. Do the seminar properly. Plan it right down to the last gnat's eyelash, and get top management's participation. But keep the quality professionals out of it.

The idea is that the audience should consist of those who actually have to do the work, and they should be hearing from those who face the same problems and pressures. It is truly a revival meeting, with witnesses telling how they were wrong once, but now they know the way and are accomplishing actual improvement.

The senior quality professional should conduct the ceremonies in order to keep the meeting moving. But the emphasis has to be on worker bees. Let an engineering manager tell about the results of establishing effective product qualification procedures. Have a marketing type tell how having less problems produces more sales. Let the consumer affairs people relate their experience in handling reduced complaints and even compliments.

At the end ask for commitments. Make the audience do something like stand up, or raise their hand, or sign a master commitment chart. Send them back to be greeted by their quality department, all prepared to implement this commitment. Before you know it, they will.

Recognize all achievements, and assist senior management in doing some recognizing of their own. But always remember that this is just a start. You will have to do it over and over again. Conduct the same type of success-witnessing seminar for quality people in the quality councils. They need encouragement and information more than their leaders. As long as their attitudes are positive, they will keep management on the right track.

A COMMENT ON MANAGEMENT ATTITUDES

I visited my old pal Dinsmore recently. He had called to let me know that he had taken over as general manager of the Flagship hotel about six months and thought that I might be interested in seeing a real hotel from the inside. He also indicated that I might learn something about the hotel business.

When I drove up to the front door, a steady rain kept me inside the car for ten to fifteen minutes. During that time I noticed that the doorman was peering at me from inside the lobby. Sensing that the rain was not going to quit, I made a dash for the doors and pushed my way in, dripping on the carpet in the process. The doorman told me I could only leave the car there for about ten minutes since it was a no-parking zone, but that the hotel garage in the next block would be glad to store it for me. He offered to lend me his umbrella in order to unload the trunk.

Accepting his offer, I retrieved my suitcase and clothes bag in order to drag both to the front desk. Announcing myself as Mr. Dinsmore's guest didn't seem to make much of an impression on the clerk, who was chattting with the cashier. She seemed a little irritated at my interference.

There was no reservation for me, but they said they could fix me up since I had said the general manager had invited me. After only three rings of the "front" bell, the bellhop came to lead me to my room, which it turned out wasn't made up. He commented that it was only 3 o'clock, and the room would probably be fixed by the time I returned from my business. I tipped him, dropped my bags, and remembered the car.

It wasn't necessary to worry because the police had just towed the vehicle away. The doorman said that he had waved to the tow truck but they hadn't been able to see him for the rain. He assured me that I could pick up the car in the morning with no problem. A cab could take me to the police lot, and the fine was only $25 plus the towing charge. The garage charged $6. He noted that it was interesting how they could move a car like that without having the key. Said they would make good thieves.

I found Dinsmore's office on the third floor. One of the elevators wasn't working so I took the brisk walk up the stairs. His secretary nodded and suggested that I move some magazines off that bench and sit down as "Elmer" would be with me as soon as he got off the telephone. She went back to her book.

After a few minutes she seemed to notice my presence again, and offered me some coffee from the percolator in the corner of the reception room. (She didn't like the hotel coffee, and neither, apparently, did Elmer.) I accepted with thanks, telling her I was still damp, having not been able to shower and change because the room was not prepared. She said I really shouldn't expect much else since, although checkout time was noon, they didn't like to push their guests out on rainy days like this. I said I thought that was very considerate of them.

I asked about my automobile, and she repeated the information I already had about the $25 fine and towing charges. Happens all the time, she indicated. The police have no class.

Dinsmore emerged from his office and greeted me effusively. Now, he told me, I was going to see how a hotel should be run. He took me into his office, cleared some reports off a chair, and offered me a cigar. After remarking on my trip, and how fortunate it was of him to catch me in an off moment, he asked how I liked the place so far.

I told him about the car, the doorman, the room clerk, the room, the bellhop, and the elevator. He told me how to get the car back and dismissed the other incidents as growing pains.

Then lowering his voice he asked me if I would mind checking out the restaurant for him. He would pay, naturally. But he wasn't sure if the restaurant manager was really operating the place right. She didn't seem to get along with the other department heads and barely spoke to Elmer. Something funny is going on, he thought. Also, the hotel occupancy rate had been dropping rather steadily. He was sure that this had something to do with the food.

Then straightening his tie, rolling down his sleeves, and putting on his favorite old hunting jacket, he took me on a tour of the hotel. He emphasized that I had only seen the front side of hotels in my travels. He was going to show me the real guts.

In the maid's room nine or ten women were involved in a discussion with the housekeeper about their assignments. Those on the lower floors had to wait until the vacuum cleaners were available from the upper floors, so naturally everyone wanted to work on the upper floors. Dinsmore suggested that they vacuum every other day; then they could share the machines on a rotating basis. The maids thought that was a great idea, although the housekeeper didn't seem too pleased.

Dinsmore remarked to me about the lack of some people's decision-making ability. He sighed that he had to make more and more decisions each day because his staff seemed reluctant to take the initiative.

We met the bell captain and three of the bellhops in their locker room discussing, with the doorman, the procedure for getting guests' bags from the front door to the desk. The problem was in splitting the tips, which were getting a little lower every day. Elmer listened judiciously and then suggested that all tips be given to the bell captain, who would distribute them on the basis of effort as he saw it. This didn't seem to make anybody very happy, except the captain, but since the four couldn't agree on anything else, it was adopted on the spot.

We toured all the floors, I mentioned the amount of room service trays that seemed to be standing in the hall. Dinsmore said that this was a normal part of the hotel scene. The guests didn't mind because it reminded them that room service was available.

The cigar and newspaper stand looked like it belonged in the subway. The old man behind the counter offered me some stale alternatives to the cigars I had requested. He was very pleasant about it. The only magazines I saw featured cover pictures of attractive girls in various stages of disrobing. "Guests don't go in for high-class books anymore," Dinsmore told me. With a nudge he reminded me that I didn't understand the hotel business.

The restaurant seemed to belong to a different world. It was packed. The mâitre d' rushed over, bowed, seated us at a window, and took our drink orders. An atmosphere of quiet efficiency seemed to blanket the room. Two drinks appeared before us while attractive menus were deftly placed to our left. Elmer didn't seem happy. The restaurant, he told me, was a concession left over from the previous owners. He was trying to buy out the leases so he could run it into a real moneymaker. At present it made only about 10 percent net. I mentioned that most hotels lose money on their restaurants. He countered by showing me how many people were there even on that rainy day, and insisting that raising the prices while cutting back on the help was bound to increase the take.

My appetite disappeared momentarily, but was reawakened at the sight of a beautifully poached trout heading for another table.

The next morning I retrieved my car, placed it firmly in the hotel garage, and returned for a farewell meeting with Dinsmore. He asked my opinion concerning his stewardship. He commented on the failing standards of today's workers, noted that he had ever-increasing difficulty in getting people who wanted to do quality work, and bemoaned the fact that the big grand hotels like his were losing out to the motels.

I just couldn't bear to tell Dinsmore the truth. He wouldn't have believed me anyway.

Last week he called again. The hotel had been sold and was to be torn down to serve as a site for an office building. It was just too old and poorly located to make any money, he felt. He was going to accept an offer from a motel chain to run their East Coast operations. He would be responsible for thirty-four inns, and he wanted me to be his guest at one of them soon.

I can hardly wait.

5

Quality Organizational Status

Suppose you were responsible for supplying towels at your club. Suppose you found that some of the members were using three and four towels each time they showered. Suppose you decided that this had to stop. How would you proceed?

Would you speak separately to the members, telling them not to be so wasteful? That would take forever, you would never find anyone who would admit to wastefulness, and you absolutely would not pick up any new friends. In fact, you would probably alienate many old ones. You would probably become known as that "towel watcher," and there would be an intense amount of mental effort expended creating original jokes at your expense. There would be speculation as to where you had learned your trade. Life would take a definite turn for the worse.

You wouldn't attempt to correct the problem on a personal basis. You would probably hang up a sign requesting that the members not be wasteful, since continued waste would make a towel-use fee necessary, and sign it "The Bath Committee."

The bath committee. What a delightful way to get attention without being personally involved. People can make up jokes about the bath committee, but who cares? Since the membership of that group changes continually, no one ever has to face the charges personally.

From such reasoning comes most of the direction you receive in your daily life. No names of people, just names of institutions: greens committee; Internal Revenue Service; United Airlines; the finance committee (if you don't pay your dues); the board of directors; and of course the greatest vagueness of all – *the company*. You have your own list of appropriate names, and you have probably used the committee approach in your managerial role.

When it comes to organizing a functional discipline in a company, particularly one with several divisions or different operations, it is necessary to issue directions and orders. It is essential that each function be established in some orderly way that can be measured and controlled. For that purpose most companies have developed a book of policies and standard practices.

Notice that I said "companies have developed"; and notice that you accepted it. Now you know as well as I do that companies are inanimate objects, with no ability to develop anything. We both know that some *individual* in an organization had to develop this approach. Attributing it to "the company" is a form of social communication that lets orders be given without personal involvement.

Quality is something that is rarely defined and directed in formal policies for companies. Somehow it is felt that such a thing doesn't really require documentation and establishment. But it does, perhaps even more than other functions, because otherwise people will feel that they can make up their own rules. A lot of problems will be avoided if you lay out a clear policy covering the entire quality operation.

The policy I recommend runs along the lines of the following example. You might want to add a little to it, but please resist the temptation to turn it into gospel. Keep it simple, and you will have the reasonable expectation of having someone read it. But make certain that it is complete. After all, policies are used to settle arguments.

POLICY

Quality Management Function

It is the policy of our company that the function of quality management shall exist in each manufacturing and service operation to the degree necessary to ensure that:

1. The acceptance and performance standards of our products and services are met.

2. The cost of quality goals for each operation are achieved.

The company general manager is responsible for obtaining agreement with the corporate director of quality on the proper degree or quality function to be established in each operation. The general manager shall issue a quality policy for the operation, quoting this document, and shall take affirmative steps to ensure that the employees understand that the quality policy of the company is to *perform exactly like the requirement or cause the requirement to be officially changed to what we and our customer really need.*

To ensure its effectiveness, the quality function must be exercised in an objective and unbiased manner. As such, the head of the quality function in each unit shall report directly to the general manager and be on the same organizational level as those functions whose performance is being measured. The head of the quality function shall represent the company in the quality councils.

The quality function shall be staffed with professionally qualified personnel, and their responsibilities shall include:

• Product acceptance at all levels

• Supplier quality

• Quality engineering
  Data analysis and status reporting
  Corrective action
  Planning

Qualification approval of products, processes,
   and procedures
Audit
Quality education

- Quality improvement

- Consumer affairs

- Product safety

The company shall produce cost of quality reports in accordance with the comptroller's procedure and will create regular quality status reports for presentation to all management personnel. Standard practices to support the details of all activities mentioned in this policy have been prepared.

SOME THOUGHTS ON QUALITY

A lot of people seem to think that God was the first quality professional, and that those who have followed Him in the business of judging what is good and what is not good do so by divine right. They know that there are two kinds of people, the good and the bad, and that the good get to decide which is which. The purpose of having an independent objective quality department is to get away from this kind of thinking – to limit such choices to those who have nothing to gain from the decision.

Quality organization is not very complicated, but establishing a good quality operation can be. If something is easy to understand and makes sense, and yet isn't always done, there has to be a reason for not doing it. There are two possibilities: (1) Management doesn't trust anyone else to make the decisions about quality. (2) Management doesn't understand the value of a good quality operation.

I prefer to think that the second is the usual one. Certainly companies who have given the subject some thought get along well with their quality departments.

Speaking about giving the quality business some thought, I feel it is time to discard a lot of the useless appendages that have made quality management difficult to understand. The word "quality" is good enough to stand by itself. We should eliminate "control," "assurance," and other modifiers that too often accompany it. These identify relatively insignificant and minute differences in approach.

The term "quality assurance" came into being during the first frantic missile years so a few astute individuals could move into higher salary brackets and at the same time be involved in more dignified work. They were soon peering over shoulders, rather than making quality happen. Certainly I have no objection to a little nest feathering, but it is possible to make an excellent living actually doing the job of quality rather than just auditing to find out why it wasn't done.

There is absolutely no reason for having errors or defects in any product or service. The concepts of quality management listed throughout this book, plus some hard, dedicated work, plus continuous exercise of personal integrity, make preventing error a realistic possibility. That in turn makes it realistically possible for the error preventer to become one of the most valuable executives in any company. You can get rich by preventing defects. You can never make much by simply "assuring" or "controlling." Police officers try to keep things under control. Lawyers often work at prevention. You have never seen a rich policeman. There are a lot of rich lawyers.

Think about it.

ORGANIZATION

Quality operations should always report at the same level as those departments they are charged with evaluating. Thus they cannot be bossed by engineering, marketing, manufacturing, administration, and so forth. But more than that, the quality manager must have access, on an ordinary basis, to the thought leaders of the company. The quality manager must be the type of person who can fit into their business circles comfortably. The most valuable actions the quality manager can take for the company involve preventing problems by heading them off and by advising restraint or redirection at the proper time. It is not possible to put this sort of thing on an organization chart, and in fact it is not really possible to direct it. That is why there is a chapter on management style at the end of Part One. Every successful quality program I ever saw was headed by an individual who knew how to communicate with, and even discipline, management groups without antagonizing them. Successful quality managers know that the way to make people quality conscious is to make them comfortable with the concepts of quality, and show them how to recognize what they can receive from loyalty to the concept. That art must be practiced in most functions. But quality is unique in that all the successes as well as failures are caused by people in other operations. The product or service is quality because of other people's fingers and minds, and the quality managers must be able to work with those people in order to handle the function properly.

The difficult jobs of management are generally considered those having to do with profit and loss of money, and responsibility for same. Headhunters look for operating people who "turn companies around," and who maximize profits. And of course there are people who do those things. There are also people who do the opposite.

What the headhunters and business writers don't recognize is that the functional jobs are what really make that sort of thing happen or not happen. Functional management is much more difficult than operations. Operations is a matter of ordering functional people around. In twenty-five years of functional management, I can count the useful directions I have received from operation types on one finger. How's that for a positive, endearing attitude?

QUALITY DEPARTMENT FUNCTIONS

Product Acceptance

Inspection. The base of every quality program is data collected through visual and mechanical inspection which permits evaluation of product or service status. Data can be the result of housekeeping evaluation in hotel rooms, a check of soldering, inspection of machined parts, or any of a thousand examinations. Each measurement has three things in common. First, they are planned evaluations conducted in a planned manner for a planned reason; second, they are conducted by professionally trained inspection personnel; and third, the inspection personnel are organizationally separate from those operations they are inspecting. Uncertainty and Awakening will give you the story that the inspectors should report to manufacturing so they "will have the tools to do the job." Actually this only gives them the tools to control the *acceptance* of the product, whether it is any good or not. Inspectors who report to line supervisors receive no professional training. They serve as sorters, go-fers, and general flunkeys. As a result, most inspection operations set up a separate quality control group to audit results. This group always finds 10 percent defectives that the inspector missed because he or she was not properly trained, informed, and led. An inspector is not a true inspector unless the inspection is independent and last.

Testing. Part of the acceptance function is accomplished with electronic or mechanical test equipment used to determine the functional integrity of the product, from components testing in receiving to systems testing at the end of the line. This function measures the performance of the product at all levels. In addition to testers who do actual testing, this function employs test engineers who assist in developing test equipment concepts and establishing testing procedures. The only purpose of testing is to determine whether or not the product will perform to the basic product specification.

Since testing includes many more variables than inspection, it is subject to more pressure. For instance if the test supervisor tells the project manager that a system has passed testing the manager will say, "Great. Ship it." However, should the report be negative, he will say, "Test it again, Sam." Whenever a product passes, it is acceptable. For that reason the test engineers must write test programs that require exact test results.

The biggest current problem with testing, particularly in electronics, is software. The computerized test equipment naturally requires computer programs that direct, and for the most part conduct, the test. There is no reason why these programs themselves should not be considered products and should not be required to meet the qualification test requirements. Testing equipment and software now represent a major financial investment, sometimes larger than the development cost of the product itself. It is wise to make certain that this important function is well controlled.

Testing itself, acceptance testing anyway, should never be performed by engineers. One time I was responsible for a weapons-system test which included testing the missile, the ground equipment, and the combined hardware. The only thing all three had in common was being behind schedule constantly. Finally we took all the engineers out of the area, installed hourly paid testers, and instructed them to follow the test procedure exactly until they got a red light. Then they would call the test engineers to the floor to determine if the fault was in the product, the test equipment, or the procedure. Slowly we worked our way through the entire system and got the acceptance equipment and procedures verified to the point where they would accept a good product while rejecting nonconformances. From then on the testing was a breeze, and I learned once again that technical people will never finish their testing if you don't exercise some control.

Supplier Quality

Just about every company purchases products, supplies, or services in an amount that is equal to around 50 percent of their sales. These materials or services entering the company on a continual basis make necessary a dedication to defect prevention and product acceptance that is usually underestimated. Remarkably little is accomplished, except in companies under government or regulatory contract.

The lowest-level purchasing agent can commit a company to expensive contracts without murmur. However, if people want to spend money on brick and mortar, they must go through the administrative wringer. The money is the same. It is just the concept that is different.

In discussing the supplier quality operation I will concentrate mostly on product or material control. But it would be wise to remember that the largest single supplier to your company, the vendor to whom you pay the most money, is probably an insurance company. When we talk of procedural control, it is necessary to think of contracts that go on for a long time and produce things that don't get inspected in the receiving operation.

Supplier quality engineering. I have always considered purchasing to be too narrow a function. Traditionally purchasing's job has been to take an order constructed by some other department and place it. The operation has not usually been involved in whether the item specified offers the best purchasing opportunity. After-the-fact dilemmas like this face quality operations in the usual purchasing situation. The shortest time lag in the operation is usually spent searching for the best supplier in terms of quality, cost, and delivery. Most of the time is spent in product development or conceptual design. Purchasing has little opportunity to do a selection job, and quality doesn't really know how to help them. A tour of potential suppliers, conducting "quality audits," is next to useless. Unless the vendor is a complete and obvious disaster area, it is impossible to know whether their quality system will provide the proper control or not. You can only know by being on the inside of the vendor's company. The Quality Management Maturity Grid can be completed only by those who know the company from having lived there for a while. The same type of situation exists with suppliers.

Just as purchasing needs time to identify, examine, and develop suppliers, so quality needs time to participate in this process with them. I have tromped through hundreds of plants on supplier audits, peering intently at calibration stickers, asking questions about control of nonconforming material and doing all the conventional things. All the time I knew that the real answer was behind the eyes of the general manager and that I would never decipher that from what could be seen in a brief visit. The general manager would swear to anything, or undergo any rite, to obtain my blessing. But once blessed, would the manager be true? Or even be there long? Who could know?

The only answer is for the supplier quality people to assist their purchasing friends in getting involved earlier in evaluating the key items that will be bought. Since quality is closer than purchasing to the manufacturing and technical operations, quality people can act as a catalyst to start this process. I wish someone in purchasing would write a purchasing management maturity grid.

Purchased goods acceptance. Acceptance inspection and testing of purchased items can take place anywhere. They do not always have to be done in a receiving room next to the truck dock. With proper planning, acceptance can take place in a supplier's plant, even during an in-process operation. It can happen in your own plant at final assembly. It can be accomplished anywhere in between. All this is a matter of planning and execution. Uncertainty does little but the most obvious receiving inspection; Awakening doesn't do much else; Enlightenment sets up sampling inspections and gives serious consideration to more quality engineering effort in this area; Wisdom is into planned acceptance work, but still believes in the dream of supplier selection by quality audit.

Obviously all acceptance operations are conducted by the same organization that conducts the rest of the quality department acceptance functions. Each inspection or test must be planned with the same technical integrity as the ones on the assembly line. The most important consideration is to make certain that the acceptance is conducted by the terms of the purchase order, not by the terms of some leftover plan. This is important because you will find that half of the rejections that occur are the fault of the purchaser—you. Either the item was not described properly in the purchase order, or the wrong requirements were put in, or the test equipment wasn't coordinated properly.

Quality Engineering

Back when I started in the quality business it was easy to identify the quality engineers. They were the ones with the shirts and ties. Now it is the other way around. But I can remember being required to wear a white shirt and tie for the first time in the plant. I slunk around avoiding my former colleagues for a week until I got over being self-conscious. I'm not really certain what this has to do with our discussion of quality engineering, but it did occur to me as one obvious way that it is different from product acceptance.

Broadly, quality engineering is supposed to be responsible for determining and planning the work of the rest of the department. They should see the overall quality responsibility for the company in terms of doing this here, and that there, to make the whole achieve its proposed results. That means they must decide who inspects and tests what, who collects data where, and what information should be supplied to the system to keep it moving.

Quality engineers should collaborate with design engineering concerning a new product's performance characteristics and meet with manufacturing engineers concerning the way the product will be manufactured. In that way quality engineers can determine how the product should be inspected, tested, and controlled during its life both in and outside of the company. Detailing these requirements, training people to accomplish them, and measuring results are what quality engineering is all about.

Data analysis and status reporting. Each inspection or test brings about two results. First, the product is either accepted or rejected; and second, the measurement itself must be recorded. By accumulating these measurement results and analyzing them, the quality engineer can determine exact and continuing status. The quality engineer assembles the data and then reports it in a form that will be of practical use to everyone involved.

Highly visible charts should be hung in the work areas. If you take the time to explain the charts to the individuals involved, they will relate to them and appreciate their being displayed. People really like to be measured when the measurement is fair and open.

Progress charts and reports allow working-level management to know if their process is being controlled. They provide information on which workers are having problems and which are doing well. Senior management needs accurate trend data to learn when action must be taken. If the quality engineering function doesn't provide such data, it will be out of business. Senior management will let quality work on the future only if it is helping them survive the present.

Corrective action. It isn't what you find, it's what you do about what you find. All the planning, inspection, testing, measuring, and other activities occurring within the quality department are a waste of time if they don't lead to preventing the recurrence of a problem. The real strength, and value, of quality engineering involves learning from the past to make a smoother future. (That would make a great political slogan.) Unfortunately most people only learn from the past for the purpose of repeating it.

Suppose you have a heart attack, and survive it. The physician tells you that you can well have another one unless you change the basic patterns that led to the first one. Specifically you are requested to reduce your weight to what you weighed when you left high school; quit smoking; alter your diet in order to lower cholesterol and triglycerides; and take action in your personal life to reduce stress. If you have learned from your experience, you will take this preventive action. If you have learned nothing, you will change nothing. Then you will deserve what happens to you.

Today most medical problems, with the possible exception of cancer, can be prevented or greatly alleviated. All that is required are some personal discipline and professional guidance.

Today most nonconformance problems, with the exception of unknown phenomena, are preventable. All that is required are some organizational discipline and professional guidance.

The best sources of information about situations requiring corrective action are observation of actual rejections and analysis of trends. Actual rejections are easiest because the evidence is so obvious. You wind up with a defective part in your hand and people to talk with. Trends are less obvious; they require detective work that may involve lab analysis and other kinds of sleuthing.

Detailed corrective-action experiences are described in Part Two. But I should caution you that people will only tell you the troubles that others cause for them. They will not reveal what they make happen themselves. Also I believe that once you put on a suit no one tells you the truth anymore.

Planning. A modern quality department in a manufacturing operation certainly pays its own way, but up front it is expensive. For that reason it is only reasonable that planning should be a key part of quality engineering. Everything that happens in the quality system must be a result, not a reaction. Many of us sit waiting for the telephone to ring or the mail to arrive before acting. Even the biggest big shots sometimes are "closet reactors," who sit absolutely dead in the water on mail holidays.

Most quality departments formally lay out their obvious planning activities to support such product activities as acceptance, data analysis, product qualification, and others. Often they ignore quality improvement programs, even though the total effect of such "off line" functions is much more significant to the success of the department than any product activity. Nothing can be left to chance. For example, one activity that should be part of each company is new employee quality orientation.

Each and every task must be listed and assigned some sort of action line, even if it is to say that nothing is going to be done about it. Otherwise all the policies, standard practices, and philosophy will come to nothing. Good things only happen when planned; bad things happen on their own.

Qualification of products, processes, and procedures. Every new thing must be tested and proven before it can be used. This includes the procedure for translating sales personnel's orders to a format that can be used in the shop; it includes the new method of programming computer tapes; it includes the new process for plating plastic with chrome; it includes new products; and it includes products whose design has been changed. Very few problems occur in any organization that are not the result of introducing a new and untried change into the life of that operation. The proving and correcting always occur eventually, if for no other reason than to correct problems that inevitably occur. But that is expensive and restrictive. It is better to make the change prove itself before sending it out to fend for itself.

Products must be made to operate in the actual environmental conditions they are designed to meet; processes should be made to show, by test, that their result is in conformance to the requirements; and procedures should be proved to be accurate, understandable, and effective. In all cases these proofs should be demonstrated to the quality department people. I think they should not actually perform the testing because that would require their becoming too closely involved with the results. There is nothing like a little parenthood to cause bias.

Finally, remember that reality is the ultimate criterion. It is one thing to watch a planning director institute a new hotel reservation procedure. It is another to witness actual reservation makers carrying the procedure out.

Audit. Few functions are spoken about more and understood less than auditing. It is often the last refuge of those who don't really know how to run a prevention-oriented life. Audit is the Bat Masterson of business. When you get into trouble, just call old Bat. He'll find all the bad guys and drag them to justice. And even if he fails to find the real ringleaders, you still look good. After all, you called in the *law* didn't you?

Accomplished properly, audit is a valuable tool. It is a planned examination of a function, carried out either by determining conformance to procedures in process or by critical analysis of the product or service that is the result of the process. That is about all there is to auditing. Meticulously done there is no method more fruitful in exposing the shoddy, inattentive, or misguided. The fraudulent are usually too dedicated to be caught by anyone other than themselves or just plain luck. Audits catch only the undedicated, bored, or careless.

A successful audit follows these few basic rules:

- Be specific about what you want audited and against what criteria the audit is to be acomplished.

- Select individuals to conduct the audit who couldn't possibly be interested in the outcome one way or another.

- Brief the audit team carefully and give them time to write a proper report.

- Do not tell them in any manner what kind of results you expect to find.

- Remember that the findings will point only to the front-line troops. The real cause of the problems lies behind the findings.

It is best to train a few key quality department individuals to lead audit teams. Select team personnel at random from a jury list of other operations. Don't insist that everyone on the team be a specialist in the function to be audited. They are guaranteed to come equipped with their own set of blinders. One of the best audit methods is to prepare a "self-audit" that applies to a specific function like environmental quality. Let the operations conduct periodic audits of themselves, list results, and act upon them. All you have to do to check them out is conduct a few measurements of your own that will give you a good idea of their integrity and competence. By monitoring self-audits on a proper basis, you can cover much more ground than by insisting on doing everything personally.

Quality Education. There is a theory of human behavior that says people subconsciously retard their own intellectual growth. They come to rely on clichés and habits. Once they reach the age of their own personal comfort with the world, they stop learning and their mind runs on idle for the rest of their days. They may progress organizationally, they may be ambitious and eager, and they may even work night and day. But they learn no more. The bigoted, the narrowminded, the stubborn, and the perpetually optimistic have all stopped learning.

The only reason I bring this up is that you have to recognize what all teachers already know: some people are just plain not interested in learning anything that will make them have to change. Therefore, quality education needs to be visibly oriented toward the product, the service, and the customer. Actually, of course, it is aimed directly at the individuals involved, but you have to go through the charade.

Quality Education takes three basic forms:

1. Orientation to the concepts and procedures of quality; the problems that have a harmful effect on the product; and the expectations of the customer.

2. Direct skill improvement in such specific things as soldering, bellhopping, computer programming, telephone handling, procedure writing, etc.

3. A continual low-level but concentrated barrage of quality idea communications to serve as reminders and conditioning, to make quality a thought always in everyone's mind. Nothing flashy, just positive ideas that are in good taste and current.

Now obviously a lot of self-improvement goes on in this type of education. And if someone comments on how their self has improved, it is a good idea to support that thought. However, don't put yourself in the business of selling self-improvement.

Quality Improvement.

It is important to list quality improvement in your policy because you must not give any operation the option of whether or not to have such a program. You don't have to do the exact fourteen-step program detailed in Chapter 8, but the operation won't be able to come up with anything better and will end up following that program anyway. Whatever the reason for beginning, history shows that once people begin a quality improvement program they stick with it because they grow to like the results and the newly found internal management communications.

Consumer Affairs

Consumer affairs is a professional quality function. The identification, investigation, resolution, and future prevention of customers' problems are actions that require the most professional experience and training. To relegate consumer affairs to a public relations function is to devalue PR by implying that it is not an honest activity. Asking someone to "jolly" a consumer along until the cause of the complaint is forgotten is no way to handle the situation.

Customers come in two types: amateur and professional. The general public as a customer is unorganized, and acts on an individual basis. The purchasing agent is acting for a company of some sort and is backed by that company. Both require equal protection. Both should be able to reach the ear of someone who is on their side.

The customer deserves to receive exactly what we have promised to produce—a clean room, a hot cup of coffee, a nonporous casting, a trip to the moon on gossamer wings. Whatever it is, real or implied, we must do or make it well. Otherwise our integrity systems concept is not genuine.

There are three basic action phases in consumer affairs:

1. *Prevention.* This involves monitoring advertising claims, taking affirmative action in providing customer information and education on using a product or service; establishing early warning systems to detect any potential problems; and, of course, running a competent and independent quality management system.

2. *Awareness.* Create "listening posts" so customers can reach you to tell you they are having a problem—by letter, telephone, return postcard, any way at all. A return contact must be made within twenty-four hours, and a communication started. Almost all complaints will require only one contact, if you listen the first time. Keep up with

consumer legislation and regulations to make certain your company does not violate the law. For a modest fee you can purchase the services of a newsletter, that will keep you informed. But industry societies, and the quality societies, will be the most active sources of information. Attend the meetings, assist in the work. It will be a good investment of your time. Most poor government regulations exist only because those who were involved didn't take the time to offer positive guidance and suggestions on the best way to legislate requirements or conduct regulation.

3. *Correction.* Satisfy the complaint fully, as quickly as possible. The consumer is not out to rip you off except in the most unusual of circumstances. I have very rarely seen even a hint of such activity. There are much easier ways to rip off the world than beating a big company out of a few bucks. Naturally your legal department should be aware of all your planned activities on a current, but not serial, basis. The system that produced the problem must also be corrected; otherwise you will go through it all again. This is vital.

When answering complaints, do not use form letters; write each person individually. In thinking the problem through, imagine that the person making the complaint is sitting across from you. This takes practice but becomes very natural after a while. Your problems will cease much more quickly when the customers feel a sincerity behind your messages. Consumer affairs, after all, is basically professional quality management and common sense. No consumer affairs person should ever have an office without pasting the golden rule on the wall across from the desk, where it will be constantly in view.

Product Safety

How can you keep your product from hurting your customer or others? Prevent those kinds of problems through planned design reviews, product qualification, and quality control. Don't be unnerved by all the horror stories about irrational jury verdicts and the intricacies of the law. Hardly any of those things occurred because of the original incident. They occurred because someone who had contributed to the problem didn't have enough sense or courage to face up to it early and get a reasonable settlement.

I have never seen a product safety problem, real or potential, that didn't get itself handled with an absolute minimum of expense when it was faced maturely. If you are wrong, admit it, correct it, and keep smiling all the time. Don't let the lawyers, or the timid, panic you. Remember just one thing: there are millions of products produced every day that don't wind up in court. People just want their rights until you try to trample them. Then they want revenge. And they just might get it.

In a way, this whole book is about product safety. The integrity systems concept is meant to produce an organization that, while producing a nice return on investment, doesn't make problems for itself or for others.

Speaking of integrity, let me make a very exact statement. I do not know of a single product safety problem where the basic cause was something other than a lack of integrity judgment on the part of some management individual. Usually the objective was to achieve a short-range goal by cutting corners. The result was a long-range and unprofitable headache.

Product safety is not a legal problem, it is an ethical one.

6

Handling Problems

The Monday morning staff meeting started a little later than usual, but the tone was set very positively before much time had elapsed. Owen Bloody, the chief engineer, began to state his feelings without waiting for any kind of call to order. In fact some of the staff had barely finished settling themselves into their seats when Owen tapped his finger on the table.

"I know this is your meeting, Jane," he said to the general manager, "but before we get started with the numbers I just have to get something off my chest. I got back from the Evansville operation last night, and I can't tell you how upset I am at the amount of quality problems we have out there. No one is doing anything but reworking and repairing all the equipment we shipped them. Didn't we bother to test anything in the factory before it left? We have to do a better job of quality control than that or we'll be out of business. I tell you it is disgraceful."

He turned to the quality manager.

"George, I know you're shorthanded, but how could you let this happen? It's just awful. All those people with soldering irons and drawings and wires all over the place. You've never seen anything like it."

George didn't say a word. He just looked at Owen. Owen

paused and then stopped. He glanced around the room, apparently looking for some sort of reaction. After a moment the general manager spoke.

"Owen do you remember about nine months ago when George and the manufacturing people wanted to hold up the Evansville product and bring the equipment up to the new level of engineering design? And do you remember that you didn't feel it was necessary, and you convinced me that the changes didn't amount to much, and we could do them in the field? Do you remember that I overruled George and we went ahead and shipped?"

Owen nodded.

"Yes I remember all that. What's that got to do with all the defective hardware out there?"

The general manager leaned forward.

"The hardware isn't defective, Owen. It looks just like the design. All the work being done out there is installing the engineering changes that you said didn't amount to much. Every bit of that mess is because you and I wouldn't give the factory a little more time to do the job right. That big "quality problem" out there is an engineering problem. It is our bird that has come home to roost, Owen. Yours and mine. I doubt if George is even interested."

There was a lot of silence. Then the general manager turned to the comptroller and said: "Let's look at the numbers."

*   *   *

No person is so exposed as when that person starts to handle a problem. At that point, as with no other, smooth, civilized veneers evaporate, and the real self emerges. I often feel that way about people who drink. The real person is the one who emerges right after the "buzz" begins.

Many people are at their absolute best when they face difficulty. Many become cooler, calmer, and clearer as problems deepen. Many shine only when there is trouble; many are, in fact, dull without it. Many do not shine.

I think that all of us might do something we could be proud of if we stood alone, between our families and harm, or if our country demanded some sort of obvious sacrifice. But situations are not always so straightforward. The less clear the challenge, and the result, the more complicated the response becomes.

Suppose, for instance, that you were standing on Fifth Avenue in New York watching a parade. Suppose in that parade an honored national figure was marching, someone you personally admired and respected. Someone whom you felt was a valuable individual in our world. Now suppose you overheard two people talking about how they were going to shoot your hero when the parade passed. You looked, and by George, they really did have guns.

Would you tell that police officer over there? Would you tell the secret service agent standing nervously with a walkie-talkie only a few feet away? Certainly you would. You wouldn't want to get involved, but after all your duty would be pretty clear.

Now suppose you didn't know they were going to do this until you suddenly noticed one of them raising the weapon and pointing it. Suppose the potential assassin was standing right next to you. Would you push him to destroy his aim? Would you yell out to alarm everyone? Certainly, or at least probably, you would. It would be an almost natural reaction.

Now suppose you could know, with absolute certainty, that you would be wounded if you did interfere? Would you still do it? Suppose you knew that you would be killed, but the parader would be saved? Suppose you knew that you would become a national hero, mourned by millions? After all, you have to go someday anyway. What would be your choice?

Let's play the fantasy out. Suppose you knew that you absolutely would save this honored person's life, but that you would be accused of the assassination attempt. Your name would go down with Czolgosz, Booth, and Oswald. You could solve the assassination problem, but would be destroyed.

What would you do?

Most company problems don't require such a specific life-or-death commitment. At least not physically. But each human conflict produces winners, losers, and observers. No one is exactly the same after being involved. Each mental or physical action we take adds to our knowledge and alters our attitude. It is said that at age fifty, people have the face they have earned. How you react to problems has something to do with the face you will earn.

When Uncertainty receives a problem, the attack is on. Problems are recognized as the enemy. They must be thrown off the ladder, and the ladder tossed down on top of them. Heavy breathing and stand-up discussions are part of this type of problem handling. If nothing else the actions have to clear a space for the next problem, which is at this moment building a ladder out there in the woods.

People who live in this environment for a while, begin to believe that yelling and screaming are what it is all about. If their rank is not high enough for them to be doing the screaming themselves, they learn to avoid the sessions— and the problems. They learn the art of excuses.

Operations that truly want to handle problems, for the purpose of solving them, must create an open society within their walls that is imbued with the basic concepts of integrity and objectivity. Integrity in this case means the general attitude that "we do things right around here because that is our policy and because it is the right thing to do." That eliminates the possibility of attaching virtue of any sort to deviousness or subversion. The open and straightforward path is the way to get ahead.

Objectivity comes with not placing the blame for problems on individuals. Aim the questions and probing at the job. The job is what failed, not the individual. It may be that the two are imperfectly matched and you have to change one or the other. Either way, the individual has the chance to improve another time, under different conditions.

Going on the premise that the job is the target, we can deal with problems in the system on a straightforward basis. Problems are announced and discussed, and reasons for them are assigned. This assignment carries with it the responsibility for true definition of the situation, for communicating with those who are involved, and for bringing out an action plan with a specific timetable.

Over 85 percent of all problems can be resolved at the first level of supervision they encounter. Of the remaining 15 percent, about 13 percent can be resolved with two levels of supervision, or two different departments, agreeing to change something or act together in a certain way. The remaining 2 percent might require as many as three operations or levels of organization. But they can be solved.

Once in a while you come up with something for which there is no solution. Then you make a judgment and accept the situation, and life goes on. Count on one or two per career.

When the Earl of Mountbatten had the task of dividing India, there was absolutely no way to fairly divide Kashmir between the new states of Pakistan and India. With the agreement of both sides, the English government selected a brilliant jurist, Sir Cyril Radcliffe, to draw the line. The key thing about Sir Cyril was not only that he had never been to India but that he knew almost nothing about the country. Armed with no preconceived notions, he drew a line that, as any line would do, caused disruption and heartache. But it was done, the wounds have healed, and there were no recriminations over the line itself.

SOME CASE HISTORIES

Specific problems require specific solutions. One company had difficulties with problem resolution, performance measurement, and absenteeism, among other things. The real situation was that the supervisors just weren't participating in the Zero Defects program. To help this company solve its problems, I wrote a special set of case histories and lectures, with the provision that they be administered and conducted by the next supervision level higher than the supervisors involved in the immediate problem. At first management wanted the training department to do it, and the source of some of the difficulties became apparent. After some persuasion, my proposal was agreed to. The results were quite dramatic. Everything improved, and the Zero Defects program really took hold.

Although the cases are very manufacturing-oriented, the thought process applies to any company and to all levels of management. They provide an example of how both student and teacher can learn from the same session.

Lecture 1: Supervisory Problem Solving

One of the great challenges to individual supervisors is deciding how to distribute their time. They must fulfill their responsibilities to their companies, their subordinates, and of course to themselves. The demands for attention seem endless: schedule control, employee administration, training, parts availability, absenteeism, meetings, quality, budgets, etc., etc. Sometimes it seems that the day is over before even half the problems have received any notice at all.

Most of us have encountered this problem and have taken steps to correct or eliminate it. Unfortunately, our best intentions often go to waste because of problems that occur out of "nowhere." Just as you are about to take a moment to bring the shortage report up to date, someone runs up with the news that the air line broke at station X. There's twenty-five minutes shot. Just when you think you'll have time to give that new employee a little extra training, you're notified that you have to attend a meeting to talk about how to improve your operation and perhaps even manage your time better. So far the only thing that has happened is that you have lost time.

As experienced supervisors, you know the danger of trying to apply one set rule of time allocation that covers every situation. We all encounter situations that are a little different, or at least we think they are. The supervisor's primary function is to direct the work of the personnel assigned to his or her operation. Yet this primary function sometimes becomes a secondary one because of our tendency to concentrate on "the problems of today." Not only are such problems vital, they are also usually more interesting than the overall system.

Therefore we are not going to say again that the supervisor should be dedicated to spending more time with each person. We have all tried that approach many times. Dedication is not enough. Rather let us decide how we can best utilize the amount of time we have available to us. If we are going to do that, we must determine what we want to accomplish during the time allocated: "What are the goals we should attempt to accomplish during the time we have available for our people and our problems?"

Class Discussion:

Attempt to obtain a consensus on at least eight goals and list them on the blackboard. Encourage discussion by remaining silent for a minute or two. Some goals that might be listed are:

- Get them to understand their job better.

- Try to learn their interests.

- Improve training.

- Find out what problems they are having.

- See how we can help in their development.

- Get them to meet their quotas.

A great number of items might be given by the supervisors. List them under the headings of *quality improvement, performance measurement,* and *employee identification with the job.)*

Resume Lecture:

Now we can take these items one at a time. Let's start with quality improvement. Just what does this mean? Quality means conformance. When we talk about quality, we are really referring to the compliance of the product. Does it look like the advertisement? Does it conform to the requirements? Will it do what the customer has been led to expect? All the effort put forth by the supervisor in schedule and budget control can go quickly to waste if the product is not produced correctly. It is vital that we as supervisors understand this and, more important, that our people understand it.

We all recognize that we need to do a better job in the quality area. Unfortunately, we may not recognize the steps required to achieve this improvement. That is the purpose of our discussion today. Nonconformance is caused by three things in an assembly area:

1. The materials and products supplied for assembly are not in conformance with their requirements.

2. Personnel and/or tools required to perform the job are not adequate.

3. The supervisor has not set high enough standards for employees.

It is not necessary to determine the order in which these causes are affecting your area. All that is required is to take a close look at the defects created, and decide which causes apply.

Let's take an example.

Case History 1

"Assembly," thought Charlie Gordon, "is just making big ones out of little ones. Why do you suppose that we are having such difficulty running a good assembly area?"

Charlie was muttering to himself as he stood, clipboard in hand, near the rework station serving final assembly. He watched as the units moved briskly through the repair process. It seemed like more of them had to come here every day. The whole line was falling behind schedule, overtime was ruining the budget, the repair foreman was yelling for more help. The quality control people were walking around shaking their heads.

Life was not very pleasant for Charlie Gordon. The superintendent had called him in for a chat yesterday. The purpose of this chat, Charlie soon discovered, was to let him know that this rework problem had better get solved and soon. Costs were going out of sight. Did Charlie have any ideas?

Charlie didn't, but he promised to look into it and try to come up with something. So there he was, with a long list of problems and discrepancies before him, staring blankly into space.

"This isn't getting us anywhere Charlie boy," he decided. "You'd better sit down and give this a good think." He returned to his office.

The figures were very clear: 100 units per hour came off the line; 14 of these units required work in the repair station, and 6 needed some sort of touchup in the line. There was a 20 percent failure rate, and each repair usually involved 2 or 3 items per unit.

Reasoning that the place to start was with the defects, Charlie began to review the list before him:

Item	Cause	Defects per hundred units
Missed operation	Workmanship	13
Paint scratches	Workmanship	9
Wrong part	Production control	12
Part failure	Vendor	2
Gaps	Workmanship	11
Misalignment	Workmanship	6

Many other items were listed, but they didn't occur often enough to be significant at this time. Charlie decided that the main item to be attacked was workmanship. Before mounting his white horse, he thought it might be a good idea to make sure in his own mind that the causes listed were correct.

He approached Ann Collins, a line leader, with the question of missed operations. "How does it happen, Ann, that we miss this many steps? Don't the people have their minds on the job?"

Ann responded: " 'Mind on the job' isn't the whole story. You have to look at everything that is put into the classification of missed operations. For instance, suppose there is a shortage when the unit moves through. Instead of stopping the line, we just mark the ticket, and the unit gets pulled off into repair when the part catches up with it. Why they call it workmanship I don't know. We did have a couple of occasions when someone really did miss an operation, but it doesn't happen often."

Charlie was beginning to feel that he was getting somewhere, so he hustled over to talk with the production control supervisor.

"Charlie," said Elvin Walker, "you have been taken. Shortages happen now and then, but not at the rate of 13 percent of the units. Really it's less than 1 in 100, and then it certainly isn't charged to workmanship. I'm afraid that those guys on the line just don't want to own up to their problems."

Charlie was becoming more confused than ever, so he decided to examine another type of defect and see if he could pick up a better understanding. The next highest on the list was "gaps", but he put that aside temporarily because several departments were involved and he could already imagine the story he was going to get on that one. Better select something less complicated, like "paint scratches."

"Paint scratches," said Ann Collins, "occur for one reason—the vendor leaves burrs on the moldings. When we make the attachments, the burr cuts the paint and produces a scratch. You get those burrs off and the scratches will disappear right now."

When Charlie approached the purchasing agent and the

supplier quality analyst, they did not agree with Ann's story.

"Sure we have a burr now and then, but the vendors have been making a lot of extra effort to get rid of them. Look at this lot we just received. I'll buy you a lunch if you can discover a single burr on any part. Why don't you tell those guys on the line to quit hitting the paint with these moldings, and their tools. That's what causes the scratches."

Charlie went back to the repair area just to make sure it was still there. The only thing he had learned today was that no one was causing a problem. If no one was causing a problem, why was the repair area full and getting fuller?

While Charlie is searching for some sort of an answer, let's examine the situation in which he finds himself. It is apparent that no one feels responsible for the defects that are occurring. All the individuals have determined that they personally are not the cause. In their minds, Charlie's responsibility is to let others see the error of their ways and make them start performing their assigned tasks properly.

Yet if no one is at fault, whose mind should be changed? The units are created by individuals, and each has a responsibility. How can they be made to see it? Surely quality improvement has no chance unless the individuals are ready to recognize that improvement is necessary.

Charlie brought the supervisors together: line assembly, production control, quality, purchasing, and industrial engineering.

"All I have learned from my investigation," he stated, "is that I do not understand the reason that these defects are occurring. Each of us seems to feel that we personally are not responsible for them. Therefore, I would like to say that I accept the responsibility, since I am charged with eliminating them. I need your help to do this. So the question before us is: How can we stop me from causing all this repair work?"

He handed them copies of the data and waited for some response.

Ann Collins spoke up first. "I think we have been listing

things as being caused by 'workmanship' too freely. You can classify everything that way if you want to, but it is too broad a term. We should start being more specific and determine things like 'tool malfunction,' 'worker error,' 'part shortage,' 'wrong part issued,' 'training lack,' and so forth. Then each category would be investigated separately to determine the real reason for its existence."

Tim Ebons, the quality control engineer, agreed. "We could do that, but it would require everyone's assistance. It is very hard to get people to agree that their area is responsible now."

Purchasing suggested that they talk with the repair people. "They should have a good idea of what is causing the defects."

They took the meeting to repair. Charlie explained the purpose of the gathering, and the head of repair was only too pleased to be included in the effort. Charlie requested that they start with the defects classified as "missed operation." Some of the items listed in this category were:

- Two parts installed backwards

- One part missing due to a shortage

- Six parts that had one screw or another attachment device missing

- Four units with all the parts installed but with the wires not connected

Ann Collins commented that things didn't seem as clear to her as they had before. She also volunteered that perhaps she had never really understood what "missed operation" was supposed to mean.

They checked out several other defects, and determined that in each case the group did not have a clear and unanimous understanding of just what the different classifications meant.

"It is apparent," said Charlie, "that we will have to develop a better method of communications in this area."

The team agreed. During the next few days each person made a contribution to Tim Ebons, who was charged with putting the analysis list together. As a result a new procedure was developed.

Each defect that occurred more than once was investigated by two members of the team in order to determine its exact cause and the method to be used in preventing its recurrence. Once the assembly personnel began to feel that the team was serious about wanting to eliminate the errors, they began to make very practical suggestions. Soon problem identification, analysis, and correction became routine. The repair area began to have less business, the schedule began to recover, and the operation was on its way to being back on budget.

None of the steps taken were remarkable in themselves; they were usually just common sense. What was remarkable was that the effort could take place so quickly once everyone started working without fear of being criticized for causing the defect in the first place.

Some of the actions taken to eliminate the defects were as follows.

Part installed backwards. It was found that the reverse installation occurred while a relief worker was on the line. (The part in question does not appear to have a different front or back, and only an experienced assembler can tell the difference. This happens very often with diodes in electronics.)

Solution: Engineering was requested to add a directional arrow on the body of the part. While the change was going through, the purchasing agent got the supplier to color-code the front end with a small paint dot.

Result: No further occurrences.

Screw or other attachment device missing. Investigation determined that these defects occurred during the final moments of the work shift. Production control had been placing the exact amount of attachment devices in the assembly bins. However, screws were occasionally dropped or found to be defective themselves. Therefore, the assembler could be short of screws and have no time to obtain replacements.

> *Solution:* Extra fasteners were placed on the line in reserve packages. When the assemblers required additional screws, they could break open the package and proceed. The line moved on, but the broken package became a signal for production control and industrial engineering to reevaluate methods.
>
> *Result:* No further occurences.

Paint scratches. It turned out that the vendors were delivering burr-free parts, but no one had told the assemblers about the change. They had little faith in the moldings from this standpoint, and therefore expected to see some scratches occur. They weren't careful in the installation.

> *Solution:* Line management took great pains to identify the assemblers who worked on each unit so that any scratches could be charged back to them and they could be instructed on better mounting techniques.
>
> *Result:* Scratches dropped off dramatically. However, the most important result was that the vendors, upon being told about the procedure, became even more burr-conscious.

Wires not connected. It's hard to believe this one, but the work instructions didn't tell anyone to connect the wires at all. They merely described in great detail how to assemble the parts. Workers who made the attachment did so only because they knew it had to be done.

> *Solution:* Work instructions were clarified.

Result: Defect occurs less than once a day.

Wrong part. The part involved turned out to be decals. Special units being constructed required decals of a different color from those ordinarily used. Also the assembler making the error was color blind and could not tell the difference between the two decals.

Solution: Assembler was transferred to another operation.

Result: Still getting one or two a day because the frequency is not sufficient to develop a habit pattern.

Gaps and misalignment. An industrial engineering analysis showed that half these defects were caused by unanticipated tolerance buildups in the tools. The other half defied analysis until one of the supervisors noticed that the assemblers in the fitting operation were using a positioning technique applicable to the model from the previous year instead of the one recommended. Questioning revealed that these assemblers had not been part of the training sessions set up for this operation.

Solution: Assemblers were retrained. The industrial engineers were asked to rewrite their tolerance guidebook.

Result: Misalignments have become very rare. Gaps, however, still exist within the tolerances of the original sheet-metal parts. Corrective action is being taken in the stamping area.

CASE HISTORY QUESTIONS

1. Why do you feel that the individual supervisors were so convinced that the defects were not their fault? _____

_____

_____

2. What changes took place once several supervisors were involved in a common effort?

_____

3. Do you think the supervisors had given understandable performance standards to their people? (Discuss.) _____

4. What is there about identifying the real cause of a problem that makes it so easy to resolve? _____

5. What do you think Charlie should do to make sure these problems do not occur? _____
_____

6. What actions should be taken to ensure continuous quality improvement? _____
_____

QUALITY IMPROVEMENT SELF-EVALUATION

The supervisor who wonders how to effect quality improvement in his or her area should ask the following questions:

Do I really understand the cause of the defects that occur? __
_____

What are the most frequent defects occurring in my area? ___
_____

What defects occurring are the most expensive to repair? ___
_____

Do I feel that any of them are the fault of my people or myself? _____
_____

If so, which ones? _____
_____

If not, whom do I feel is responsible? _____

Have I talked with the other departments involved about the defects that concern me? _____

What was their reaction? _____

If I could eliminate three problems, what would they be?____

_____

Do I feel that I am personally responsible for causing any of these three problems?_____

_____

Suggestion:

Select one of the three problems listed and analyze it in depth. Guideline questions:

How do I know the problem exists?_____

_____

What is the apparent cause of the problem?_____

_____

What do the other people involved say the apparent cause is? (Does it agree with yours?) _____

_____

Have I asked anyone not directly involved to look at it? What did they say?_____

LECTURE 2: PERFORMANCE MEASUREMENT

Supervisors like explorers, must know where they have been to know where they are so they can plot the course to get where they want to go. To put it another way: Unless you know how you are doing as you move along, you'll never know when you're done or if you have succeeded. Each characteristic that makes up your project must be considered.

The broad characteristics that interest the supervisor are schedule, cost, and quality. Of course each of these areas can be further broken down, since they are only end results of a total effort. We must be able to identify these component parts and measure them before we can know how our schedule, cost, and quality are doing.

For instance, schedule is affected by such things as parts shortage and absenteeism. Quality will be affected by training and attitudes. Cost will be affected by wages, and repair. Let's list some other items that affect each of these characteristics.

Class Discussion:

Here, follow the same procedure as that described in Lecture 1. Obtain a consensus and write the items on the board under the headings *schedule, cost,* and *quality.*

How many of these items have a dual or triple effect? Absenteeism, for instance, affects schedule by reducing the amount of work that can be done; it affects cost by requiring additional overtime; quality is jeopardized by the possibility of untrained personnel having to be put into specific jobs. There are several other items with multiple results.

What is the point of recognizing the tie-ins? As you will see in the accompanying case history, the supervisor can learn to predict what is going to happen to established controls by understanding the relationships shown in trends. No single measurement is sufficient to provide this knowledge. Using this information is part of the supervisor's technique in allocating time properly. If you know the areas of potential weakness, you can concentrate on them. If you wait until the water begins to pour in through the roof instead of taking action when the first leak appears, it may be too late. Things move too fast. People like to think that they shape events, but in reality it is the other way around.

Proper usage of our time depends on how well we are able to understand events that are occurring and how we attempt to mold them to fit our own desires.

Case History 2

"It seems to me," said Charlie Gordon (to himself), "that the only time the old man ever invites me for a 'friendly' chat is when he has a tough problem to give me. This time I think he has overextended the 'friendly' bit. All I have to do is to show George Thomas why his line is behind schedule. George was my first boss when I came here, and he's probably the most senior supervisor we have. George isn't going to like this. But we'll give it a try. Wonder if I should put on my suit of armor?"

Much to his surprise Charlie was warmly received when he stepped into George's small office. "I'm glad the old man (who was 10 years younger than George) sent you down here, Charlie. Maybe you can help me get him straightened out on this thing."

Charlie opened his mouth to start his pitch, but George was not to be denied. He waved him off and launched into his own analysis of the situation. "My line is off eight units an hour – that's eighty a day. It's running my costs way up because I'm having to work overtime on the weekends to get close to breaking even. On top of that the defect rate is rising, and I've had to expand my repair area. All of this came on us very quickly without any warning.

"Now I know what is wrong, but I haven't been able to make the old man understand. That's why I asked for you to come down here. I've made a list of what has to be done to fix the problem. Now you take a look at these, and then let's talk about what is the best way to present these to our management. If we're going to have Zero Defects around here, we all have to help."

George leaned back to light his pipe as Charlie picked up the typed list. The recommendations were four:

1. Reduce the schedule requirements of the line by 15 percent. (Justification: The people we are able to get today are not interested in doing a good day's work; they are just not able to handle the present line speed.)

2. Retrain the inspectors in order to improve their judgment. (Justification: Inspection is overly

aware of minor defects on basically sound items. They are continually writing up almost invisible marks and gaps.)

3. Reorganize the production control operation. (Justification: Parts shortages are a continual headache. We like to stay at least two hours ahead of requirements, and current parts shortage practice is one hour.)

4. Crack down on the vendors. (Justification: We have had several shortages in the past few weeks that required us to store units until parts arrived. The quality of vendor items has not been very good either.)

Charlie peered at the list and placed it back on the table with a sigh. George laid down the pipe.

"OK Charlie, Let's see how we are going to convince the old man to take these actions. If he really moves in, we'll be back on schedule before you know it."

"I don't think he'll buy it George," said Charlie. "I think he feels that we should have known about and prevented our situation before it occurred, and I'm pretty sure that he won't accept the first three recommendations. He is working on the fourth one, but our studies have shown that it really isn't too big a problem. Perhaps we should take a look at the charts to see if we can determine how we got into this situation. Maybe we can figure how to get out of it if we find out how we got in it."

George obviously didn't care much for this suggestion. He thumped his fist on the table. "Charts, charts! What do they tell you? I don't need them. I can stand near a line and tell you the output just by listening. I used to be in production control, and I know when inspectors are nit-picking. I know all their tricks. What are these charts going to tell me?"

Charlie was wishing he had accepted that offered transfer to Europe.

"Well it won't hurt us to take a look at them will it, George?" he asked. "When we go see the old man, he is sure to want to know how we feel about the current trends. . . . We can hardly say that they haven't even been reviewed."

Grudgingly George agreed, and, after some poking around, his secretary managed to find the neglected charts. Charlie selected the ones that described schedule performance, defects per unit, absenteeism, and shortages.

"The cost charts can be of use to us later, but let's start with these. If we place one above the other we will be able to see what was happening at any specific time."

Both men moved around to the conference table and began to examine the papers.

"Let's look at the schedule performance first. You have been over the 100 units required on five different weeks."

"That's right," said George. "I always like to get a little ahead."

"OK, but look what happened to the shortage and defect per unit charts after that. You know that the parts are programmed in at the specific rate of 100 per hour. When you produce ahead of that figure, you are requiring the issue of parts programmed for the following day and purchased for that purpose."

"These new systems don't make much sense. But what are you trying to say?"

"Well, you'll notice that the absenteeism peaks follow the schedule peaks? And that the defect-per-unit peaks precede the schedule low points?"

"So?" said George.

"Doesn't that indicate that a major reason for your schedule delinquency is the defect rate? When you have defects, you have repair. When you have repair, you have less people available for the line, which places a greater strain on the line people. They get tired, or disgusted, and stay home to rest once in a while. Your total absenteeism is on an upward trend. The way this chart looks you and I will be the only ones here in ten more weeks."

"I think you're trying to convince me of something by

using hindsight. Anyone can say what made something happen after it has all happened. Look at the stockbrokers. I never thought you'd be a Monday morning quarterback, Charlie."

"I'm not pretending that you can know the future just by plotting the past, George. But you must admit that some trends do repeat. Here I think it's a clear case of cause and effect. Let's look at our status today and see if we can determine what is going to happen to us in the next week. If we can predict that, then you'll have to admit that the trend charts have some value to the supervisor by letting us know what things to take action to prevent."

"Now, that's a sporting proposition. I'll tell you what. You write down three events that you think will happen within the next six work days and we'll seal it in an envelope. At the end of the six days we'll list what actually happened, and then we'll open your envelope. If you're right on two of them I'll buy us both dinner. If you're wrong, you help me convince the old man to get a little more practical."

Charlie began to have a mental picture of himself in the unemployment line, but he was too far committed to stop.

"OK," he said. "You get a new copy of these charts every week. I'll take this set and use them to predict what is going to happen next week. We'll put the charts in the envelope."

The agreement was made, and Charlie marked the charts. They were then locked in the file cabinet, with appropriate ceremony. At the end of the next week Charlie and George got back together. George had his new charts clutched to his chest. "Open the file and let's compare. That will give us time to get up to see the old man this morning."

After a detailed comparison George sat back in his chair with an air of amazement. "You hit three out of four, and you didn't miss the fourth by that much. How did you do it? Is there some new technique that I don't know about?"

"No new technique George. Same old stuff. You can do it as well as, and perhaps better, than I can. The only problem you have is that you haven't taken time to study the charts to get the overall picture. I think you have a mental block about them. All you have to do is recognize that the days are gone when one person can keep all the data mentally. In fact, I'm sure you could develop some new measurements and teach us how to use them. That's what our Zero Defects program is all about—prevention. If we can learn how problems happened in the past, then we can learn how to prevent them in the future. I took your charts and listed them in a different order to compare what has happened in the 20 model weeks. I marked the "take action" points with an asterisk."

Charlie and George looked at the figures together (see accompanying table).

Cost Data for Case History 2

Week	Output	Absenteeism, %	Shortage	Defects per unit
5	96	0.5	None	3
6	104	0.5	None	2
7	106	0.4	None	2
8	103	0.4	None	6*
9	97	1.5*	0.2	5
10	97	2.0	0.8	4
11	93	0.4	None	4
12	104	0.4	0.4	10*
13	104	1.0	0.6	8
14	97	2.0	0.2	11*
15	93	1.4	0.6	15*
16	87	3.0	0.8	7
17	87	3.0	0.4	5
18	87	1.0	None	8*
19	92	1.4	None	12*
20	92	2.4	None	15*
Charlie's predictions:				
	84	3.0	2	17
Actual:				
21	84	2.8	2	17

"Now," said Charlie, "the important thing to consider is that, within the limits of your control span, schedule is a result of the other three measurements. Absenteeism goes up and down on its own sometimes, but it can be traced to defects per unit in your area. Defects slow the work, cause frustration, and force people into the repair area and into overtime. If you'll notice, absenteeism increases following defect-per-unit increases, as does parts shortage. You have to take immediate action any time defects start to rise. And if you'll really get behind the Zero Defects program, maybe you can eliminate defects altogether, or at least come closer."

George decided to give it a try. In a few days Charlie was pleased to report to his boss that the situation was much improved. However, his boss gave him another assignment. Seems the planning people were being driven up the wall by all the data requests that were coming from the line supervisors after George had finished talking with them. Would Charlie see what he could do about it?

Discussion Questions

1. How valuable do you feel performance measurement data are to you in conducting your job?

2. Do you feel that you can predict trends?

3. What additional data would you like? Who should provide it?

4. What are your favorite indicators?

5. What specific actions do you take when you detect an unfavorable trend in any of the indicators?

LECTURE 3: EMPLOYEE IDENTIFICATION WITH THE JOB

It is an old phrase but true: "The supervisor is a person who gets things done through people." There isn't any other way. So as we consider our time allocation, we can easily see that one of the prime considerations is our relationship with those who depend upon us for guidance, leadership, and support. In this age of machine technology the supervisor-employee relationship is even more important. As people's jobs become more specialized, they become more difficult to replace and to train. The days of placing a tool in an individual's hand and pointing that person to the job are over. Too much depends upon the interrelationship between the specific job and the specific person.

Many supervisors today feel that their people are interested in the job only as a source of income. They can find "proof" of this all about them if they wish to do so. Such proof is easy to find if you search for it and if you have made up your mind before you start that you will find it. If you start with a more objective viewpoint, you won't find evidence supporting the view that workers care only about salary. Let's consider just a moment. What do you work for, personally?

Class Discussion:

List some of the reasons that the supervisors in the room work, taking care to point out that they obviously expend a great deal more effort, both on and off the job, than is required by their specific job descriptions. The list, after you get past the erroneous chorus of "money," will include such things as feeling of accomplishment, recognition, achievement, personal satisfaction, and security. Point out a few things that people won't do for money, such as hit a friend, leap 40 feet into the air, sell their families, etc. Money is a score-keeping mechanism that tells how well you are meeting your personal objectives. It has not proved very successful as a motivator in industrial environments. (Aristotle said that the purpose of working is to provide for leisure.)

Now if these are the reasons we are interested in working, why should we consider that our employees are much different? I have seen supervisors work many hours without pay in order to get a job finished on time. I have seen them return to the plant, long after their shift, just to make sure personally that something was going right. Why do they do these things?

Class Discussion:

Ask for some reasons, and perhaps list them on the board. Here the answers will revolve around job dedication, desire to complete things they are responsible for, promises that they made to superiors, and just general job dedication.

If all employees had the level of dedication we have just discussed, we would rid ourselves of problems such as absenteeism, lack of attention to detail, and lack of job interest. Perhaps we should examine some reasons why employees often do not have the same level of job interest as their supervisors.

Class Discussion:

Ask for reasons. If the group is with it, they should offer items like: they don't feel as important; their job is pretty cut-and-dried day after day; they don't have the same opportunity to know what is going on that we do; they don't get that much association with upper management; they don't have the same dedication to the company. If you get answers like "They are not interested in progressing or doing a good job," ask them how they know.

Absenteeism, for instance, is usually a good indicator of job interest or the lack of it. One of the responsibilities we have as supervisors is to help employees identify with their jobs. Perhaps there are some things that should be accomplished by management at all levels in order to increase employee job identification. What sort of things should be considered?

Class Discussion:

The items brought up can be categorized under the heading *employee communications.* Where all the items are listed, try to select those that are the responsibility of the supervisors themselves. There will probably not be too many in this category. Discuss this point and try to point out other specific items that the supervisors can do. For instance, the supervisor can find ways of showing employees how they are performing, and give them an understanding of where the work they do originates and who gets it after they have finished. Supervisors can encourage employees to tell their work problems to the supervisor so a way can be found to solve the problems.

In the final equation, the supervisor is the person the employee sees as "the company." The type of work accomplished and the attendance maintained by employees are very much indications of their relationship with their supervisors. That is why some areas have high absenteeism, while others have less. The supervisor needs and deserves support in these relationships, and the comnpany must consider methods of assisting. But in the end, it is up to the supervisor to assist the employee to develop job identification, and it may be the supervisor's most important job.

SELF-EVALUATION ON EMPLOYEE JOB IDENTIFICATION FOR SUPERVISORS

1. Do you know the first and last names of your people?

    Yes No

2. Is your absentee rate lower this month than last?

    Yes No

3. Could you make a listing of your people in order of their job proficiency? Yes No

4. Could you make a listing of your people in terms of job interest? Yes No

5. Have more than 10 percent of your people participated in the suggestion program? Yes No

6. Do your people ever ask specific questions about the growth of the company or its goals? Yes No

7. If so, do they receive specific answers? Yes No

8. Do you feel that you have given them a performance standard that they understand? Yes No

9. Do you show new employees the end result of their work (such as a tour of the area it goes to when they are finished)? Yes No

10. Do you feel that your people have as good a relation-
    ship with you as you do with your boss?   Yes No

Rating (Number of yes answers)

10   Should run for President

 9   Could be Secretary of State

 8   Would make a good ambassador

 7   Should run for vice president

Case History 3

Elmer Currant peered over his coffee cup. His daughter
was hastily making some notes as she finished her
breakfast.

"Got a history report today, Dad," she replied to her
father's unspoken question. "I forgot to make an outline, but
I have a study hall first period so it'll come out all right."
She gulped her milk, waved kisses at her family, and disappeared out the door.

"I don't know," Elmer said to his wife. "Kids just don't
seem interested in their work these days. They wait till the
last minute to do everything and then they don't do a good
job. It's like most of these people we have at the plant now.
They just do what they have to, and don't seem to take much
interest in really doing a good job. Seems like I have to drive
my group harder every day just to get the minimum output.
Things aren't like they used to be."

His wife placed the pancakes and sausage in front of
Elmer and permitted herself a little "I've heard this before"
smile.

Elmer continued his analysis between bites.

"When I first started on the line, there was a sense of
teamwork. We knew that if we didn't do our job, we'd be
letting the other people down. It took everyone to produce.
We were a team. Today everyone works for himself. Why

the other day a part dropped on the floor and two guys walked around it for an hour without making any effort to pick it up. When I asked them why they didn't move it, they told me they didn't drop it. We didn't do that when I was on the line.

"It's just like your daughter. When I had a history report to do I didn't wait until the last minute. That teacher would have killed me. We had to work a lot harder, and we did."

Marilyn Currant stared at her husband.

"Elmer Currant," she said, "I went to school with you for eight years. I happen to know what your grade average was, and I happen to know what your daughter is achieving. She gets almost all A's, and has never had less than a B. She does at least two hours of homework every night, plus music lessons, plus band practice, plus Girl Scouts, plus Youth Fellowship. How can you say she doesn't work hard? I don't remember you doing all those things."

"Well, perhaps I was a little hard on her. But you must admit that things are different in the plant. I remember my first boss—we all worked extra hard for him and for the company. We were always the top area. Nobody cares about that now. You should see our absentee lists. Why nobody ever missed a day then unless they had a broken arm or something. I remember Ev Brown trying to come to work on crutches once just because it was the rush period."

"What do you think is different now, Elmer?" asked Marilyn.

"I'm not sure. They just don't seem to think the job or the company is all that important. Like the fellow said the other day in the management training class, 'They don't relate to the job.' I guess it's just the times, everything comes too easy."

He pushed his chair back and reached for his coat. As he started to the door, his wife asked him: "What was his name, your first boss?"

"Paul Terrace. Why?"

"Where is he now?"

"He's retired. Moved upstate after he left the company

about two years ago. He was manufacturing director when he left. Why do you ask?"

"I was just wondering if he would think everything had changed. You know, I was wondering if he would think that people couldn't 'relate' anymore."

"I can answer that," smiled Elmer. "His retirement dinner was the biggest one ever held around here. People came from all over the country, mostly people with big jobs who had worked for Mr. Terrace at one time or another. When he made his little speech that night, he said that people never change, only situations change. He said that people always want to do things right and that the primary tools of management were involved with relationships, not with procedures." He frowned. "I remember telling you that right after the dinner that night."

"I know," she said. "I was just wondering if you had forgotten it."

As he drove toward the plant that morning Elmer thought about his wife. "I guess I know I have been given a lecture," he decided. "Maybe I have forgotten. But even so, what can I do about it?"

The first task Elmer faced that morning was making out his overtime plan for the following week. To do this he had to determine the hours scheduled, hours worked, and units behind schedule. The discussion with his wife was still on his mind as he completed this routine task. Suddenly he came upon the name of Jane Hampshire and for some reason he stopped. Hampshire, he noted, had been absent two days the preceding week and one day so far this week. What bothered him was that Hampshire was one of the people he had mentally identified as having a growth potential. She was a hard worker, always busy, and seemed to take a real interest in her job. Why would she be taking off?

Elmer got up from his table and walked over to Hampshire's station. "Morning Jane," he smiled. "How are things moving along?"

"Moving pretty well this morning Mr. Currant. We had a couple of shortages on some units, but the equipment came along just now and we managed to catch up with the shorted units and fix them. At least there are two cases where they won't have to go into repair."

Hampshire returned to her task as Elmer stood staring at her. "How," he thought, "can a person that interested in the job take off three days out of eight?"

"Say Jane," he said, tapping her on the shoulder, "if you can find a relief man for a few moments, how about stepping over here? I have something I'd like to discuss with you."

When Jane came over, Elmer asked her about her absences and at the same time offered the comment that he didn't see how a person showing such job interest could be absent so often.

Jane smiled. "I guess I should have discussed it with you before this, but there never seemed to be the opportunity. You see I have been studying nights for a real estate license. The state examining board met last week and I needed the two days to take my tests. This week I took off to attend the oral examinations. Of course I won't know the results for a few days, but I think I passed."

"Does that mean you'll be leaving us?"

"Not right away, but I plan to make my career in real estate and if I get the right opportunity I guess I'll have to leave. I must say that I like it here, but I have to think of my future."

When Jane returned to her job, Elmer began to feel that he was getting somewhere. People wanted opportunity, that was the secret. There was a lot of that around here, no need to go outside. He made a note to have personnel talk with Hampshire. "We probably have real estate people too," he thought.

Armed with this new knowledge he repeated the interview with the next person on his list: Joe Thompson. Asked about the reason for his six absences in four weeks Thompson replied: "I needed a rest so I went fishing. Didn't like to leave the job, but we have to be there when they're biting."

The next individual reported:

"My boyfriend was home from college and we went up to

see my family. We're thinking of getting married."

By this time Elmer was getting a little confused, but he plodded on:

"I had the flu."

"Had to take the kids to the doctor. My wife works and she can't get off."

"All this overtime we've been working wore me out. I needed to relax."

"I had a union meeting, didn't you get notified?"

"My grandmother has been very sick."

"I went for an interview at the college to see if I could get back in next year."

Elmer finally quit his interviews and returned to the paper information. By a quick calculation he was able to determine that the majority of absences occurred on Friday and Monday. He figured that this was to permit extended weekends. However, he noticed that very few people missed two Satudays in a row. "That must be because of the over-time," he thought.

Still searching for some hard answers, Elmer circulated through the work area speaking to his people. He encountered a few new employees whose names he didn't remember and reintroduced himself. But his main mission was seeking information. He asked them questions to determine if they knew what the schedule rate was supposed to be, to examine their views on the importance of quality, and to see what identification they had with the company.

Finding that most of these items were not foremost in the minds of his people, he called the programming and quality departments to ask if they would post status charts in the area. It took some convincing, but that afternoon the charts were posted and Elmer made sure that everyone understood them:

"It's a start," he thought, "but I sure wish I knew how to reach these people."

Although discouraged by the lack of reaction, Elmer continued his discussions for the next ten days. No significant changes were noted, although the absenteeism did improve. In fact the superintendent came by one day to tell Elmer that his area had gone from the number 10 to the number 5 rating in absenteeism in only one week. He wanted to know the cause of this improvement. Elmer couldn't tell him. The super asked him to pass the information along if he ever found out.

Somewhat encouraged but still bewildered, Elmer decided to take a new step. He contacted the supervisor of the area next to his in the line and suggested that they work out a people swap for a few days.

"I'll trade you three of my people for three of your people for a week. Then we'll bring them back. Maybe it will help them get a better idea of the whole job."

The other supervisor was not enthusiastic about the exchange, but agreed to try it if the super agreed. The super started to question Elmer, but changed his mind and told him to go ahead.

The operation went smoothly. The employees seemed to obtain a better understanding of the results of their work on the one hand and the difficulties of total assembly on the other. In fact, they started to volunteer for the exchanges.

Elmer's absenteeism began to drop even further, and, even more remarkably, the amount of rejections decreased dramatically. Schedule delinquencies began to disappear.

Elmer also found that his workers began to seek him out, to discuss their problems and ambitions. Several who he had felt were listless workers indicated their desire to enter supervisor training, and he was able to send a few others to career guidance discussions in personnel.

When the super invited Elmer to his office to explain the change in his area to other managers, Elmer found it hard to explain just what *had* happened. He listed all the activities he had instigated and reviewed the results. But he could not say which one seemed to do the job.

"It was all of them, Elmer," said the super. "I think they are responding to the attention and the genuine interest you have given them. We are going to give you some support in this area. I think we have been so busy doing the job one day at a time that we have forgotten to establish the proper relationships with our people."

CASE HISTORY QUESTIONS

1. Do you think the super's analysis of Elmer's success was correct?

2. What support actions could be taken?

3. Do you feel such relationships are important?

4. Why did exchanging operators cause improvement?

5. Why did the actions Elmer took make people feel more necessary?

6. What other actions do you think could be taken by the supervisor?

7

Cost of Quality

Let's eavesdrop on the Management Monthly Status Review of our favorite company. The comptroller is providing his overview:

"Inventory increased $270,358 this month for a total of $21,978,375.18. This is still $9981 below budget, but I think it requires a good look because the rate of increase is getting steeper."

"Good point," says the boss, who then directs purchasing to see if they are bringing material in quicker than needed and asks material control to give him a detailed report on in-process versus finished-goods inventory.

"Sales are directly on budget except for the hotel operation, where occupancy is falling off. During the week occupancy is running 98 percent, but this is dragged down by the weekend rate of 35 percent."

"Hmmm," says the boss. "Marketing better get hopping on putting together some weekend specials. 'Take the little lady away from it all' sort of thing. Give them a special rate and a bottle of bubbly. That should take care of it."

"Employee compensation is overbudget. We've been paying too much overtime in the foundry and electronic test operations. This is caused by delinquent schedules in the assembly group. They got 2 days late last month and haven't been able to catch up." "Production," frowns the boss, "hasn't been paying enough attention to scheduling. I think it's all due to that new and expensive computer operation. Set up a task team to find out what's wrong and give me a daily report."

"Our quality is falling off—we've had several customer complaints."

"There's no excuse for low quality. The quality department has to get on the ball," growls the boss. "Maybe we need a new quality manager. I want high quality. Meeting adjourned."

Now you'll notice that everything in the above report is quite precise, even down to the last 18 cents of inventory. All things are measured, evaluated calmly, and dispositioned. All, that is, except quality, which is merely "falling off." How come that portion of the company is not reported in numbers? Why is it left dangling in midair? Why is the quality manager suddenly considered inadequate when the other functional managers who have troubles are not? Why wasn't he there?

How come there wasn't a report on *quality*? Something like this:

"Our receiving inspection rejection rate has climbed from 2.5 to 4 percent in the last month. This is due to purchase orders on standard hardware not calling out the proper plating requirements. Printed circuit board rejections have risen from 4 to 6 percent due to untrained assemblers being placed on the line. Production has pulled them back for training. Customer returns have dropped from 3 to 1.2 percent, but this has cost us $35,491 in overtime due to the additional testing required. An engineering error was responsible for the defect. Changes have been issued and the problem will be corrected by the 18th of next month. The cost of quality is running at 6.1 percent of sales, and we plan to meet the year-end objective of 5.9 percent."

"Great," beams the boss. "As long as we can find these situations early and take action, we will be able to have confidence in our conformance. Quality is doing a fine job."

Quality is free, but no one is ever going to know it, if there isn't some sort of agreed-on system of measurement. Quality has always suffered from the lack of an obvious method of measurement in spite of the fact that such a method was developed by General Electric in the 1950s as a tool for determining the need for corrective action on a specific product line. I remember a case history in a course I took that compared two product lines using the cost of quality as the basis of comparison.

The quality profession, however, clings to the very management concepts that allow them to be inadequate, so cost-of-quality measurement was never really implemented except by a radical here and there. The first instance of using a companywide quality measurement, actually calculated and reported by the comptroller was probably in the ITT program we instituted in the mid-60s.

By bringing together the easily assembled costs like rework, scrap, warranty, inspection, and test, we were able to show an accumulation of expense that made the line management listen to us. This led us to install more sophisticated quality management programs, which uncovered costs in areas such as change notices, installation, and supplier in-plant operations. At present we are learning how to measure "service" costs of quality. This applies not only to operations like insurance or hotels, where there are no milling machines or printed circuit assembly areas, but to manufacturing plants themselves. It took a long time to get around to the realization that half the people in the most manufacturing of manufacturing plants never touch the product. And of course, as individuals we are all service people. Unless we are blood donors—then we are manufacturing plants.

A detailed explanation of how to use the cost of quality to get an improvement team moving is given in Chapters 10 and 11. Here I cover some general details on the things that go into the cost of quality (hereafter often referred to as COQ).

All you really need is enough information to show your management that reducing the cost of quality is in fact an opportunity to increase profits without raising sales, buying new equipment, or hiring new people. The first step is to put together the fully loaded costs of (1) all efforts involved in doing work over, including clerical work; (2) all scrap; (3) warranty (including in-plant handling of returns); (4) after-service warranty; (5) complaint handling; (6) inspection and test; and (7) other costs of error, such as engineering change notices, purchasing change orders, etc. It is normal to obtain only one-third of the real cost the first time you try it.

Many quality management people start out with the thought that it is a good thing for them personally if the company has a very low figure for cost of quality. They tend to come up with readings like 1.3 percent of sales. Then they run to the boss for applause. A few years later their successor finds that it is really 12.6 percent of sales and embarks on a well-rewarded campaign to reduce this needless waste. The first person just refused to understand that the cost of quality has little to do with the operation of the quality department.

To make the total calculation more understandable to other managements it is a good idea to relate it to a significant base. Most people use a percent of sales. However, if you are in a company where there are unusually high costs of distribution like the food industry, you may want to measure COQ as a percentage of cost of sales, or just plain manufacturing costs. In insurance, banks, hotels, and similar businesses the cost of operations makes a good base. What is really important is that the number be something that quality management can use to communicate the importance of the concept. That is what the whole business of COQ is all about.

Many managers wait, and fiddle, and never really do get a workable COQ system installed. They collect endless lists and classifications of things that should be considered. They are too concerned with trying to obtain an exact cost figure, and don't really understand the reason for doing the calculation in the first place.

All this just delays the rest of their program. As I said, the purpose of calculating COQ is really only to get management's attention and to provide a measurement base for seeing how quality improvement is doing. If managers spend all their time getting ready and attending endless conferences searching for the secret, they will be disappointed.

Once an operation knows its COQ, or a good approximation, goals for reducing that cost can be set. Ten percent a year is a good, attainable goal that people can relate to. As you go along, and become more adept in determining things that belong in the COQ, you will find the base number growing. This means that you must go back and apply this information to figures obtained in the past if you want apples to look like apples.

All calculations should be produced by the accounting department; that ensures the integrity of the operation. Naturally, they are going to ask you for a list of those costs which must be included. The following list should be of some help, although you will have to add any items that are unique to your business. These three categories should be sufficient at first; don't search for additional details until you absolutely need them. That is what creates bureaucracy.

Prevention Costs

Prevention costs are the cost of all activities undertaken to prevent defects in design and development, purchasing, labor, and other aspects of beginning and creating a product or service. Also included are those preventive and measurement actions conducted during the business cycle. Specific items are:

Design reviews
Product qualification
Drawing checking

Engineering quality orientation
Make Certain program
Supplier evaluations
Supplier quality seminars
Specification review
Process capability studies
Tool control
Operation training
Quality orientation
Acceptance planning
Zero Defects program
Quality audits
Preventive maintenance

Appraisal Costs

These are costs incurred while conducting inspections, tests, and other planned evaluations used to determine whether produced hardware, software, or services conform to their requirements. Requirements include specifications from marketing and customer, as well as engineering documents and information pertaining to procedures and processes. All documents that describe the conformance of the product or service are relevant. Specific items are:

Prototype inspection and test
Production specification conformance analysis
Supplier surveillance
Receiving inspection and test
Product acceptance
Process control acceptance
Packaging inspection
Status measurement and reporting

Failure Costs

Failure costs are associated with things that have been found not to conform or perform to the requirements, as well as the evaluation, disposition, and consumer-affairs aspects of such failures. Included are all materials and labor involved. Occasionally a figure must be included for lost customer credibility. Specifics are:

Consumer affairs
Redesign
Engineering change order
Purchasing change order
Corrective action costs
Rework
Scrap
Warranty
Service after service
Product liability

Once you and the comptroller have calculated the COQ for your operation, the next step is to figure out what to do with it. This calculation is the only key you will ever have to help your company properly implement quality management. Seize an opportunity and make a speech like the following:

A prudent company makes certain that its products and services are delivered to the customer by a management system that does not condone rework, repair, waste, or nonconformance of any sort. These are expensive problems. They must not only be detected and resolved at the earliest moment, they must be prevented from occurring at all. To give you an idea of how expensive these problems are, let me show you some of the actual costs we are incurring at this moment. (At this point, show them.)

To remove these costs and to prove that quality is free, we must implement our quality management system to its fullest. That way we can turn what is sometimes considered a necessary evil into a profit center. Our cost of quality is now X percent of sales. It only needs to be Y percent of sales. The difference is pretax profit.

Thank you.

Used as a management tool for the purpose of focusing attention on quality management the COQ is a positive blessing and serves a unique purpose. Used as an accounting measurement, like the calculation of nuts-and-bolts inventory, it becomes a useless pain. When the concern becomes which operation has come up with the most accurate figures, the purpose of keeping the figures gets lost. It is like someone on a tight budget keeping neat records of overspending. Make certain you keep your eye on the true reason for the calculation. Don't get lost in statistical swamps.

8

Quality Improvement Program

The most difficult lesson for the crusader to learn is that real improvement just plain takes a while to accomplish. The urgency of the need, the obviousness of the cause, and the clarity of the solution have little to do with getting things straightened out.

That is why government programs almost always fail and are scrapped whenever a new administration takes over. The disappointment and disillusionment of the previous administrator are all too obvious. The administrator blames a lack of funds, cooperation, timing, or whatever for the failure. Yet no matter what the program was, or however well it was directed, its success potential hinged on events entirely separate from the executive's efforts.

Quality improvement programs have similar problems. Because quality improvement sounds like such a great idea, and because it is usually so necessary, managers often feel that merely announcing its conception is the signal for arranging a victory dinner.

I have yet to attend a quality meeting where someone didn't comment to me that they had been unable to "really reach their management," or "get the people motivated," in order to put quality improvement over the top. They claim that they have taken the actions any well-oriented professional would expect, and yet they are disappointed. Those colleagues who have faithfully implemented the fourteen-step quality improvement program worry about an inevitable falloff in "enthusiasm," and search for new means of keeping the program on a high intensity level.

Each time I hear these things I am shocked. I am always surprised that they are surprised. Why should quality be different from the real world? After all, the method of preventing smallpox had been discovered and tested many years before the devastation of plagues ceased. Why wouldn't people take the necessary steps to protect themselves from such a painful and ugly disease? Why did they ignore the simple and inexpensive act of vaccination in the face of absolute evidence that it worked? Why do people continue to smoke tobacco when even the tobacco companies admit it is a clear danger? I smoked for thirty years, enjoying every puff, before being forced to quit. Now that I am free I recognize what a truly messy business smoking is and am not tempted to return to it. But that may be hindsight. Basically, we are slow to change because we reject newness. The world is a complicated and unsettled place. Each individual treasures the few things he or she can depend upon. "Perhaps it is better to take my chances on the pox rather than go over and let these strange people scratch me." If you think this is old-fashioned, just consider how much difficulty the government has had in getting people to take flu shots. Why? Well, for one thing we know for a fact that the flu shot is going to make us ill for a while. And we might not catch the flu even if we don't get the shot (particularly if everyone else takes it).

Take another example: urban redevelopment. It has cost more money than any domestic program in the history of the United States except defense. However, you could say that both operations have similar effects: the subjugation of cities and their populations. The difference is in the location of the cities.

Obviously the goals of urban redevelopment are above reproach. Tear out the old and inefficient and replace it with the new and efficient. Create jobs in the process and improve our way of life. Very rarely has that happened. Poor people have been uprooted, middle-class people have fled the cities, and the urban patterns built up by centuries of slow development and real living have been destroyed in a few years. Whose fault has it been? Not the politicians—they really didn't have time to do it right because they had to get reelected or they had to spend this year's budget this year.

There is always some reason given for failure, but it is rarely the real one. The real one is that you have to lead people gently toward what they already know is right. Otherwise they just will not cooperate. If you have any doubts, ask those who have tried to stamp out the "adult entertainment" sections in cities, assuming that the population is against such things. But the basic assumption is wrong. The population isn't against adult entertainment. It just doesn't want it next door. After all, nothing lives unless the people support it. It is not the "kooks" who support such enterprises, it is real people with real money.

The most practical way to establish your frame of reference when you decide to start an improvement program is to put it in very personal terms. Pretend that you are a company. Presumably you know yourself well enough to know how you will react under certain circumstances. Then announce to yourself that for your own good you must take up a new sport. Let us say that you have selected golf. Millions of people play the game, there are courses everywhere, and there is probably more information available about the details of this sport than any other. Perhaps someone has even written a book on the fourteen steps of golf improvement through defect prevention. In that case it is only necessary to announce your commitment, agree upon the measurement criteria, and go forth to meet your goals. Maybe you can even have some banners made in order to "motivate" yourself.

You could set up goals based on improvement, and could reward yourself for achievement. But it is going to take a while. There is a lot more to golf than having the equipment and the intent. You must work hard at it, and you must stay at the wheel for a long time, if you ever want to play a really good game of golf.

A company quality improvement effort has a lot of the same elements. It must be well thought out, and it must be implemented according to a plan, over a long period of time. It requires a "culture" change; it must become part of your life-style. And it requires that you never relax your attention. You have to stay at it continually.

You as a manager have an obligation to demand continual quality improvement from your operation, whether you are in the accounting business or a machine shop. You as a manager have an obligation to provide thoughtful and imaginative leadership. What you put out is what you get back.

It is not possible to take shortcuts in an attempt to keep from involving yourself. Everyone can tell whether or not you are being sincere. Experiments in "job enrichment" have shown this clearly. The technique of having one group of individuals completely assemble a car, in order to build their pride in their work, did not noticeably improve quality, interest, or productivity. The people knew they were being used.

People who have to put improvement programs of any kind into their company always feel that others are not for it. This is entirely normal, and reflects the natural shyness of the organization bird. We don't really like to get out front with too much unless we are absolutely certain it will be properly received. But my experience has been that improvement efforts, properly explained, are always received correctly. It's the "proper explanation" that takes some effort. So in searching for a way to convince the quality manager at ITT, I came up with the Quality Management Maturity Grid. The Grid has its own uses, as described in the previous chapters. But in the case of the quality improvement program it is even more important just for itself. The question you have to ask yourself is: "What would the boss, and the rest of the managers who report to him or her, have to do to convince you that they really want a quality improvement program?" The answer, of course, is that they would have to convince you that they personally feel the need for improvement in the operation. And that is what you use the Grid for. Send them a copy, ask them to read it, and then go see them to discuss it. Have each of them rate the company as they see it according to the Grid. Don't be too heavy with them. If they think something is Wisdom and you think it is Awakening, don't argue too much. Just leave room for improvement.

Once you have discussed all their judgments on an individual basis, you can bring them together to discuss the overall program (which is spelled out in the case history presented in Chapter 10 and 11, which thoroughly covers the installation of a quality improvement program). And if anyone is reluctant, you can point out that their personal evaluation showed the need for improvement.

At this time it is a good idea to move right into the basics of quality. Help them to understand what real quality means, emphasizing the absolutes of quality management:

- Quality means conformance, not elegance.

- There is no such thing as a quality problem.

- There is no such thing as the economics of quality; it is always cheaper to do the job right the first time.

- The only performance measurement is the cost of quality.

- The only performance standard is Zero Defects.

Explain the Zero Defects concept (see Chapter 10). Have them take the test, and leave out nothing. Answer all their questions, and keep it all simple and untechnical. Tell them again that quality is free.

They really want to believe, and they really want it to happen. But their life is one continual scene of people bringing them plans and schemes that will help them succeed, cut costs, fly to the moon, and a thousand other things. Like you, they know that most things don't work like they are supposed to work.

The main task you have at this key moment is to show them that the program has worked for other companies and it will work for yours, if they participate. But you also have to help them understand that although there will be instant improvement as soon as you start the effort, it will be a long while before it becomes permanent. It is hard and rewarding work. It will bring recognition to all of them.

As for yourself, remember that the product that you are selling, and they are buying, is quality improvement. The result of quality improvement is improved everything else, from sales to absenteeism. But it is a result. So don't tie in a bunch of marketing motivation activities, the blood bank, the savings bond drive, or the annual barbeque. Keep quality improvement in the front of your mind each time a decision has to be made.

THE FOURTEEN STEPS

Step One: Management Commitment

Action. Discuss the need for quality improvement with management people, with an emphasis on the need for defect prevention. There are plenty of movies, visual aids, and other material available to support this communication. (Do not confuse "communication" with "motivation." The results of communication are real and long-lasting; the results of motivation are shallow and short-lived.) Prepare a quality policy that states that *each individual is expected to "perform exactly like the requirement or cause the requirement to be officially changed to what we and the customer really need."* Agree that quality improvement is a practical way to profit improvement.

Accomplishment. Helping management to recognize that they must be personally committed to participating in the program raises the level of visibility for quality and ensures everyone's cooperation so long as there is some progress.

Step Two: Quality Improvement Team

Action. Bring together representatives of each department to form the quality improvement team. These should be people who can speak for their department in order to commit that operation to action. (Preferably, the department heads should participate—at least on the first go-around.) Orient the team members as to the content and purpose of the program. Explain their role—which is to cause the necessary actions to take place in their department and in the company.

Accomplishment. All the tools necessary to do the job now are together in one team. It works well to appoint one of the members as the chairman of the team for this phase.

Step Three: Quality Measurement

Action. It is necessary to determine the status of quality throughout the company. Quality measurements for each area of activity must be established where they don't exist and reviewed where they do. Quality status is recorded to show where improvement is possible, where corrective action is necessary, and to document actual improvement later on.

Nonmanufacturing measurements, which are sometimes difficult to establish, might include the following:

Accounting:
   Percentage of late reports
   Computer input incorrect
   Errors in specific reports as audited

Data processing:
   Keypunch cards thrown out for error
   Computer downtime due to error
   Rerun time

Engineering:
Change orders due to error
Drafting errors found by checkers
Late releases

Finance:
Billing errors (check accounts receivable overdues)
Payroll errors
Accounts payable deductions missed

Hotel front desk:
Guests taken to unmade rooms
Reservations not honored

Manufacturing engineering:
Process change notices due to error
Tool rework to correct design
Methods improvement

Marketing:
Contract errors
Order description errors

Plant engineering:
Time lost due to equipment failures
Callbacks on repairs

Purchasing:
Purchase order changes due to error
Late receipt of material
Rejections due to incomplete description

There are innumerable ways to measure any procedure. The people doing the work will respond with delight to the opportunity to identify some specific measurements for their work. If a supervisor says her area is completely immeasurable, she can be helped by asking how she knows who is doing the best work, how she knows whom to keep and whom to replace.

Accomplishment. Formalizing the company measurement system strengthens the inspection and test functions and assures proper measurement. Getting the paperwork and service operations involved sets the stage for effective defect prevention where it counts. Placing the results of measurement in highly visible charts establishes the foundation of the entire quality improvement program.

Step Four: Cost of Quality Evaluation

Action. Initial estimates are likely to be shaky (although low), and so it is necessary now to get more accurate figures. The comptroller's office must do this. They should be provided with detailed information on what constitutes the cost of quality. The cost of quality is not an absolute performance measurement: it is an indication of where corrective action will be profitable for a company. The higher the cost, the more corrective action that needs to be taken.

Accomplishment. Having the comptroller establish the cost of quality removes any suspected bias from the calculation. More important, a measurement of quality management performance has been established in the company's system.

Step Five: Quality Awareness

Action. It is time now to share with employees the measurements of what nonquality is costing. This is done by training supervisors to orient employees, and by providing visible evidence of the concern for quality improvement through communication material such as booklets, films, and posters. Don't confuse this with some get-motivated-quick scheme. It is a sharing process, and does not involve manipulating people. This is an important step. It may be the most important step of all. Service and administrative people should be included just like everybody else.

Accomplishment. The real benefit of communications is that it gets supervisors and employees in the habit of talking positively about quality. It aids the process of changing, or perhaps clarifying, existing attitudes toward quality. And it sets the basis for the corrective-action and error-cause-removal steps.

Step Six: Corrective Action

Action. As people are encouraged to talk about their problems, opportunities for correction come to light, involving not just the defects found by inspection, audit, or self-evaluation, but also less obvious problems—as seen by the working people themselves—that require attention. These problems must be brought to the supervision meetings at each level. Those that cannot be resolved are formally passed up to the next level of supervision for review at their regular meeting. If a specific functional area does not hold such meetings, the team should take action to establish them in that department.

Accomplishment. Individuals soon see that the problems brought to light are being faced and resolved on a regular basis. The habit of identifying problems and correcting them is beginning.

Step Seven: Establish an Ad Hoc Committee for the Zero Defects Program

Action. Three or four members of the team are selected to investigate the Zero Defects concept and ways to implement the program. The quality manager must be clear, right from the start, that Zero Defects is *not* a motivation program. Its purpose is to communicate to all employees the literal meaning of the words "zero defects" and the thought that everyone should do things right the first time. This must be transmitted to every member of the team. In particular, the ad hoc group should seek out ways to match the program to the company's personality.

Accomplishment. Improvement comes with each step of the overall program. By the time ZD day is reached, as much as a year may have gone by and the initial improvement will be flattening out. At that point the new commitment to an explicit goal takes over, and the improvement begins again. Setting up the ad hoc committee to study and prepare the implementation ensures that the goals of the program will be firmly supported by the company's thought leaders.

Step Eight: Supervisor Training

Action. A formal orientation with all levels of management should be conducted prior to implementation of all the steps. All managers must understand each step well enough to explain it to their people. The proof of understanding is the ability to explain it.

Accomplishment. Eventually all supervision will be tuned into the program and realize its value for themselves. Then they will concentrate their action on the program.

Step Nine: Zero Defects Day

Action. The establishment of ZD as the performance standard of the company should be done in one day. That way, everyone understands it the same way. Supervisors should explain the program to their people, and do something different in the facility so everyone will recognize that it is a "new attitude" day.

Accomplishment. Making a "day" of the ZD commitment provides an emphasis and a memory that will be long-lasting.

Step Ten: Goal Setting

Action. During meetings with employees each supervisor requests that they establish the goals they would like to strive for. Usually, there should 30-, 60-, and 90-day goals. All should be specific and capable of being measured.

Accomplishment. This phase helps people learn to think in terms of meeting goals and accomplishing specific tasks as a team.

Step Eleven: Error Cause Removal

Action. Individuals are asked to describe any problem that keeps them from performing error-free work on a simple, one-page form. This is not a suggestion system. All they have to list is the problem; the appropriate functional group (e.g., industrial engineering) will develop the answer. It is important that any problems listed be acknowledged quickly—within twenty-four hours. Typical inputs might be:

- This tool is not long enough to work right with all the parts.

- The sales department makes too many errors on their order entry forms.

- We make a lot of changes in response to telephone calls, and many of them end up having to be done all over again.

- I don't have any place to put my pocketbook.

Accomplishment. People now know that their problems can be heard and answered. Once employees learn to trust this communication, the program can go on forever.

Step Twelve: Recognition

Action. Award programs are established to recognize those who meet their goals or perform outstanding acts. It is wise not to attach relative values to the identification of problems. Problems identified during the error-cause-removal stage should all be treated the same way because they are not suggestions. The prizes or awards should not be financial. Recognition is what is important.

Accomplishment. Genuine recognition of performance is something people really appreciate. They will continue to support the program whether or not they, as individuals, participate in the awards.

Step Thirteen: Quality Councils

Actions. The quality professionals and team chairpersons should be brought together regularly to communicate with each other and to determine actions necessary to upgrade and improve the solid quality program being installed.

Accomplishment. These councils are the best source of information on the status of programs and ideas for action. They also bring the professionals together on a regular basis.

Step Fourteen: Do It Over Again

Action. The typical program takes a year to eighteen months. By that time turnover and changing situations will have wiped out much of the education effort. Therefore, it is necessary to set up a new team of representatives and begin again. ZD day, for instance, should be marked as an anniversary. Nothing more than the notification may be necessary. Or a special lunch for all employees might be given. The point is that the program is never over.

Accomplishment. Repetition makes the program perpetual and, thus, "part of the woodwork." If quality isn't ingrained in the organization, it will never happen.

9

Management Style

"Management style" may be the wrong title for what I intend to discuss in this chapter. However, it will have to do because "style" is a word that is often used in our culture to describe certain subjective measures of performance.

The concept of executives needing a sort of "flair" first came to light when Clark Gable invested his last $20 for a "sincere" tie to impress Sidney Greenstreet in a long-ago movie about advertising called *The Hucksters.* Since life really does imitate art, all the outrageous actions taken in that film are now routine procedure. Gable got the job, and we got the message about the need for style.

I don't mean to disparage the concept. There is a definite advantage in knowing what you want to do, and carrying it off with élan. It *is* an advantage, say, to be continually poised under fire, to always have a ready and incisive remark, to keep your head when all about you are losing theirs and blaming it on you. It is an advantage, and much of it can be learned. All that is necessary is that you understand the situation we are all in as managers—and understand yourself. You can try to understand yourself by going through a checklist which I will enumerate shortly. Understanding situations requires a recognition of both the state of the times and the responsibilities of management.

Until recently the career history of successful executives was fairly predictable. They spent the first twenty years learning the business from the ground up. They spent five or ten years in increasingly senior jobs, learning broader and more complex aspects of the industry. They spent their last fifteen years running the show, while developing better and more effective ways of tracking the beaver back to its cave. They retired, and were a pain in the whatever to their successors.

All of this was possible only because there was little fundamental change in markets, products, methods, or concepts over the years. Certainly technology advanced at an alarming rate, certainly the unions deftly separated management from some of their choices, and certainly the vagaries of the economy alternatively pinched and flooded the money supply. There were these and other problems, but they had all been written about somewhere. All had been experienced before, in one form or another. The blueprint for coping had been filed. At least one could know what wouldn't, or hadn't, worked.

Each generation peers at its predecessors and remarks that things are certainly different today. This generation can look at itself and make the same comment. Ten years ago the market for an American company was the United States, Europe, and a small part of Latin America. Nobody bothered about the Middle East. Nobody thought about Africa. Economists had three charts: United States; Western Europe; and Other.

Today the wealth of the world is slowly draining off into part of that "other": the oil-rich Middle East. United States companies must sell like mad in order to get some of it back. The new investors are people whose difficult culture is being rapidly learned by those who have property to sell. The really big houses in Beverly Hills, the big new hotels with international clientele, the minority interests in basic industry companies—all are being purchased by this new money. What should modern management do about this?

Ten years ago, who ever heard of currency translation?

Many people still don't know what it is. But if you are involved with a company that operates internationally, you know. This accounting practice requires translating some assets (debt, accounts receivable, etc.) into local currency value each quarter.

It isn't necessary to actually sell the assets, or do anything with real money; you just have to take that local currency figure and change it to United States currency according to the current conversion rate. Then you drop that figure to the bottom line. If it is more than it was the last quarter, you have to declare the difference as income. If it is less, you have a loss. If the United States dollar has softened as compared with the local currency during the quarter, you have lost profit. And there is absolutely no way to control it. You can't plan for it except by creating reserves. Either way, you have lost a voice in the financial control of your company.

Employment, or just plain labor, has changed dramatically and is continuing to do so. In the late 1940s and early 1950s, the great concern of labor leaders was that "automation" was going to destroy the labor force by replacing it with artificial arms and wheels. This didn't happen. The mechanization of assembly lines just lowered costs and increased sales. Labor grew along with the sales.

Now, however, it is beginning to take fewer hands to produce many products. The construction of telephone switching equipment once involved thousands of people who assembled mechanical relays. Now the equipment is solid state. Relays can be grown chemically. Building the product takes less hand labor. The labor costs lie in testing and selecting, and much of that is becoming automatic.

As a result of social expenses (fringe benefits, early retirement plans, etc.), areas that formerly were sources for low-cost labor, like parts of Europe and Japan, now provide only high-cost labor. Many companies making products throughout the world are beginning to find, to their surprise, that the United States is their least expensive producer.

African and Middle Eastern countries are hiring Western companies to "create" instant economies. Contracts are being made whereby a company will build a plant, a town, and an industry for an underdeveloped country. Local citizens will be enticed from the fields, hills, and deserts to learn to work in the factories, live in the towns, and grow into the new century. (Presumably they could then save enough money to retire into the desert and do what they are doing now.)

These are interesting experiments. They offer a great opportunity for "improving" life-styles that haven't changed for hundreds of years. I'm not sure they will provide improved happiness. After all, a lot of cultures have moved from farms to industries, and the change hasn't created contentment. I was raised in West Virginia, where the "factory town" was a way of life. There is no way I would live in one now.

The executive's problem in understanding and utilizing the labor force is compounded by the fact that people are not interested in doing something just because they have been told to do it. Communication has to be established and continually reinforced in order to keep employees informed and participating. Several big corporations found to their surprise that hard-nosed practices involving a lot of order giving just didn't mix with young, educated workers. It isn't enough to design a whizbang assembly operation; you have to help people want to participate in running it.

There are no clear-cut differences among the various levels of an organization when it comes to understanding the purpose and work of the company. No one can be left out. Orders sent out to be obeyed may come back with questions that need answers. And it is the executive's responsibility to see that answers are provided. Personnel professionals are the least likely to give good answers to people inquiring about the quality program. They are usually one generation behind in their thinking. However, that is still at least one generation ahead of most senior people.

Another significant change that requires management consideration is energy. Our modern industrial society has been built on energy, primarily from fossil fuels. Oil embargos, increased prices, and transportation problems have made us finally admit that there is an end to these supplies. Someday we are going to run out. In the meantime our total dependence on these sources has done more to change the economy of the world than anything since the Flood. I personally think we should pay the price to buy their oil and leave ours in the ground until we need it. That way we will have the last light.

Other sources of fuel are available. Each day the sun transports, free, more fuel than we can possibly use. Underground steam exists. I can visualize the day when individual sources of fuel will be available for individuals. It will be like the beginning of the computer age.

When computers first became economically available, every company, university, and government had to have one. The bigger the better. The idea was that every organization would have one of those huge machines that could do everything. Then they could rent time to other people to pay for the machine. This created an information revolution that hasn't quite been handled yet.

New technology now permits minicomputers to do the jobs once handled by the giant computers. The payroll department can have its own computer. The research people can have one. Departmental ownership eliminates waiting, scheduling — and empire building — by people who share the unintelligible language of software. And the price is coming down. Soon every home can have computers tied into their telephone lines and TV screens. Instant information and communication. Pay your bills by telephone. Let your eyes do the walking.

This same pattern can emerge in the energy field. Every home or community center can have a power source taking energy from the sun and distributing it for use as electricity. This means that automobiles can at least do their local traveling on storage batteries, requiring gasoline only for long distances. We can survive and even grow in a world like this, but only if we learn new management concepts.

If you put these changes together, you have managerial headaches that you weren't taught about in business school. You have situations for which there is no precedent. They can be handled, but only by someone who really has a lot of management style. We need people who are in complete control of themselves, people who are able to think creatively and to implement their ideas at the same time, and stay loose enough to anticipate and avoid whatever it is that is lurking behind the next hill.

Some of that style is a function of the amount of potassium concentrated in adjacent brain cells, and that is something you can't do anything about. But a great deal of it can be learned. You can use the following ten-item management style checklist to rate yourself as ordinary, super, or spectacular. You decide what to do with it all.

Listening	Implementing
Cooperating	Learning
Helping	Leading
Transmitting	Following
Creating	Pretending

There are other important characteristics, like integrity and compassion. Vital and fundamental facets of character, they cannot be learned or vastly improved from without, but you cannot succeed in the management business without them. As a matter of fact it is difficult to think of any profession you would want to be part of that wouldn't demand a great deal of integrity and compassion. However, they are not style.

The purpose of examining any aspect of your management style is to determine how to make it work for you. If you want to accomplish what you want accomplished in this complex world you have to be more up than the next person.

You don't have to be unfair, or unanything. But you have to take advantage of the assets you have.

LISTENING

When I did a promotional tour for the book *The Art of Getting Your Own Sweet Way* (McGraw-Hill, 1972), most interviewers were interested in the ten laws of situation management. The list provided a format that neatly fit the time allocated for the interview. It worked out very well. I would not be thrilled at the idea of going through all that again, but it was an interesting and educational opportunity. The law everyone liked best was number ten: Nobody really listens. We all have something to say, and we keep searching for someone to listen to it. After all, if a pearl of wisdom drops from your lips when no one is about, and is lost, it will have no value.

You can pay people no greater honor than to actually absorb the content and intent of what they have to say. Not just the superficial stringing of words together. Most of us are able to handle that much. No, you must concentrate on what is behind the words. Really listen into the transmitter. Is the person in trouble? Does she want help? Is he saying one thing and meaning another? What is really going on?

Most of us wait patiently for the speaker to finish so we can do our own talking. If you doubt this, walk up to a fellow golfer and say, "I hit myself in the toe last week and broke it." He will say, "One time I almost busted my knee." He will not ask how your toe is until much later, if at all. Tell a horror story about something that happened to you in the stock market, or even in the parking lot. Your listener will tell you another, and probably grander, tale.

In spite of this you must listen and question until you are sure you understand the message. Frankly I have to warn you that you will discover a whole interesting new world. Once people find that you are willing to take the time to understand them, they will take the time to arrange thoughts into concepts that are easier to comprehend. You may even create some listeners of your own. Then you can reach a state where true communication takes place. You are actually transmitting, and receiving, real meanings.

Once you have a basis for eliminating or preventing misunderstandings, success is at hand. Nothing is more important than true understanding, and nothing is harder to come by.

COOPERATING

Being part of a team is not a natural human function; it is learned. Participants in a contact sport, such as football, learn quickly that the rest of the team evaluates personal worth by evaluating a team member's determination to cooperate. The player must not only cause plays to be executed, but protect others as well.

During World War II, bombers learned to fly close together so they could take advantage of multiple air defense systems. There was no room for showboating in the air. Basketball players who take shots indiscriminately will not get the ball very often. The hunter who scares the game will not be invited again.

To cooperate with others in accomplishing a task is one of our nobler achievements. It is also one of the more productive aspects of the manager with style. The whole really is greater than the sum of its parts. Synergism really does work, if you will let it. And the more you carry, the more they will appreciate you.

Cooperation does not mean that you have to abandon any personal standards. You can leave one team and join another if yours decides to raid the treasury. Make certain that the team is worthy of you, just as you must be worthy of the team. Expect only the best. Don't settle for less. A surefire way to successful cooperation is to help build a winning team from one that is not doing well. Bring people together;

return to the basics; manage; lead. The same principles apply in relationships with individuals. Those who are known to work with others for a common goal become known as trustworthy people. Trustworthy people acquire no worthy enemies as they go about their labors. That is a great advantage.

But most of all, do not be *un*cooperative. That guarantees that you will be ignored. Ignored managers cannot cooperate with anyone.

HELPING

Helping and cooperating are not the same. Helping involves giving, without direct expectation of immediate return. It is letting someone lean on you without getting to lean back. In cooperating you are both, together, leaning on something for mutual support.

In corporate life, helping has to do with smoothing the road for others, whether they know you are doing it or not. It is being available when someone needs someone; it is putting in a good word for someone who deserves it; it is not putting in a bad word for someone who deserves it. It is telling someone the awful truth, like they have bad breath. It is offering a discrete personal loan without making a big deal out of it.

To help in a positive manner, you must be genuinely interested in people and results. You can't fake this one even if you try because true help is truly unselfish. And, of course, you must have the patience to wait until the individual recognizes that he or she really does need assistance. Otherwise you can cause a lot more harm than good. Help must be carefully thought out, like a Rockefeller Foundation grant. One interesting example of misguided aid is the way alcoholics have been "helped" by their families over the years. By being supportive, by covering up the incidents, by arranging "second second" chances, families have encouraged the victims to become more dependent on the drug, and have actually contributed to their downfall. In the case of alcoholism or other drug abuse, help becomes those actions that force the individual to face up to reality.

In business life it is difficult to show your friends that the systems they are installing are counterproductive. It is hard to let them know that they are on the wrong path. If you are prepared to offer such assistance properly, you can slip into "meddling" quickly. But if you are confident that your efforts to help are based on a genuine concern for the individual, and are not to further your own ends, then the help will be accepted.

TRANSMITTING

More is done about personal transmission, and less is accomplished, than any individual function I know. Speech therapy, personality improvement courses, transcendental meditation, body language—these and many other activities have been undertaken by people in the hope of improving the way they transmit. Usually they achieve a better understanding of themselves, which is what most of these activities are all about, but they fail to improve their transmitting. They don't understand or believe a fundamental truth: you have to have something to say.

I deliberately chose the word "transmitting" for this characteristic because there is much more to conveying your thoughts than just speaking. Your clothes, your physical manner, your weight, your cleanliness, and many other things transmit a lot about you, often so clearly and loudly that the words you choose to say may not be heard at all.

There are three basic transmission actions: writing, prepared speaking, and conversation.

Writing is like putting. Short and straight is best; long and curving is undesirable. Writing helps you bring your thoughts together so that others can understand them. It may be that you produce ringing phrases and memorable content; enough to send armies marching. It may be that stonemasons consider you one of their primary assets, since they are so busy engraving your words on marble walls. More than likely, though, you are like the rest of us and struggle continually to make yourself understood. If you believe that, you are on the way to improvement. Writing is the hardest of the communication arts. When you speak to an audience, you can get a little feedback as you go along. You can detect confusion, boredom, or drowsiness. Reading is a private act, and you can never know if someone understands what you have written unless that person shows evidence of having understood — or misunderstood. Being understood is hard work. But if you are successful at it, you can achieve more than you ever dreamed.

Prepared speaking is a rewarding, and at the same time wearing, communications method. It always amuses me that a really good speech doesn't seem prepared, and yet it takes so long to produce one. Not preparing formally for any speech is the biggest ego trip of all. It is a direct insult to your audience, and they always know. They are liable to march on the stage rather than go to confront the enemy.

In the last fifteen years or so, individual audiences have become quite sophisticated about what to require from those who address them. The exposure to political compaigns on TV, the growth of the lecture circuits, and the discussions on talk shows have opened their eyes. For this reason alone it is necessary that you obtain guidance early in your speaking career. Toastmasters International is not exactly a professional organization, but it offers by far the best method of learning how to be acceptable to an audience of real people. Professional help is advised for learning how to construct a speech, but Toastmasters is best for building confidence and fellowship.

Conversation is the one thing we are all certain we can handle. It is not the best subject for many, perhaps because they feel it requires little preparation and attention. Smart managers listen to themselves and learn how to improve. They learn things like how important it is to look into the eyes of the other person; like when to touch them and when not; like when to not be clever or funny; like when just to remain silent.

All these transmission factors — writing, speaking, and conversing — project a picture of you on everyone's mental wall. What they see is what they think you are. You may feel that you are something else, and may actually not be what is projected. But what appears to be usually is. Think of the people you know who are objectionable to you in some way. You probably think they are doing it on purpose. They aren't.

CREATING

There are those who feel that creative ability is a matter of genetic structure. You either are, or aren't, creative. I suspect that this is a correct analysis when it comes to pure art, and even sports activities. But in the world of management you can learn to be creative.

You can create solutions to complicated problems by being the only one to break that complicated problem down to its basic causes. Once these causes are exposed, a creative solution appears — if you can recognize it. Unfortunately, most people give up before that.

Problem solving is an acquirable skill; many techniques and concepts for learning it are available. The most practical technique, however, is to go ask the people who are involved with the problem on the front lines. Not management people, but working people. I have made a good living for years by walking directly to the test or inspection position and asking what the problem really is. The operators are delighted that someone cares about their opinion. They share with me the fact that errors are increasing because untrained people are being put into the areas; or that the new test equipment hasn't been calibrated yet; or that the people are teed off at the line manager. They'll tell it like it really is and help make a solution obvious. Naturally you should make certain they get any credit that is due, and you must absorb any disgruntledness.

One other source of creativity is to expand on the ideas of others, or to take old ideas and update them. But be sure you pass the credit out; there will be a lot to go around.

The most important aspect of creativity for management style is not to get into the habit of stating your lack of creative ability. Someone might believe you. Probably less than one-tenth of one percent of the people in the world are truly creative, that is, able to develop an original concept from an original thought. It is not necessary to feel left out if you don't happen to be one of that group. They are often misunderstood, underestimated, and mostly alone anyway.

IMPLEMENTING

The most valuable manager is one who can first create, and then implement. So few of these exist that if you find one you should keep it a secret. More available are those who can implement another's concept or add their own improvements to already existing methods. They are worth their weight in Arabian oil rights. Most managers can only follow directions (which is not a bad value in itself, although unimaginative), and real implementers are respected, appreciated and well paid.

Every boss dreams of finding subordinates who can accept an assignment, figure out how to do it, and then come back with the accomplished result: A person able to handle something like: "Get that inventory down to last year's level" or "We need to enter the capacitor industry" or "These waiters are too slow, get them speeded up."

Just stepping up, ferreting out the basic problems, determining a practical solution, selling everyone on it, and then getting it done. No big deal, no special authority, no questions. Just step in there and be Mr. or Ms. Reliable.

Quality improvement programs are like that. Many quality management people get hung up because they want absolute authority—plus a signed commitment that everyone will cooperate. If you could get that up front, you wouldn't need to do any managing. You would probably also be in the wrong place. If they could provide that, they wouldn't need you.

LEARNING

It always makes me wonder when people ask, "What did you study in college?" What difference can it make? People don't do for a living what they learned in college anyway. Management, unless you are in a true professional field such as chemistry, medicine, metallurgy, and the like, is very much a general knowledge thing. The more information you have about everything, especially people and money, the more you can accomplish.

Therefore it is essential to never cease learning. Taking formal learning courses whenever possible is one sure way of learning something. But it is more important to just read and listen. Read everything. Read at least one magazine every day and three or four books a month (on any subject from history to sex). Dig up several good conversations each week. And don't get hung up on the same routine for recreation. Keep alive and uncommitted.

It is not possible to know what you need to learn. Therefore you have to constantly seek out new experiences and exposures. Some of the new magazines, or movies, or cultures may turn you off. But they are real. They need to be understood a little, if only so you can know how to deal with them or the effect they create. You can't shut out the parts of the world you don't like. It helps a lot when you can relate modern actions to those of the past. Just about nothing is new, and almost everything used to be worse.

It is also a good idea to learn a new major activity every five years. Learn to play the organ; take up tennis or cross-country skiing; paint. All these are stimulating and challenging; they continually exercise the learning muscles in your head. It keeps you from becoming that person you know so well who has a negative answer for every new idea and a lost enthusiasm for life. That person stopped learning, probably at about your age. But it is impossible to stop things worth learning from happening.

LEADING

Many times leading is simply finding out where people are going and then hopping out front to yell, "Follow me." Many times it is not. Leaders communicate by giving understandable direction and by setting evident example. Leading means stating objectives in a way that is precisely understood, ensuring the commitment of individuals to those objectives, defining the methods of measurement, and then providing the impetus to get things done. It is very hard and unending work. You have to keep everyone busy. The leader who runs out of jobs for the led to do will soon be replaced by someone more interested in working hard.

You know, of course, all the conventional thoughts about the problems of being a leader: the long hours; the agonizing as to whether all the bombers will return; the problems of choosing between those who are coming up and those who are going down. You will survive such problems somehow.

The thing you may not survive is something which destroys most leaders. That something is a continually growing belief in their individual infallibility, the thought that only they can see the light which is hidden from everyone else. "Why am I the only one who knows how to do anything?"

The cause of this is a constant changing of the rules on the part of the leader. If the leader is the only one who knows what game is being played, then the leader is obviously the only one who can win. Very few people set arbitrary rules deliberately. It is the natural result of a process in which they are thinking ahead in a direction unknown to their subordinates. Since the subordinates don't know the compass reading, they may be thinking equally hard in another direction. The inevitable disclosure of the difference causes a loss of confidence on the part of the leader. This produces hesitancy on the part of the led and everything such hesitancy builds. The result is a disease that paralyzes the organization.

Open-mindedness — an open approach in which ideas are floated and guidelines are proposed openly — is the only cure. A closed leadership does not grow. Both Napoleon and Hitler, who were absolute masters of their political system, left the same legacy. Absolute zero. Nobody picked up their political banner and carried it forward. They had completely shut off all circulation. It was a solo show in both cases, and their programs died with them.

FOLLOWING

It is not easy to be a good follower. Servile — yes. Obedient — easy. But good? That's difficult. A good follower has to want the same results that the leader wants. The follower doesn't necessarily need to have identical goals, but the desire for the same results must exist.

A good follower takes time to make certain that he or she understands the intent of the boss's request as well as the words. Good followers do not "translate" the boss to others, and they stick to their own areas of activity. All this is not for the purpose of restricting effectiveness or curtailing inventiveness; it is merely a requirement for reducing confusion.

Good followers, who want to expand their sphere of influence, get promoted and move into higher activities. They don't spend their time carving a piece out of the leader's cave. They expand into an area where there is little happening, and do it with the full understanding of the boss. Internecine conflict usually accomplishes nothing, except to delay the accumulation of divisible spoils.

The art of following should not be looked on as something to be learned just to fulfill a temporary obligation on the way to becoming supreme exalted rooster. You never, never get away from being a follower. You may reach a level where your leader is a board of directors, or you may become so high that the only remaining leader over you is "the people." But, as you know, the people have a way of reminding political leaders just who runs things.

Study following. Leading will take care of itself.

PRETENDING

This is a skill best left undeveloped. There is always a time when you forget what it is you are pretending to be. If you want to be an actor, be a good one. But pretending all the time is a terrifying management style to adopt.

SUMMARY

Listening. You can convey no greater honor than to actually hear what someone has to say.

Cooperating. You don't just cause plays to be executed, you protect others in the process.

Helping. Let someone lean on you without expecting to lean back.

Transmitting. How you come across to others should not be left to chance.

Creating. Original solutions are a result of hard work in uncovering unoriginal problems.

Implementing. There comes a time when someone has to actually get the job done.

Learning. When you have an answer for everything, you know you have stopped learning.

Leading. Leaders start to fail when they begin to believe their own material.

Following. You never reach the stage when you aren't working for someone, so learn to be good at it.

Pretending. If you're going to be an actor, be a good one, but stay out of management.

MANAGEMENT STYLE: BALLET OR HOCKEY?

Your management style should be both natural and deliberate. A natural style is the most highly desirable and useful. However, you may possess a few natural characteristics that are neither lovable nor useful. Identify them and get rid of them. But most of all, prepare. Be ready when the big opportunity comes. Know what you would say if Walter Cronkite stuck a microphone in your face and said, "What would you do?"

Consider the difference between ballet and hockey.

Hockey is a game requiring the instant application of learned and natural skills to an ever-changing situation. The puck is dropped, and an original event begins. Action continues until a score is made, the game ends, or a whistle blows. The player must know when to be aggressive, and when to pull back. There is no script; there is no respite. Only action, force, and player against player. Hockey is an exciting sport, and its style is exciting. But it is not a good management style.

A ballet is deliberately designed, discussed, planned, examined, and programmed in detail before it is performed. The placing of each prop, the timing of each movement, the disclosure of the plot, the beat of the music—all are carefully thought through and planned to the last detail. Yet because of the creativity of the artists and the orientation of the audience, each performance is an original. Ballet is a communications medium . It is also a practical and effective management style.

Suppose that an organization discovers that many of the current problems it suffers are being caused by new employees who are not being properly trained before being put to work. Obviously the organization is going to have to require that the operating departments be more careful about training in the future. Armed with the assignment to correct this situation, Hockey writes a memo for the general manager to sign stating in no uncertain terms that "in the future employees will be assigned to perform actual work only after their skills have been verified by the quality department." The result is several days of hurt feelings, conflict, and ultimatums, and perhaps the hiring of several people to "approve skills."

Ballet, on the other hand, asks the affected departments to meet to discuss the subject. Showing the evidence clearly and unemotionally, Ballet helps the group reach the decision that "we haven't been training the new employees properly prior to releasing them to the operations." After a discussion, those involved agree on a more controlled discipline. The quality department is asked to monitor progress on a regular basis, and the problem team meets regularly until the problem is resolved. Ballet has let these departments know that the jig is up; they are going to have to do what they should have been doing in the first place. No fuss, no feathers flying. Just positive and productive results.

If you are able to consider the situation and work out a specific way of ending a specific problem, you will be respected. If you flail about, squashing the problem while damaging the walls and spectators, you will be classified as dangerous. Hockey receives frantic telephone calls, memos, visits, inquiries, attacks, and continuous activity. Short vacations, abbreviated trips, and long hours are normal for the hockey-type manager. There is the satisfaction of having approached and resolved many problems, but most of them have to be "solved" anew each time they occur. The ballet school of management receives few unplanned interruptions. Goals are met regularly, vacations go as planned, and overtime is not part of the vocabulary. Problems that do arise are put right quickly—with the competence of a British nanny.

Hockey is detection; ballet is prevention. Both styles are possible within the conventional framework of quality management. But only prevention brings you the rewards and satisfaction you deserve. Top management wants their quality function to prevent problems entirely. It wants problems that do erupt to be dealt with at once, without emotion, turmoil, or expense. It is not interested in continually having papers thrust under the imperial nose to be signed as evidence of "support." They want quality made certain. So must you.

Quality is free. But it is not a gift.

PART TWO

The Doing: The HPA Corporation Quality Improvement Program

The biggest problem managers face comes when they are actually expected to accomplish all the things they have been saying could be accomplished if only everybody would listen to them. They must put action where their ideas have been. But it always comes out right if they take the time to learn from the experience of others. In all the hundreds of quality improvement programs I have witnessed over the years, I have never seen an unsuccessful one when the operation followed the fourteen steps—even vaguely. The HPA case leads you through a real-life example that shows how to set up and implement a quality improvement operation. You may recognize some of the management types in the story. You will certainly recognize the attitudes. You will be pleased to know that it all turns out all right.

The case has been conducted as a teaching aid with many diverse groups of managers and professionals from every persuasion. Acting out the roles and discussing the various steps, they have learned in advance how to handle situations. As a result they have gone back to their company, implemented the program, and become big heroes.

All the attitude tests, all the discussions, and all the meetings necessary are contained in the case. Part Three contains the instructor's guide. I suggest you read the case through first, examine the guide, and then read the case over again, asking yourself the questions in the guide.

The case history is supposed to be fun to read and accomplish. Think of your own company after you have read it once. Then move out. Quality improvement is waiting for you.

And now on with our tale. . . .

10

History of the Project

PERSONNEL INVOLVED

Hugh Gibbon—Vice President and general
    manager, HPA Appliance Division
Sally Gibbon—His wife (not employed by HPA)
Will Ellis—Director, manufacturing
Otto Meyer—Manager, purchasing
Harry Williams—Director, engineering
Ralph Lowell—Manager, field service
Katherine Norton—Director, marketing
Allen Fielding—Director, quality
Dr. Marian Nelson—Manager, personnel and indus-
    trial relations
Alice Wagner—Comptroller
Bill Ranson—Program administrator
Sharon Ranson—His wife (not employed by HPA)
John Halden—Quality engineer, HPA corpo-
    rate headquarters
Tom Wilson—President, union
(Various employees and family members)

Hugh Gibbon, vice president and general manager of the
HPA Corporation Appliance Division for three years, had

been dragging the old-line manufacturer and distributor of small appliances toward a breakthrough in its traditionally thin border of profitability. He had instituted modern management approaches, and felt the division would soon reach the point where it might make some real money. Somehow it just never seemed to happen. There was always a brightly unique problem emerging from what had formerly appeared to be brightly polished woodwork.

Two years ago it was the sudden discovery that the components being used in the personal TV line had been mysteriously "downgraded," resulting in an accelerated early failure rate in the field. This brought the field service manager, Ralph Lowell, screaming into Hugh's office. Ralph had barely finished pleading for an additional thirty-five people to handle the problem when the marketing manager crashed aboard. Katie Norton usually swept more than crashed, but anger evaporates poise. "Dealers are suspicious of us now," she stated, "and we better get going on our quality, or we are in big, big trouble."

The quality manager, Allen Fielding, had reacted to the problem by immediately calling the marginal components out of the stockroom and installing corrective action with purchasing. He was sure it wouldn't happen again. In addition, his quality engineer had written a new repair manual for the field people that simplified the repair jobs. It could have been worse, they agreed.

Six or seven months after that, another bubble popped to the surface. This one concerned a sudden accumulation of finished goods inventory in toasters and table broilers. Exhaustive investigation by the manufacturing manager, Will Ellis, showed that two separate errors in the production control computer program had caused the erroneous production of these units. Marketing had to move them out somehow, and they did — at a significant loss.

Small fires burned brightly, were stamped out, and then reappeared again in some other part of the operation. Staff meetings became recrimination sessions. Everyone was to blame but no one was responsible.

Productivity was dropping, and rejections were slowly

rising throughout the operation. The salespeople were "down" on the product. Being emotional souls anyway, they reacted to the specific problems they had seen and magnified them to perhaps something bigger than real life. There was no denying that the salespeople were really unhappy, and it was beginning to show . "No unhappier than me," thought Hugh.

Dealers were also reacting negatively. HPA sold through individually owned hardware and appliance stores, and thus depended on the goodwill of these independent dealers. Said goodwill, in turn, revolved around the credibility and performance of the product. Although HPA maintained repair facilities in major market areas, and a staff of field service people, the recent problems had overwhelmed their efforts. Thus, as the laws of mathematics require, repairs began to fall further and further behind.

At Hugh's last staff meeting Allen, the quality manager, presented the status of current corrective action programs and the overall quality status. There was an improvement in several lines but a drop in others. All in all the situation, while not getting worse, was not improving. Fielding expressed the view that they were beginning to get a handle on it and perhaps would see a turnaround in the next few months. The manufacturing people backed this statement, and an air of optimism began to pervade the meeting. Hugh asked tough questions about the corrective action steps being taken. He satisfied himself that the teams Al had set up were beaming in on the right aspects of the problems. He received the impression from all the staff that this was the right thing to do.

As a result of this analysis, Hugh decided that he should take some positive steps. The annual sales meeting was scheduled for the following week. Hugh had planned to make his usual thoughtful speech about the future of the small appliance industry in general and HPA in particular. But this time, he told Kate, he would talk about quality and how the positive actions being taken would eliminate the problems they were suffering.

The idea was received with enthusiasm. Al put together

some charts to use in the presentation; the comptroller, Alice Wagner, plotted some growth curves; and the speech was written.

The salespeople really liked the speech Hugh made. It was just the kind of reassurance they needed. Kate was happy, Al was delighted, and Hugh was reassured. Only Ralph Lowell was not completely sold.

Pulling Hugh aside in what was for him a quiet gesture, he asked what Hugh intended to do about the problems. He pointed out that all the actions being taken were to resolve problems already existing. He emphasized that they could have been prevented. The field manager admitted he didn't really know what to do about it, but he felt that there must be some way of heading the problems off at the pass before they got into the valley and knocked off the ranchers.

That ruined the meeting for Hugh.

What really bothered him was that the whole thing was so obvious. If you can find problems when they are little, you can remove them with almost no effort or expense. Better still, if you can figure out why you have them in the first place, you can avoid the whole uncomfortable business.

Suddenly it became apparent to Hugh that his "get well" program was totally inadequate. He would spend the rest of his days careening from one crisis to another. There had to be a better way. He resolved to think the situation out.

A few days later Hugh called the quality manager into the office. After making sure they wouldn't be disturbed, Hugh began to talk.

He said, "Al, I think we have a situation on our hands that we have not been treating properly. Let me be sure that you understand that I am not blaming you. You have been doing everything I have asked you to do, and doing it very well. The teams you set up have been clearing up our product and service problems. And I think your status reporting is accurate and useful.

"However, we have a problem that I think is up to the two of us to solve. This problem, as I see it, is two things.

First, the whole company is oriented toward patching things up rather than preventing. Second, I think we of the top staff have the wrong attitude toward quality. We're trying to do just enough to get by. Is that correct?"

Al didn't quite know how to react. He privately agreed with Hugh but was not sure that it represented good common sense to show it. Al was not a martyr at heart. So he nodded noncomittally. Hugh, lost in his own thoughts, didn't seem to notice. He continued while the increasingly uncomfortable quality man wiggled.

"We have to recognize that we need a change of attitude around here, and we need to make sure that attitude change is positive. We need to get everyone interested in defect prevention. Now, I think that is the quality manager's job to implement and I think it is my job to start. How do you feel about that?"

Al thought a moment and replied.

"Hugh, if you are talking about a quality improvement program as I think you are, it would be a wonderful thing for this company and for my work in particular. Is that what you want?"

Hugh nodded and replied, "Exactly. I want to get started on getting people interested in doing things much better than we have been and I'd like to do it as quickly as possible. Can it be done?"

"Certainly it can, Hugh. certainly it can. I have been reading up lately on a fourteen-step program for installing the attitude of defect prevention. It seems to work where it is properly applied, and it has produced great results from what I can read in these papers."

Hugh stood up. "Great, that's what we'll get started. Let's get the rest of the staff in here now and tell them what we're going to do. We can get the program moving tomorrow. You're in charge of it. We'll motivate everyone."

Al stood too, but held up his hand to Hugh.

"Whoa, hold it a minute. That's got to be the wrong way to begin. I think you and I need to make sure we understand the situation, the program, and just what is involved before we can get everyone else involved. Can I have a few more minutes of your time?"

Hugh sat back down, looking at this quality manager with a new view. He cocked his head, thought a moment and then smiled. "I'm beginning to get the feeling that you are trying to figure out a way to tell me that I'm part of the problem, and that if I rush off on a motivation crusade I'll screw it up even more. Right?"

To Al's consternation he blushed a little at the comment and, having done so, realized that no reply was necessary. Hugh sat up straight at the desk and pulled his note pad to him.

"OK, what do we have to do? Let's start with what you need from me. First orient me, and then give me a summary of those fourteen steps you were talking about so I can read over them tonight. Obviously I don't understand quality improvement and motivation. Elucidate please, sir."

Al thought a moment and then decided the best approach was to let it all hang out. He leaned forward so he could look his boss right in the eye and began.

"OK. Well Hugh, as I said, I have been studying this business of quality improvement. While I'm at it let me make something clear also. Until just recently I've had the wrong idea about the whole thing. For instance, take Zero Defects. I always thought that Zero Defects was some sort of motivation concept where you were supposed to show people posters and make a few speeches at them so they would sign a pledge. Having done this you could sit back and let everything get better. Since that is what I thought, I figured it was just a bunch of nonprofessional foolishness. Most of the literature in the quality profession supports that belief.

"However, it became apparent to me that some companies were having a lot of success with ZD, and that the success was continuing over a long period of time. So I figured there must be more to it than that. Believe me there is. ZD is the key to quality improvement, and it starts here in this office."

Hugh leaned forward. He was really interested.

"Do you mean you want to motivate me with some posters and speeches?"

"Not hardly," smiled Al. "Not hardly. What I mean is that we have to set a very clear standard of performance for our people and we have to do it in a sincere way. Sincerity starts with our commitment to it. Motivation has nothing to do with it. Those who have used ZD programs over a period of time say they never understood how the idea got started that it was a motivation program. It is merely setting performance standards that no one can misunderstand and then starting a two-way communications exercise to let everyone know about it. As you said before, we are all working diligently on the wrong thing. We can work just as hard on the right." Hugh frowned.

"We can't afford to get everything gold plated, or give away the whole store. If you're going to have zero defects in everything we would have to hire 300 inspectors. The people would get frustrated just from failing once in a while. It sounds impractical to me."

Al tapped his finger firmly on the desk.

"It's not that way at all, Hugh. What ZD is is the *attitude* of defect prevention. It means 'do the job right the first time.' That's all. Do what you said you were going to do when you came to work. If everyone will do that, we will be way ahead. Most of the problems we have are just lack of attention. We as management have not insisted on things being done right. Look, I have a short tape recording that spells out the ZD concept as it was originally intended. After you hear that I'll give you the list of the steps involved in getting up to the day we have a companywide ZD program, and tell you about the actions that follow after that to support it. Agreeable?"

Hugh nodded.

"That sounds like a good approach. But before you play the tape, let me ask you one question. Assuming all this makes sense to me, how soon could we begin our formal quality improvement program?"

"Boss," grinned Al, "we have already begun." He went

quickly down the hall to his office, returned with the tape recorder, and put on a tape:

The products of industry are good not enough. Customer complaints are rising; there is too much waste. Those products that work trouble free do so because of an investment in test, inspection, and service that is out of proportion. Many companies spend 10, 15, and even 20 percent of their sales dollar on scrap, rework, warranty, service, test, and inspection. The errors that produce this waste are caused directly by the personnel of the company, both employees and management.

To eliminate this waste, to improve the operation, to become more efficient, we must concentrate on preventing the defects and errors that plague us. The defect that is prevented doesn't need repair, examination, or explanation.
The first step is to examine and adopt the attitude of defect prevention. This attitude is called, symbolically: Zero Defects. Zero Defects is a standard for management, a standard that management can convey to the employees to help them to decide to "do the job right the first time."

People are conditioned to believe that error is inevitable. We not only accept error, we anticipate it. Whether we are designing circuits, programming a computer, planning a project, soldering joints, typing letters, completing an account ledger, or assembling components, it does not bother us to make a few errors, and management plans for these errors to occur. We feel that human beings have a "built-in" error factor.

However, we do not maintain the same standard when it comes to our personal life. If we did, we would resign ourselves to being shortchanged now and then as we cash our pay checks. We would expect hospital nurses to drop a certain percentage of all newborn babies. We would expect to go home to the wrong house by mistake periodically. As individuals we do not tolerate these things. Thus we have a double standard—one for ourselves, one for the company.

The reason for this is that the family creates a higher performance standard for us than the company does.

In short, we must determine if we as management have made our desires clear to those who look to us for guidance and direction. We must provide an understandable, constant standard for quality performance.

Consider the three basic areas of performance in any organization: cost, schedule, and quality. All these are vital for success. Each requires the establishment of a performance standard that cannot be misunderstood.

Take cost. Everyone understands what $2.35 looks like. There may be some argument about what to do with the money, but everyone understands its substance. A budget is set, and the standard is to make the job and the funds come out together.

Schedule also has an understandable common base: time. We all use the same standard calendars and clocks. Delivery and completion dates are specified in contracts and requirements. We either meet the dates or we do not.

Now what is the existing standard for quality?

Most people talk about an AQL—an acceptable quality level. An AQL really means a commitment before we start the job to produce imperfect material. Let me repeat, an *acceptable quality level is a commitment before we start the job that we will produce imperfect material.* An AQL, therefore, is not a management standard. It is a determination of the status quo. Instead of the managers setting the standard, the operation sets the standard.
Consider the AQL you would establish on the product you buy. Would you accept an automobile that you knew in advance was 15 percent defective? 5 percent? 1 percent? 1/2 of 1 percent? How about the nurses that care for newborn babies? Would an AQL of 3 percent on mishandling be too rigid?

The Zero Defects concept is based on the fact that mistakes are caused by two things: lack of knowledge and lack of attention.

Lack of knowledge can be measured and attacked by tried and true means. But lack of attention is a state of mind. It is an attitude problem that must be changed by the individual.

When presented with the challenge to do this, and the encouragement to attempt it, the individual will respond enthusiastically. Remember that Zero Defects is not a motivation method, it is a performance standard. And it is not just for production people, it is for everyone. Some of the biggest gains occur in the nonproduction areas.

The Zero Defects program must be personally directed by top management. People receive their standards from their leaders. They perform to the requirements given to them. They must be told that your personal standard is: Zero Defects.

To gain the benefits of Zero Defects, you must decide to make a personal commitment to have improvement in your operation. You must want it. The first step is: Make the attitude of Zero Defects your personal standard.

After the recorder switched off, Hugh sat there for a moment. Then he turned to stare at Al. His voice was calm and quiet. He almost muttered. "Well, I'll be darned. If 'the product looks like the management,' and we're having all this trouble, then the problem or at least a large part of it must be me and my staff. OK Al, I think I have the message. Leave that material with me, and come back tomorrow morning at 8:15. You and I should have a meeting at that time each morning to go over the steps one at a time while we're laying out the program."

"See you in the morning."

(The material Hugh took home with him was titled "Quality Improvement through Defect Prevention." The program contained the fourteen steps that should be familiar to you by now, steps which were outlined in Chapter 8.)

Talking to his wife, Hugh commented on the program and the problem.

"This program sequence certainly sounds logical, and the experience reported by these other companies is realistic and well documented. But the whole thing still bothers me. It seems like the program isn't, well, I don't know exactly what it isn't."

"I know what it isn't," remarked his wife. Hugh looked up in surprise and amusement.

"How could you know? You haven't even seen it."

"I know you. The problem you have is that the program doesn't look complicated enough to accomplish all those things, in fact it looks like something you should have thought up yourself. Isn't that correct, oh mighty industrial tycoon?"

Hugh had to admit to himself, and eventually to Sally, that the simplicity and directness of it bothered him. Make a commitment to a standard, communicate it, recognize performance, and then recycle. And be honest about it.

The commitment part was what really bothered him. He guessed his feelings were hurt. As a dynamic and interested manager he felt that he had always given his people the challenge to do the job right the first time. He thought that he had always demanded top performance. But in honest retrospect he realized that in his intensity to deliver on schedule, meet the budgets, and keep a smooth operation, he had let things get off course.

Just six weeks ago he had raised Cain with the final test people for delaying acceptance testing on some rotisseries while their equipment was calibrated. He thought at the time that he had been punishing them for lack of foresight. Now he realized that he had been telling them that testing wasn't important.

Anyway he had to settle down and accept the task of really making it clear to his people that he was serious about quality. He would do that when the program formally started. Sighing a little, he turned to the booklet, determined to do the damn thing one step at a time if that was what it took to get the outfit moving again.

11

The Program

STEP ONE: MANAGEMENT COMMITMENT

Purpose:
To make it clear where management
stands on quality.

It is necessary that we consistently produce conforming
products and services at the optimum price. The device to
accomplish this is the use of defect prevention techniques
in our operating departments: engineering, manufacturing,
quality control, purchasing, sales, and others. No one is
exempt.

It is much less expensive to prevent errors than to rework,
scrap, or service them. The expense of waste can run as
much as 15 to 25 percent of sales, and does in some
companies.

The first action that must take place in improvement is that
the management of the company must take a moment to
understand what is needed, and make the decision themselves that they indeed want to improve. This decision is
made when they decide to adopt the attitude of defect prevention as their personal standard.

The reason that this is important is obvious but bears repeating. It is a matter of the quality policy.

The quality policy of an organization is too important to be left to those responsible for the acceptance of the product. The quality manager, or the inspector, asked to judge continuously whether the product is good enough or not, will bias the product or service according to his or her own background and personal attitudes.

What is the quality policy?

It is the state of mind held by the company personnel concerning how well they must do their jobs. It is this policy, whether it has been stated or not, that determines in advance how successfully the next job will be done.

If a formal policy is not established by the management of the organization, then the personnel will select their own—individually. This policy must be stated and established by the top executives of the organization, much in the same manner as the financial policy. To delegate this function to the quality manager, or other vertically oriented executives, is dangerous.

To determine what this policy should be, we should first examine some things it should not be:

1. It should not be a treatise on the "economics of quality." Quality means conformance. There is no such thing as the economics of conformance; it is always cheaper to do the job properly. There are economic levels of inspection, testing, laboratory equipment, secretaries, food servings, and other functions, but there is no economics of quality.

2. The quality policy should not have a number in it. Stating allowable nonconformance is no way to get what you want because no one notices the number for what it is. They just know it is there and allow for it.

3. It should not indicate any method of deviating from the policy. If it does, immediately there will be a procedure written on that method, and meetings will be held to train

people extensively in the procedure—to the reduction of the original intent.

4. It should not delegate the responsibility for evaluating performance to the policy. This must be the prerogative of the chief executive, even though the executive will have others gather the information.

5. The policy should not be hidden in a book reserved for executive personnel only. It should be stated, restated, and publicized until everyone knows, understands, and believes it.

The policy statement recommended is: *Perform exactly like the requirement . . . or cause the requirement to be officially changed to what we and our customers really need.*

The statement of this policy, and its explanation to the management team, will properly set the stage for quality improvement.

Comment: It is vital that each member of operating management understand and agree with this policy, and more important—implement it.

Hugh turned to his desk and wrote the policy as it was stated. He toyed for a moment with adding a comment like "if you have any questions, consult your supervisor" but decided that this would just reopen the gate. If you were going to stick to the published requirements, then you were going to stick to them. It might be interesting to find out whether or not the products could be made to what he and others thought they ought to be.

He did add that this policy applied to all employees of the company and would be enforced not only in the manufacturing operations, but everywhere. That, he thought, ought to get the marketing types going.

Promptly at 8:15 Al Fielding walked into the general manager's office. Hugh handed him the proposed policy statement. Al read it several times, smiled, and handed it back.

"Short and to the point, Hugh. 'Do what you're supposed to do,' that's the way it has to be."

"Good, I'll have it issued today and we'll at least be past step 1. However, I think it would be a good idea if we told the staff why we're doing it. How about setting up a meeting for 3 o'clock this afternoon, and we'll go over the whole thing?"

"No problem," said Al.

"Now, my friendly quality manager, we have to come to grips with the rest of this program. You have already begun step 13, quality councils, so we don't have to worry about it at this time. How's it going, by the way?"

"Very well. The biggest problem I'm having is that they're not really sure yet that we're serious about the whole thing. I think this policy will help in that line."

"Boy, have we lost that much credibility? Perhaps it would be a good idea if I met with them. Can we arrange it?"

"We're having a meeting next Wednesday after work. Suppose I make it a dinner instead. You can come and say a few words, and then – if you don't mind – let's just open it up and let them ask any questions they want."

Hugh obviously liked that idea.

"If it works out, maybe we should do the same thing with the other departments. Now, the next step in this program is number 2: quality improvement team. You should be the chairman, shouldn't you?"

"I don't think so, Hugh," replied Al. "If you read the instructions, they don't specifically recommend the quality manager. I think if it was that obvious, they would have done so. My feeling is that if you make the quality manager responsible for the program, it becomes 'just another quality drive' to most people."

"OK. Well, let's read the concept of the step a word at a time and see if we can figure it out. Apparently the choice is up to us, because we need to find the person in our organization who can be the most effective strictly from a quality improvement standpoint."

STEP TWO: THE QUALITY IMPROVEMENT TEAM

Purpose:
To run the quality improvement program.

Since every function of an operation is a contributor to defect levels, every portion must participate in the quality improvement effort. The degree of participation is best determined by the particular situation that exists. However, everyone has the opportunity to improve.

The quality improvement team is strictly a part-time job for the members except the chairperson, who will become rather deeply involved. Therefore, the selection of the chairperson is an important step. There are really only two requirements:

1. The chairperson should be a mature member of management who understands the need to improve and agrees with the concept of Zero Defects and defect prevention.

2. The general manager and the manager's staff must have confidence in the person chosen.

No special skills are involved. Some companies have selected their quality manager, and some have used executives from industrial relations, manufacturing, engineering, or finance.

The chairperson should assemble a team representing each department, and together they should examine the purpose of the program and the concepts involved. Then this group runs the program.

The responsibilities of the members are:

1. Lay out the entire quality improvement program.

2. Represent their department on the team.

3. Represent the team to their department.

4. Cause the decisions of the team to be executed in their department.

5. Contribute creatively to the implementation of the improvement activity.

Although the team has the responsibility of creating and directing the program, it must be stated emphatically that the individual departments are held responsible for developing their own programs and causing them to occur.

The team should develop its plan and then present it to the general manager and the general manager's staff for acceptance and support. Firm dates should be set for each step's accomplishment, and progress should be reviewed at each staff meeting. This constant emphasis will ensure success.

Comment: The establishment of this team and the organization of the improvement program does not represent an additional expense for the operation. It is really pulling together and organizing things that are happening in one form or another at the present time. By formalizing it and centralizing the effort, it is possible to eliminate duplication of effort.

"That's not one whole hell of a lot of help as far as picking the person goes," muttered Hugh.

Al scratched his chin. "Maybe we missed it, but it seems to me that they'd make a big deal out of which function should organize the project. They don't even give you an organization chart or a time schedule, except to say that the initial program should cover a year and the steps should be staged to occur when you're ready for them. It seems to me that we're left to decide who would care the most about it."

"By George, I think you've got it," said Hugh.

"Huh?"

"Who is hurting the most in this whole quality thing? Me, of course, because if we don't produce I'm out, and you, because you're supposed to be in charge of it according to the organization chart. All true. But the one who is really hurting is our intrepid marketing department. They are actually embarrassed at the junk we're putting out. Kate is dying inch by inch and she knows it. She is the chairman, or is it chairperson?"

"Chairwoman?"

"How about team leader?"

"Leaderette?"

"Seriously, Kate would be the logical choice. She is experienced in the business, she's tough, and she has high personal standards. In addition, everyone respects her personally and professionally."

"I don't think she'll take it. She feels, I think, that the factory is the only problem. She won't be willing to have an improvement program in marketing. Let alone run the whole thing."

"Sure she will. You just don't understand marketing people. She thinks she has the most efficient operations in the whole company; therefore, she will accept the assignment in order to bring the rest of the place up to their concept of performance."

"You're probably right. Anyway, I agree with the idea of trying it. How about Bill Ranson as the administrator of the program? He is young, very bright, good with people, and has been going to Toastmasters. I think he would like the chance to show you and the other members of the staff what he can do."

"OK. Let's invite him to the meeting today. He might as well be in on the whole thing from the start."

Hugh went back to his work and Al set off to arrange the staff meeting.

Al introduced Bill Ranson to the staff as each person arrived, explaining that Bill was going to be the administrator of the new quality improvement program. Everybody was friendly, but you could tell that it didn't register that they were going to have to do something personally in this new program. Ralph and Kate both, as a matter of fact, made comments about how Bill should feel free to call them if he needed any information about the problems in the factory.

Hugh started the meeting about 3:15.

"I'm glad you could get here this afternoon on such short notice. What I have to say is very important to all of us, and involves the business of establishing a formal quality improvement program for HPA. Let me briefly run down our situation.

"We are in command of a company that manufactures small appliances and provides service for privately owned hardware and variety stores. We find ourselves in a market that is expanding, while our share is shrinking. Two years ago our sales were $55 million; last year they were $56 million; this year sales should come out to $54,360,000. That's as flat as you can get. Our profit this year will be $815,400, which is 1.5 percent return on sales. Return on assets is 1.7 percent. When you figure the investment opportunities available today, it is apparent you could do a lot better with your money than put it in HPA.

"The very clear situation we face is that we have to improve our income and we have to do it without raising prices. In addition we need to increase sales so we have a broader base.

"Now let's take a look at where the money goes—the $54,360,000 we receive from all sales:

Compensation to employees	$26,092,800
Suppliers of materials and services, etc.	25,971,800
Federal, state, and local taxes	1,480,000
Income	815,400
Total	$54,360,000

"I know that is an unusual way to look at a company's financial breakdown, but I think it does indicate that we either have to restructure the company to the level that will give us 8 percent after tax on a smaller volume of product, or we have to reduce costs internally and improve our quality enough to let us obtain a better gross margin in the marketplace.

"We have a total of 2718 employees. I asked Marian Nelson to provide you with a breakdown of their distribution in the company."

Nelson rose and walked around the table, handing each attendee the following list of personnel assignments:

Marketing	136
Field service	281
Management staff	65
Quality	187
Design	92
Purchasing	16
Manufacturing	1825
Personnel and industrial relations	52
Comptroller	64
Total	2718

Hugh let everyone absorb the information and continued: "While we have multiple problems involving the products themselves, we also have a frightening tendency to do jobs over in the administrative and paperwork areas. Al ran some special analyses for me, and they tell some interesting stories. It looks as though as many as 25 percent of our people are involved in doing jobs over a second or even third time. Incidentally, that doesn't seem to be unusual in industry."

There was a collective gasp in the room.

Kate shook her head. "Hugh, I have a hard time believing that. Do you mean that my salespeople are saying the wrong things to customers or taking the wrong orders or going back to the wrong places or what? That is a serious accusation."

Hugh seemed a little startled.

"Kate," he said in a quiet tone, "it is not an 'accusation.' It is a comment based on the information that I have been able to put together very quickly. But I can give you an example. We have an order-writing group consisting of two people who are part of your operation."

"Right," said Kate. "They take the orders as they come in and turn them into shop requests so that the inventory, shop time, and everything else can be programmed. It saves a lot of time and effort for the manufacturing people." She looked to the manufacturing director for confirmation. He nodded.

"I understand the system," stated Hugh. "But we had one of the quality engineers spend the day in the production control department seeing what happens to those orders. He reported that of the eighty-seven received from order writing last Thursday, sixteen had to be returned because of wrong part numbers or other errors. In determining how frequently this happens, he learned that production control has one person whose full-time job is to coordinate with the order group because of the large number of errors found in the past."

"Why wasn't I told of this?" said the now-irritated Kate.

"Because we have a lousy internal communication and corrective action system, that's why. That is one of the things we have to correct. You're only a part of it—the trend is all around us. We find in field service that the repair people don't send in the results of their repair analysis because they have found that no one does anything about their recommendations in terms of redesign or change of manufacturing process. They even have informal manuals on how to fix all the known problems."

Ralph Lowell flushed. "We've tried to get people interested in these reports, but it is very hard."

Harry Williams, the chief engineer, turned in his chair. "We used to look at the reports, but most of them are the fourth carbon or some other hard-to-read material. Besides, we really don't have the personnel to search through them."

Will Ellis, from manufacturing, cleared his throat. When silence was obtained, he commented, "My rejection rates have been steadily increasing over the last three years. I attribute a lot of that to the turnover in people we've had and to lack of proper training. But I think saying that 25 percent of them have to do things over full time is a little exaggerated."

"Might be, Will, might be," nodded Hugh. "But we're going to find out and we're going to fix it. Before we start talking about the program in detail, let's assume for one moment that the guess is right — that one-fourth of our people are not productive in the true sense of the word. That is 6.5 million bucks we are paying in our own house to do things over. That is a target worth shooting for."

"You know, Hugh," said Otto Meyer, the purchasing manager, "if you project that same thought to our suppliers, and figure that about half of what we pay them is for labor, that is another $6.5 million. Altogether we could have a $13 million dollar target if we did it right."

"That's the message, Otto."

"It sounds a little dreamy to me," remarked Kate. "How's all of this going to help my problem with the quality of the product?"

"I think it would be better if we took some time now to examine the proposed quality improvement program itself, and to have Al and Bill give us a half hour seminar on quality. If we all understand what it is and isn't, we'll be in better shape to decide our actions for the next few weeks. Al, go ahead. Kate, I think you'll get your answer out of this."

Kate didn't look too convinced.

Al stood at the front of the room and began. "It is difficult to talk about quality because everyone has his or her (Kate smiled finally) ideas on what it is. So I'm going to give you a self-grading test to serve as an agenda. After that we'll review the absolutes of quality.

"We can have a more meaningful discussion once we are through this period. Bill, would you please hand out the questions ? They are all true or false. Circle your answers and keep the sheet."

Bill passed around the ten-question test.

1. Quality is a measure of goodness of the product that can be defined in ranges such as fair, good, excellent.

T   F

2. The economics of quality requires that management

establish acceptable quality levels as performance
standards.   T   F

3. The cost of quality is the expense of doing things
   wrong.   T   F

4. Inspection and test operations should report to manufacturing so they can have the tools to do the jobs. T   F

5. Quality is the responsibility of the quality department.
                                                             T   F

6. Worker attitudes are the primary cause of defects. T   F

7. I have trend charts that show me the rejection levels at
   every key operation.   T   F

8. I have a list of my ten biggest quality problems.   T   F

9. Zero Defects is a worker motivation program.   T   F

10. The biggest problem today is that the customer doesn't
    understand our problems.   T   F

(Answers begin on Page 271)

One by one the staff members completed their marking, laid
down their pencils, and looked expectantly at Bill. (It is
interesting, by the way, to watch how aggressive, successful
managers react to being tested. Without conscious thought,
they go eagerly to their classes. Having been excellers all
their lives, they are used to achieving high grades, and they
are usually not afraid of tests. However, once in a while
they run into a test that is "tilted" a little in order to gain
their attention. The questionnaire Bill handed out was that
kind of test.)

When everyone was obviously finished, Al went to the
blackboard where he wrote the numbers 1 through 10 in
vertical order.

Lowell gave a kind of well-controlled growl and asked
Al, "Do we really have to go through all of this, Al? We've
all been in the business for some years. We know all these
things. Let's start talking about some of our real problems."

Al reflected for a moment.

"OK, Ralph, I'll make a deal with you. If everyone got
number 1 right we'll forget the rest of the exercise. How
many wrote 'true' as their answer?"

Four hands were raised. Marian, one of the hands, smiled the quiet smile of superiority for a brief moment until she began to realize that "true" may not have been the proper response.

"Are you setting us up?" she demanded. "I've always used the word quality as an indication of worth, or, as you put it, 'goodness.' What's wrong with that?"

"Nothing is wrong with it in a literary sense—nothing. The problem comes when you have to measure it or make a living controlling it. We start confusing quality with elegance, brightness, weight, and other subjective things. Then even those get compared when we talk about good quality, bad quality, high and low quality, and all those things. So far today we've used the word quality fifteen or twenty times, and each meaning has been different. If we're going to have a quality improvement program, we have to agree on what the word means. We don't want an elegance improvement program, do we?"

As Al spoke, Hugh began handing out the policy he had written.

"Look at the policy that Hugh is issuing to each of you. It states that we will *perform exactly like the requirement*. That means we should conform to the requirement. Conformance is what quality needs to mean to us. We have conformance and nonconformance. If we want something more elegant or less elegant, or heavier or more powerful, or whatever, we have to make our specifications clear. We have highly educated people involved in this company. We should be able to identify some requirements more clearly than by saying we want 'good' quality."

Kate pointed her pencil at the quality manager.

"How about our customers? Do you plan that we don't talk to them unless they learn to look at quality as conforming to the requirement only? They talk about quality all the time and they mean it as goodness."

"We don't have to insist that they follow our rules, but I think they would be happy to learn that we are dedicating ourselves to making the product like it says it is supposed to be in the literature we give them. They could certainly "count on that."

Also, we can get them to tell us more specifically the things they like and don't like about our products. Then the engineering people can make changes for improvement."

Kate smiled. "It would be a pleasant change to be able to guarantee that our product will always look exactly like the specifications."

"You can't go around guaranteeing that," said Will Ellis. "It would require us to spend millions of dollars on inspection and testing. Why, we'd be wrapping a $20 bill around every toaster we sent out of here."

Hugh look puzzled.

"How do you mean that, Will? I thought we were interested in preventing defects rather than culling them out."

"Sure you can prevent errors, Hugh, but there are bound to be a certain amount getting through. How do we keep the customers from getting those?"

"I agree," stated Ralph. "Every day we see the same problems over and over again. It has always been that way and it probably will continue until I get my gold watch."

"Conforming gold watch," noted Otto Meyer.

Al nodded patiently. "I think this brings us to the next question. The economics of quality requires that management establish acceptable quality levels as performance standards. That, of course is false."

Alice Wagner, the comptroller, spoke for the first time.

"I didn't answer this one, Al, because I didn't understand exactly what an 'acceptable quality level' is. Are we talking about some sort of agreement on how good, excuse me, how *conforming,* things have to be?"

"That's what we're talking about, Alice. That's why the answer is false. If you set up a standard that says 1.5 percent of the product is allowed to be nonconforming, then you have agreed before you start that you're going to do at least that amount incorrectly."

"But Al," said Ralph, "We know that very few things in life get done right all the time, so why not be practical about it? Besides, it must cost more to get the last few percentage points correct than it did to get the first 98 percent right."

"I've heard that a lot, Al," said Hugh. "Is it true that the last few steps of improvement or attainment cost as much as all of the first ones?"

"It might be in some cases, I guess, Hugh, but no one has ever been able to show me one in a factory. This issue we are on right now is the most important part of the whole exercise. We have been raised on the cliche that "nothing ever goes right," and so we plan on failure. When we get to the Zero Defects part, I think you might see some of the logic that helps us banish this thought. But let's talk about the economics of quality and acceptable quality levels for a moment.

"The 'economics of quality' is based on the thought that you can't afford to make things too good. You can't 'gold-plate' everything. We're not talking about the matter of specifying the requirement. That, for our purpose, becomes a marketing and engineering problem. We are concerned about conformance, and therefore we are saying, 'Is there an economics of conformance'?

"Is it best to do something over several times, or is it more practical to try to have it done right the first time?"

Otto interrupted, "Obviously it is less expensive to have things done right the first time, but not necessarily more practical. That's where AQLs come in. They've been around for years."

"True," Al replied, "but they have been misunderstood and used incorrectly by management people. 'Acceptable quality level' is a statistical term coming out of the methods of quality control sampling inspection. They originally had an entirely different meaning from the one they have popularly received over the years. The way they are used now, managers literally agree on the output quality level of a new plant before the first worker enters the door."

"I find that hard to believe," said Kate.

"Unfortunately, it is very true," murmured Will. "I'm beginning to see what Al is driving at. It could be that the output of our own plant is keyed along these lines without our even knowing it."

"How can you establish the quality level of a plant without even knowing it?" asked Marian. "It would seem to me to be a deliberate act based on an analysis of the machine tolerances, the design criteria, materials, and similar factors."

Hugh smiled. "That's what the textbooks would like you to believe, Marian, but real life is a lot different. I don't think any study like that has ever been completed before the plant has been in operation for a generation. It just is not part of real life."

"So where do these standards and AQLs come from then?" inquired the industrial psychologist. "Are they picked from a hat?"

"I don't think it's quite that crude," commented Will. "Where they come from is the operation itself. One day a line or setup begins to run at what the managers think is an acceptable level. So they don't try to improve anymore because they believe that this step will cost as much as the first ones and so forth. So they concentrate on not letting it get worse. Hell, we give awards for that."

Arthur turned to Al.

"Would it screw up your procedure in educating us if we discussed this Zero Defects business now? I must admit that I'm confused."

Al nodded to Bill.

"All right, let's play the ZD concept tape and then discuss whether ZD is a worker motivation program. The answer is, ZD is definitely *not* a motivation program."

"That's not the way I've always heard it," said Ralph. "Everything I've read uses the word 'motivation' in every paragraph."

"Well, listen and see if you can find that word in this recording."

Bill played the Zero Defects tape that Al had played for Hugh in their initial discussion (page 170).

After the tape had been played, there was complete silence; each person was lost in private thoughts. Bill Ranson stepped to the front of the room.

"I know what most of you are thinking," he commented. "The reason I know is because I have just completed the same thought process myself in the past few days. I, too, found it hard to accept the thought that I might be part of the problem and that I had perhaps not been thinking about this business of performance in the most useful way. Of course, I haven't been at my job as long as most of you," (Al winced) "but I think I am beginning to understand why something so obvious was not clear to me before."

Ralph Lowell interrupted him. "Think I know what you're going to say, Bill. I think you're going to say that we here established the problem, we control the problem, and we are the only ones who can fix it. Is that right?"

"Right," replied Bill. "Right in the essentials. We certainly have to identify the specifics of the problem and cause it or them to be fixed. The only additional aspect I would add is that it really is a joint effort by all of us. If any of us don't sincerely think it can be done, and should be done, then it won't happen."

Will nodded, "I agree with all of that, and I have no problem with the ZD business as you and Al have described it. But what I really need to know is how come most of what I've read about ZD is negative in the journals, yet when I talk with people who are doing it they are very enthusiastic."

Al stepped forward. "I can answer that. It was bothering me also. I came to the conclusion, after a lot of discussion, that the quality and manufacturing people misunderstood it at first. They had the impression that it was some sort of magic formula which you used to entice people to do good work by giving them prizes and fun and games. Obviously, the point was missed that the persons needing the 'motivation' were the management, not the workers. Also, I thought it was only for the manufacturing people; I hadn't thought about the fact that half the people involved don't handle the product."

Kate cleared her throat. "OK, I think confession time is over. It should be evident to all that we need to get moving on this thing. Al, how long does it take to install this program?"

"If you start now, Kate, I think you would have it installed in a few days. ZD day is probably six months from here."

"What do you mean, if *I* start now?" She turned to Hugh.

Hugh smiled weakly. "We were hoping that you would head up the improvement team — with Bill to provide you with full-time help, of course."

"But I don't know anything about this business," she said.

"I think we just found out that no one does," said Will. "I think you'd do a great job. We're behind you all the way."

"What would I have to do? Before you answer that let me ask another question. Would I get to pick my own team?"

Hugh nodded. "Absolutely," he said, "I wouldn't have it any other way."

Kate thumped the table with enthusiasm. "OK, I agree and I pick this team right here. All except Hugh. We'll call him if we need him."

It was easy to tell that not everyone was ready for that assignment. But after a moment there were smiles all around and nods of agreement.

Kate pointed her finger at Bill. "Bill, you have the rest of today to get me educated. You keep all the minutes and you keep us straight. Call a meeting of the quality improvement team for 5:30 tomorrow evening. I'll only keep you for thirty minutes but we'll start moving."

She turned to the industrial relations director. "Marian, how about contacting the union president and asking him to sit in the meeting tomorrow with us?"

Marian didn't appear to like that idea at all. "We could be asking for trouble, Kate. I'm not sure the union wouldn't look at this as some sort of job speedup or something. Perhaps we should wait until our plans are more complete?"

Kate looked toward Al, who nodded support, and then to Hugh, who smiled.

She turned back to Marian Nelson. "How about if you

and I meet with the union people tomorrow and try the whole thing out on them?'"

Marian smiled. "You smooth-talking salespersons are all alike. How's nine o'clock?"

The Dinner

As Al and Hugh entered the quality council dinner meeting, Hugh commented that if this quality improvement drive did nothing else it was going to get him to meet more people then he had ever met before. He also noted that the whole program had a positive scent about it.

The quality council members were already in the room when Al and Hugh arrived. Al had quietly arranged it this way so his people would have the opportunity to get conversation started before the big boss arrived. Fortunately for the success of the meeting, he remembered his past. You could spend a lot time in a plant without meeting the brass. Most of the people would be a little shy, and would welcome the chance for some unpressured time before the meeting. However, Hugh handled the introductions well. He talked with each of the twenty-three people individually until he was sure he had established clearly in his mind what each person did and how they felt about their job. He was privately pleased to note that one supervisor and four of the quality engineers were women.

What amazed him even more was that they got to pay for their own drinks. Al had suggested that the usual quality council format, including the Dutch bar, be continued, although Hugh wanted the company to pick up the whole tab.

"It's the way we started out," commented Al. "We're used to being on our own."

When the time came for dinner, Hugh was a little surprised to see that there was no head table and that the receiving inspection supervisor, Norm Tate, opened the meeting. Norm noted that the general manager was there that night and that the council was honored. After dinner

Hugh would say a few words and then the meeting would be opened for questions. "Any questions at all," he emphasized.

During dinner Hugh kept up a lively discussion with the group at his table, which didn't include Al. He couldn't refrain from asking why Al hadn't opened the meeting.

"He's not the council chairman," he was told.

"Al insisted that we run the councils on the basis that the members determine what they want to do. He gets one vote like the rest of us. That's why we have the privilege of paying for our own drinks. It is one right we wouldn't like giving up."

By the time dessert was being served, both Hugh and the council had gotten used to his being there and everyone was comfortable. Norm settled everyone and then introduced Hugh as the speaker for the evening. After commenting that several department heads had met with the group in the past and that it had all been useful, Hugh spoke.

"I'm happy to be with you tonight, not just because speakers are supposed to put that in their remarks but because I am always happy to spend some time with professionals.

"As you know, we are not in an easy business. We have low margins, tough customers, and complex problems of quality. However, I guess that any general manager in the country speaking to a group of key people would be saying the same thing. So let me forget all that platitude business and get right down to brass tacks.

"We are having a difficult time from a quality standpoint. Our failure rates are too high, our field service expenses are outrageous, the customers are losing confidence in us, and there are no silver linings in our clouds.

"Most of you know this, and many of you have opinions on how things should be approached or changed to get better. But, as you also know, we must learn to do these 'get better' things in an organized manner. So we are setting up a quality improvement team. The members of that team, representing each department, are the department heads. The head of the team is Ms. Norton, the marketing director;

Al Fielding is a member, of course. In fact, he's the brains of the outfit, although we don't admit it publicly. Bill Ranson will serve as administrator, which means he will do all the work.

"Now I realize that you can say 'these are the people who got us into this mess in the first place.' There might be some truth in that. But they are also the ones charged with getting us *out* of the mess — and it can only be done with your help. You have to tell us how to do it, you have to help execute the actions the improvement team decides upon, and most important you have to measure and report the results.

"While all this is happening, you have to keep on grinding out the product, making it like the print, and insisting that the standards be met.

"It is apparent that we, and I am the biggest culprit, have managed to put forth the impression that we can be satisfied with less than Zero Defects. Let me clarify my position on that right now. With me it is Zero Defects or bust."

Hugh stopped at that point, thought a moment, and smiled at Al.

"Gee," he said with a smile, "once you say it out loud it isn't all that tough."

The group burst into spontaneous applause.

The rest of the meeting went smoothly. Hugh answered questions for a half hour and then everyone left.

Al was delighted, and Norm offered Hugh the opportunity to return anytime he wished.

The Union

Kate Norton and a nervous Marian Nelson waited in Marian's office for the union representatives to appear. Kate had never dealt with the union before, and really wasn't as calm and cool as she tried to appear. However, she anticipated that it could only be an interesting session. Tom Wilson, the president, and Mark Elliott, the business manager, arrived promptly at nine o'clock and were introduced to

Kate. Tom worked in the machine shop on the one and only screw machine. Mark spent most of his time servicing several unions in the area and so was dressed in a business suit. He good-naturedly told Tom to stay on his side of the table and not brush any grease on his new suit.

After introductions Kate began to explain the proposed quality improvement program, emphasizing how important its success was to the future growth of HPA.

After fifteen minutes Tom held up his hand.

"Mrs. Norton, if you're asking for permission to have a Zero Defects program, I'm sure that it is well within the rights of management to have one. If you're asking our opinion about having one, it's about time."

"Well then, Mr. Wilson," smiled Kate, "will you help advise the quality improvement team?"

Wilson glanced at Elliott. He obviously hadn't expected this sort of approach. Mark tried to look as noncommittal as possible. Serving on management committees was not the thing they were encouraged to do.

Sensing Wilson's discomfort, Kate began on a new tack. "I'm not looking for a way of getting automatic union approval on everything the team does. I would like you to participate as an individual. Perhaps you might want to recommend one or two other employees who should be part of the program. This is probably the most important thing we are up to in this company right now."

Wilson nodded. "OK, I'll check with the executive committee about working with the improvement team. There should be no problem; they have been concerned about our quality for a long time. You might want to ask the guards to appoint a representative even though they don't belong to the union. Also, although I would personally be happy to do it for free, the contract requires that I be paid overtime when my eight hours is over. If that's a problem, I'd be willing to go on the second shift for a while. We'll work something out."

After the union men left, the two sat quietly for a while. Finally Kate said, "I think I'm going to learn something out of this business."

Bill's Problem: A New Philosophy

Bill Ranson strolled out on his back porch and stared vacantly into the back yard he hadn't been able to mow the previous weekend. The neighbors would soon be joshing him about it. His yard was as neat as any other working man's in the world. But how could he have known he was going to wind up with a retired farmer on each side of him? Besides that was about number 14 on his problem parade at the moment.

This new assignment of being administrator for the quality improvement team was a great opportunity for getting exposed to the big brass. Gibbon had laid his huge paw over Bill's shoulder that day and noted that it was he, Bill, who was going to make the thing work or fail. He had specifically told Bill to come and see him without hesitation if he felt that things were going off track. Bill realized that things *could* easily go wrong, but he had not worried after the meeting. It appeared to him that everyone was approaching the situation in a practical and honest manner.

So what was bothering him?

His wife Sharon arrived on the porch with two glasses of beer and an offer to sit down and talk about "it."

"What do you mean 'it,' " exclaimed Bill.

"When you walk out in the middle of our favorite rerun, and you don't go in to write something, then it is my duty as a member of the Imperial Order of Wives to find out what's up. After all, I used to be an engineer myself until the twins happened along."

Bill had to grin. Her straightforwardness made their marriage work. He barely had time to start brooding over a problem before she brought everything out in the open.

So he filled her in on the latest developments, with specific emphasis on his being appointed administrator for the team.

"It sounds like the opportunity you've always wanted. A chance to really make a difference through your personal contribution. Is that what's bothering you, the visibility?"

Bill thought a moment. "I think that isn't my problem. I'm ham enough to want to be out front, as you know. I think my problem, if I have one, is that it all appears to be going along so easily. There is no opposition, and nobody's building roadblocks. It isn't like normal. Perhaps I'm just being a cynic."

"No," mused Sharon, "I think you'll see all those things happen after the newness wears off. People are still people. However, the whole idea seems so positive, and is being carried out with so little finger pointing, that I can't see where you would get too much conflict."

Bill straightened up. "You know, Sharon, I think you may be on the verge of exposing what's been bothering me even though I didn't know it. Everyone thinks we are involved in a technique rather than a concept, and that's why there is so little of the normal conflict."

"What's the difference between a 'technique' and a 'concept'? I always thought that sort of discussion related only to philosophy class."

Bill pulled his chair closer to his wife. "Philosophy is the thing I mean. That's what this program is, a philosophy concerned with improvement. It's getting people to do what they should be doing anyway, and accomplishing it in an organized fashion. For instance, eating is a concept, cooking is a technique. Love is a concept, sex is a technique. Improvement is a concept, team management is a technique."

Sharon cocked her head. "So what you're saying is that you are involved in installing a new behavior concept in the company, but you have to pretend that all that is involved is a technique of program management."

"That's about it. The key negative aspect is that the people can get the idea that the system will work regardless of how much personal effort they put in or don't put in; if that happens, I'm in trouble. That's why I have to make all this as personal as possible.

"Take the steps of the program. We've already done management commitment and quality improvement team. We have to move quickly into measurement. We have a lot of measurements available for the product itself, both in-plant and out-of-plant. However, I'm going to have a real problem when it comes to measurements on areas like marketing and finance. And how about personnel? That is going to be the first tough test. What am I going to say when engineering people ask me how I could possibly measure their precious designers?"

"Why not," said Sharon, "ask them how they know who their best people are and how they know when someone rates a raise? If they can't answer that, then you've got a bigger company problem than you think you have."

STEP THREE: QUALITY MEASUREMENT

Purpose:
To provide a display of current and potential nonconformance problems in a manner that permits objective evaluation and corrective action.

Manufacturing Measurement

General operation. Basic quality measurement data come from the inspection and test reports, which are broken down by operating areas of the plant. By comparing the rejection data with the input data, it is possible to know the rejection rates. Since most companies have such systems, it is not necessary to go into them in detail. It should be mentioned that unless these data are reported properly they are useless. After all, their only purpose is to warn management of serious situations. They should be used to identify specific problems needing corrective action, and they should be reported by the quality department.

Quality measurement is only effective when it is done in a manner that produces information people can understand and use. Therefore, the operating and reporting methods should be straightforward and expressed in terms such as "defects per unit," "percent defective," and so forth. In addition, defects singled out for their frequency, or problem potential, should be classified as to *seriousness, cause,* and *responsibility*. This eliminates the necessity of spending time on less significant items while more important worlds are waiting to be conquered. The best method of properly utilizing the information is to concentrate on two types of reporting for each area:

1. Trend charts. These charts, posted on a weekly or monthly basis, show the running status of the area. Management can use them to determine if things are getting better. The best specific use of these charts is to establish improvement goals and to expose these charts and their goals constantly to the personnel. Display charts can be created inexpensively from wood or paper and colored tape. They should be large enough so they can be seen from any place in the area. Miniatures of these charts can be supplied to managers on paper.

2. Problem identification. The quality engineer assigned to each area should provide a daily listing of the items causing the most important or frequent defects. By classifying these as to seriousness, cause, and responsibility, the quality engineer sets the stage for corrective action with the personnel involved. Those items which do not get resolved promptly can be moved further along the corrective action cycle (see step 6).

Data acquisition. Noncomplex forms should be supplied to inspection and test personnel so they can record the results of their measurements. The basic information required is:

1. Part name and number; date; name of inspector and operator

2. Amount checked

3. Amount found defective

4. Specific description of the defect

5. Operation and area where detected

The quality supervisor or engineer should review each defect and assist in classifying it.

Collected data are compiled, and status charts are posted. Problems identified are listed in order according to frequency, and this information is supplied to the supervision of the area as well as to other management people. The trends or situations exposed should be immediately placed into the corrective action system.

Comment: There is really no excuse for someone not knowing what is happening.

Service Measurement

Planned programs of improvement in quality, productivity, profit margin, and so on are usually concentrated in the manufacturing areas. There the people are physically well organized, the work is measured and analyzed, and the management is resigned to the necessity of continually doing better. Thoughtfully conceived and conducted programs always produce results. We know a lot about improvement in manufacturing. Yet in manufacturing plants at least half the employees are "white collar" or service personnel who never touch the product. In "pure" service companies like insurance, finance, education, or hotel, almost all the employees meet this definition. The implementation of improvement programs in these types of industries is not usually formalized because of the difficulty of measuring current status and thus the difficulty of recognizing improvement or its lack. Yet these are the jobs that absorb the majority of compensation costs, generate expenses, order things, pay the bills, communicate with the customer, and direct the actions to be taken in the company—all through marks on paper. This "software" makes the company "happen," or not happen.

Studies show that over 85 percent of these pieces of paper contain an error—*at least* one error. None of these errors is necessarily highly significant, or a disaster in itself, but it needs to be found and fixed. This fixing changes the process of the operation and starts a chain of waste. The cost of this fixing runs at least 25 percent of the operating expenses of any function. That means that one dollar out of four is spent doing things over and, in the process, not doing something that should have been done. To figure this "cost of time," multiply the time spent by each employee involved in the occurrence by 3. The 3 comes from counting the time taken to do it in the first place, the time taken to fix the error, and the time lost that could have been spent on a new task. This doesn't include the cost of finding the problem, which may be bigger than the cost of time itself. Eliminating this waste through local management actions is a big source of profit for a company in a day when profit sources are drying up. Consider a few typical cases of "paperworkmanship" problems:

- An order-writing group takes the salesperson's input and produces a shop order that tells manufacturing the specifics on the product ordered. Because the order writer checked "green" instead of "blue," the customer gets the wrong item. All the time spent making sure the order is manufactured exactly like the requirement was wasted. The requirement was wrong. Worse, the real cause of the error may not be found until a lot of unnecessary actions are taken.

- Accounts payable people placed the wrong information on the computer input card. Therefore, the company could not take the discount reduction.

- A new product released to manufacturing has 231 engineering changes to be accomplished. An examination shows that all but three are mathematical errors, drawing goofs, or nonscientific normal-type mistakes that we have lived with for years.

- Welfare officials state that clerical errors cost them more money than any other source.

- The hotel clerk sends a guest to an unmade room. As a result, the clerk, the bellhop, the housekeeper, the maid, the reservations clerk, and, of course, the guest all spend an unscheduled fifteen or twenty minutes doing something that didn't need to be done.

- Because someone pressed the wrong key on a teletype a very busy person wasn't met at the airport.

To overcome this waste, and to bring the problems out where you can get at them, requires three things:*

1. *Recognition* by management that the situation exists. This step is up to management.

2. A method of *Measuring* current status. This is always felt to be the most significant problem in improving paperwork and service areas. In manufacturing shops every step is monitored by quality control people, and performance is calculated to the last digit. It is not this way with paperwork and service areas, and it is perhaps necessary that it should be. However, everything can be measured if you have a basis. In the case of paperwork the basis is change caused by unplanned deviation from procedure.

3. A *program* for correcting present problems and preventing their recurrence. Every activity makes mistakes at one time or another. These mistakes must be corrected. The correction may be *formal*, for example, a purchase order change notice, a computer punched card, or a certified letter. Or it may be *informal*, for example, replacing, erasing, or destroying. However it is done, the people in the area know about it, they know how to do it, and they know how to count it. All you have to do is ask them to help identify the correction method so it can be used to quantify measurement procedures. Charting these measurements provides the method of recording progress or its lack. Having agreed-upon measurements cannot be overrated in an improvement program. Without them there is nothing. The difficulty in developing measurement is the reason such programs have not

---

*All these are contained in a new program called *Make Certain,* which is outlined in detail in Chapter 13. Developed specifically for "software" and service operations, it is proved, practical, and uncomplicated and can be conducted during or after the fourteen-step program. Implemented by supervision, it produces cost elimination, and, what is perhaps more important, develops a positive sense of participation and accomplishment on the part of employees and management.

been implemented more often in administrative areas.
Now measurement can be uncomplicated.

Kate asked Bill to brief the team on the requirements of
the measurement step and its purpose, and to add whatever
background material he felt they needed. Bill stated that
the measurement step was probably the most important aspect of the entire program because it let results be known,
for better or worse.

"It is particularly important that we establish our measurements and record them at this time so we'll be able to
know if we're doing any good.

"There are two things we have to make certain get
taken care of: First, we have to make arrangements to have
agreed-on measurements for each department, and second,
we have to have a method of displaying the measurements
where everyone can see them."

Otto leaned forward. "You don't intend to have some
kind of chart on the defect rates of different areas hung up
where everyone can look at them, do you?"

Bill nodded in the affirmative.

Otto shook his head. "I don't think that's the way to do
it. I'm sure my buyers wouldn't like everyone to know their
problems — at least when they weren't in a position to know
the reasons. And I really am sure that our suppliers
wouldn't like their names all over our plant. After all, that's
what we're measuring in purchasing, the goodness of the
companies that supply us."

"Well, we have all the incoming products checked in
receiving inspection, and we know exactly how much is accepted and how much is rejected, so why couldn't we use
that as the measurement?" asked Will Ellis.

"That's what I was saying, Will," replied Otto. "We have
several thousand suppliers. It would be impractical to have
a chart for each one of them, and, even if we did, the people
here wouldn't relate to it. They'd just talk about 'those dumb
suppliers.'"

"I've been doing some investigation in this area, Otto,"
commented Allen. "I think there is a method you might

think about. It is called a 'buyer rating.' All you do is charge against each purchasing agent any supplier-caused error. This provides a defect rate. From what I know about the system, it shows pretty clearly that some buyers are just not as careful as others, and this brings it all out in the open. Why don't you think about it?"

"It might take a lot more than thinking. I'll talk it over with the buyers and see what they say."

"I think," Bill said, "that we are all going to have to have department discussions to determine what type of measurements will be specifically made. We have no problem with manufacturing because, true to the concept of the 'manufacturing ghetto', everything is measured there. We'll just have to pick up the ones that need to be emphasized. Personnel, marketing, and the other true service departments will have to give us their input later this week. I might point out that your supervisors are measuring their people every day. If they don't know what to put on a chart, just ask them who their best people are and then ask them how they know."

Kate leaned back. "Now let me get this clear. You are saying that we should have some kind of measurement chart that is highly visible — perhaps hanging from the ceiling in each area — that we'll use these charts to measure the progress of the quality improvement program?"

Bill nodded.

"Then that means we have to be careful about what we pick and make sure it is meaningful. We have to have performance measurement that relates to the success of the company."

Ralph Lowell interrupted. "We have all this field failure information, Kate, and it has never really been analyzed. Suppose we dissect it. That will let us know what areas we need to emphasize. It could give the departments some ideas."

Kate beamed. "Now that is a great suggestion. Can the quality people help?"

"Yes. We'll work with the field service group immediately. I might suggest also that we use the results of this analysis as the starting point for the improvement program. In other words, we can say that this is where we stood when the team began operation."

"Done. Now we can break up the meeting. I am going to give you information about measurement and about the next step in the program—the cost of quality. That is also measurement of sorts. I hope you'll take time to read this little outline on the cost of quality so we'll all understand it the same way. It is what the whole thing's about."

As the group begn to rise and leave, Alice Wagner, the comptroller, sat quietly as though lost in thought. Noticing this, everyone sort of paused in their exodus. Kate, a little concerned, asked Alice, "What's bothering you, Alice? Is that accountant's mind of yours running a balance sheet on us?"

Alice smiled.

"No, Kate, as a matter of fact I was just thinking how well everything is going and how I have confidence that it is all going to come out the way we think it should. Particularly the cost of quality thing. ı ve known about that for some time, and I must say that I couldn't get anyone interested in it. However, that is beside the point. And speaking of points, as long as you're all standing there staring at me, I guess I might as well make mine."

Most of them sat down. Ralph and Allen leaned against the wall. Wagner rarely spoke about anything in the staff meetings unless prodded. She had already talked more in these few moments than in the previous year. Obviously she had been thinking about something and now had decided to part with it.

"The thing that has been bothering me since we started to do this quality improvement program is why we needed it at all."

She raised her hand as Allen started to lean forward. "I understand all about the poor products and service we have been inflicting on our customers. And I recognize that actions need to be taken to correct the situation. As a matter of fact, they are very long past due. I recognize all that. What gave me trouble was why we had to go into this unusual formation to solve it. Why do we have to have a team, and a set of inflexible steps that have to be followed in order. After all, we are only going to do what we should be doing anyway.

"The setup obviously isn't for the employees; they are pretty much willing to go along with whatever we want. The boss has already taken the blame for the whole situation, so we aren't looking for a scapegoat, and we aren't all pulling on a rope together, so there is no load to move."

Ralph stirred. "You mentioned a point."

"Right. A point. Well, the point is this. It is apparent to me that most managers, us included, are so concerned with today, and with getting our own real and imagined problems settled, that we are incapable of planning corrective or positive actions more than a week or so ahead. This team, and the long-range improvement concept, forces us to plan ahead. It requires a commitment from us and, most important, creates an environment in which we can all be completely honest with each other and work together without feeling we are going to be criticized or competed against. I think we have to recognize that we have been placed in this position for a purpose and that the success of this team may very well be the success or failure of the division.

"With that I am going to give you some advance information. As I said, I have been interested in the cost of quality for some years, and a few days ago we ran a calculation on it. I would like to report that our cost of quality is 20.2 percent of sales. To spare you the mathematics that is almost $11 million per year. My point folks, is that there is nothing more important for us to do than to reduce that to the 4 percent of sales, or $2.1 million, that the quality professionals say is reasonable if not lovable. The difference is just $9 million! We could add an easy four megabucks to our profit by doing this right.

"So I am going to meet with my staff tonight. We are going to figure out a way to measure accountants, timekeepers, auditors, and everyone else in a way they will respect and appreciate."

There was a small silence. Then Ralph said: "$11 million for doing things wrong? Do you have this all broken out?"

"Thought you'd never ask," smiled Alice. "I have copies here for all of you. Note that there is no heading and very little explanation. I wouldn't want this kind of information to get out where the competition could get at it. Most of the costs I have are for labor of one sort or another. I didn't count engineering changes or rework done by the white-collar people. However, almost everyone is there.

"I took a figure of $17,000 per person to cover salary and burden. In some cases, that figure is too high, but in most it's too low. But overall it is fair. In my opinion the entire picture is understated." She gave them the figures:

- Field service personnel (all of
  whom exist only to repair
  and replace products at
  the customer's place)   281 / 17K = $4,777,000

- Quality department (most of
  whom we wouldn't need if we
  did things right)   187 / 17K = 3,179,000

- Manufacturing personnel
  involved in in-house rework   62 / 17K = 1,054,000

- Warranty costs   1,269,750

- Scrap   620,241

    Total $10,900,000

There was a long silence as the numbers sank in. Finally Ralph asked if this meant that the entire field service department was the target of the improvement program.

"Not hardly," replied Al. "But as we improve our outgoing quality, there will be fewer field services to perform. At least as the work is structured now. But don't feel bad; my whole department is a contributor too."

There was a moment of silence. Then Will spoke.

"If we solve the problem right, we will grow enough to keep all our people, but we have to remember that we are trying to repair the health of the company. If we don't get that done, and done right, the choices will be taken from us."

"Meeting dismissed," said Kate.

STEP FOUR: THE COST OF QUALITY

Purpose:
To define the ingredients of the cost of quality, and explain its use as a management tool.

General Operation

1. The cost of quality is composed of the following:

Scrap	Purchase order changes
Rework	Software correction
Warranty	Consumer affairs
Service (except regular	maintenance) Audit
Inspection labor	Other costs of doing things
Quality control labor	wrong
Test labor	
Acceptance equipment costs	
Engineering changes	

2. This total expense should represent no more than 2.5 percent of your sales dollar.

3. If your cost of quality is more than 2.5 percent, you have a direct opportunity to increase your return on sales by the exact amount you can reduce this expense. This reduction is most efficiently and quickly taken by concentrating on preventing the defects rather than on reducing the amount of acceptance operations, since it constitutes only a small part of the cost.

The following are reasonable expenditures for quality cost.

Rework. The amount of direct labor, burden, and material required to correct nonconforming material.

Allowable   0.25% of sales
Your actual   ————

Scrap. The amount of unplanned scrap produced in dollar value, plus the added value of labor and burden to the point of discard.

Allowable   0.25% percent of sales
Your actual   ————

Warranty, service. The dollar value of sold items returned by the customer for nonconformance, and the expense of replacement, repair, or service.

Allowable   0.2% of sales
Your actual   ————

Acceptance labor. The salary and expense of the inspection, quality control, test, and audit personnel who measure nonconformance and similar functions.

Allowable   1.8% of sales
Your actual   ————

Sharon couldn't wait to find out how the meetings went that day, and Bill couldn't wait to tell her. This no-wait policy led to a lot of rapid interrupting until Bill finally held out his hands and asked for calm.

"Let's take it from the top, and I'll tell you the whole thing. We got together today for our weekly meeting and discussed the measurement system briefly and then I started to bring up the awareness activity. It's time we got started on it, although I'm not sure everyone is too interested in hanging posters all over the place. Every time I turned to that subject someone would bring up the cost of quality again. I just can't tell you how big an impact that number, and the revelation that it existed, has had on these managers. They really didn't believe they were playing for such big stakes."

"I don't understand," said Sharon. "Doesn't every company figure their cost of quality like that? Is ours so much higher? What is the big surprise?"

"The surprise, my dear, is that very few people figure it with the deadly entirety of our comptroller. In every company I've known about, they have cut it down as small as possible. For instance, they only include the salaries of the people doing rework, not the burden, and they don't count the supervision involved. Yet if you didn't have those people, you wouldn't need the supervision. It really points out that we were heading for an extremely difficult financial situation."

"I think there is another reason everybody was so shocked," smiled Sharon. "I think a lot of them realized that they haven't been doing all that great a job of managing the company. They could have made operations a lot more profitable."

He looked at her in surprise. "That's just what Will said. He made it very clear that if we could cut our defects down to zero we would have all that money to grow on and that we could use the people for that. It isn't a matter of decimating the operation; we are going to need good people to expand. This has been hanging like a rock around our pocketbook. We couldn't grow because our products needed so much work and attention. If we get our products right, then the way is clear."

"I think you should call this the 'new attitude program' instead of 'quality improvement.'"

"You're absolutely right. But you can't let the team know that; they think they invented the whole thing. Let's eat, I need my strength."

"Hunger is an attitude too, you know," remarked Sharon. "I have this feeling that we don't think enough about attitudes. Most of the people I know who have problems seem to me to create most of their problems through their attitudes. They feel this way or that way about things, they are bigoted or not, and all of it seems to be unconnected, like it is just a pattern of thought they picked up during their life."

"I have noticed that negative attitudes seem more contagious than positive ones."

"That's right. The other night I watched a minister on TV who healed people by touching them. I don't understand it all, but there have been cases of lame people walking, deaf people hearing, and so forth. I am all for these cures, whether they are God's work or whatever. But I sure wish that we could do more about healing attitudes. That would do a lot more good for peace and prosperity than any limpless foot."

She paused.

"OK, attitude healer. Come on and eat."

Note: The cost of quality is the catalyst that brings the quality improvement team and other management people to a full awareness of what is happening. Before that, often they are only going through the motions of the program just to give the right impression. After all, modern companies are filled to the brim with programs: savings bonds; blood donor drives; value analysis; Buck a Day; United Appeal; cleanup inventory control; cost reduction; and on and on. The cost of quality takes the business of quality out of the abstract and brings it sharply into focus as cold, hard cash. Suddenly the potential for achievement is there. Suddenly, it really is a profit maker instead of a negative thought.

Don't get so involved with the techniques of calculating the cost of quality that you forget what it should be used for: to call attention to the problems and as a way to identify those areas needing corrective action.

STEP FIVE: QUALITY AWARENESS

Purpose:
To provide a method of raising the personal concern felt by all personnel in the company toward the conformance of the product or service and the quality reputation of the company.

General Operation

1. By the time you are ready for the quality awareness step,

you should have a good idea of the types and expense of the problems you face. These will have been revealed by the quality measurement and cost of quality steps.

2. The idea of quality awareness is to show everyone the need for improvement and prepare them for eventual commitment to the Zero Defects program.

3. The quality awareness activity has two essential ingredients:

   a. Regular meetings must be held between management and employees to discuss specific nonconformance problems and to attempt to arrive at some steps that can be taken to remove these problems. These meetings should not only be between workers and their supervisors but also between the supervisors and their managers. Meetings should be short, positive, and to the point. They must take place on a regular basis, and promises made must be kept.

   b. Information about the quality program must be communicated through posters, articles in the house organ, and special events. The purpose of this is to provide reassurance that the company is serious about the emphasis on quality and to keep the message constantly in front of the people. The material necessary is quite inexpensive and can even be homemade. Some companies run quality poster contests for the employees and their families, giving small prizes for the winners while at the same time amassing a huge supply of free posters.

The quality awareness portion of the program should be planned by the improvement team. However, they should lean heavily on public relations, personnel, and similarly skilled functions.

Comment: Quality awareness should be low-key and constant—a consistent stream of events with no real start or finish.

As the program began to take shape, the team communications became more complex. Bill Ranson decided to begin a series of status memos to make certain everyone was receiving the same information.

Memorandum to: Quality Improvement Team
From: Bill Ranson
Subject: Measurement

We now have the primary measurement categories planned by each department as well as the preliminary status of field failure causes. Unless I have word from you to the contrary, these will be our benchmarks in describing the situation as it exists today. Detailed reports will be sent to you on the field problems. This is just to summarize what the customer is seeing:

1. Product Measurement

Item	Customer Rejections	Primary Problems
Toasters	8.6%	Open coils Wrong handles Shipping damage

Comment: Coil problem has been traced to poor soldering at vendor. Handles were to drawing but both were obsolete. Shipping damage cause not clear yet.

Item	Customer Rejections	Primary Problems
Personal TV	14.3%	Wrong color received Component failure

Comment: Color of set case and the color marked on the box don't correlate occasionally; the reason is not known. Repair technicians find that components have been placed in the wrong position; final test in factory is suspect and is being checked.

Electric skillet	6%	Flaking plating Stencil blurred

Comment: Handle paint is chipping off; reason not known yet. Stencil blurred was the main rejection reason, apparently due to sloppy handwork in-plant.

Other products will be detailed in accompanying report.

2. Department Measurements
   Manufacturing. Line charts now in use provide defects per unit and percent defective measurement in all areas. In addition the personnel involved have decided that they would like to have the improvement goals placed right on the charts and the charts hung over the work areas on 3- by 4-foot boards so everyone can see them. All charts will be this size except in office areas, where they will still hang from the ceiling but will be 2 by 2.67 feet.

   Engineering. Drawing change notices for each group as well as errors found in drawing checking, will be a major source of measurement.

   Computer programming. Calculate computer time needed to "clarify" programs, and "arithmetic" errors found in program checking. Also measure any downtime caused by punching errors.

   Comptroller. Measure accounts receivable overdues and ledger errors found in audit. Make random arithmetic inspections on timekeepers sheets. A suggestion program is now being conducted to determine ways to make more personal measurements.

   Quality. Compute customer rejections, defects repeated after corrective action, and errors found attributed to a previous department. Review board action taking more than one day.

   Purchasing. Calculate receiving acceptance product defects that are attributed to the buyer instead of the supplier. Also, find any omissions of proper specifications, etc., from purchasing order.

   Marketing. Calculate errors in order documents, misstatements of product specifications in response to bids, price notifications missed, etc.

Field Service. Identify repeat failures, illegible reporting forms, workmanship audits.

Guards. Note failure to punch location clocks. Identify security violations.

Personnel. Measure tardiness of workers. Analyze contract grievances by the union. Note delays in processing transfers and training program completions.

Kate stood in front of the quality improvement team. "The important thing we have to remember about the awareness step is that we have to reach every employee, and they have to be reached by their supervisor with their peers. These are the people who are really important to them."

Harry Williams asked, "Why can't we just have one big meeting and get the message to everyone at one time? Then we could get the whole thing over with sooner and get started on recovering some of that money we're wasting."

Kate looked toward Bill, suggesting that he answer this question.

"We probably should take that approach when we get to Zero Defects day because then we are looking for a commitment from everyone to accelerate the program. However, at this point, it is necessary that we explain the situation carefully to each individual and that each person hear it from the supervisor. Otherwise they might not feel personally involved enough to make the suggestions and take the actions necessary to reduce the errors.

"Perhaps we better review the next few steps to see how they fit together. Awareness is to let people know that we are emphasizing quality and its importance. The supervisors need direction in taking this problem to their people. We are going to have to do some supervisor training.

"After that we establish the corrective action system formally. Actually it does already exist, but it needs rebuilding. After all, if we are going to ask people to solve problems, we have to have a corrective system that works.

"Then we can plan for the Zero Defects program. Once we have launched it, we will start error cause removal and then go on to goal setting and recognition."

"Why don't we just go into Zero Defects right away? After all, that is our goal. Why fiddle around with these other steps?" said Harry.

Al spoke up. "We are after a permanent improvement program, one that will become part of the culture of the company. To do that we have to make sure it is well established. We will get a large amount of improvement out of the steps we are taking prior to ZD. If the figures of other companies can be believed, we should reduce our errors about 40 percent through those actions. In effect we are knocking off the easy ones—obvious things like improving solder workmanship, being more careful with writing process plans, and double checking the packaging.

"But when we talk to our people about ZD and ask them to do every job right the first time, we have to be able to respond to them. People take a request like this seriously. When they look at their job to see what is standing in the way of perfect performance, they want to be able to pinpoint the cause of error. All they need to know is the problem. It is up to us to find the solution."

"Let me see if I have this clear," said Otto. "We are going under the assumption that the people of this company have never had it made clear to them that we expect every job to be done right every time. Therefore, we are going to tell them that slowly so they don't get too shocked. Then we are going to help them perform to that standard by fixing the problems they tell us they have. All this is going to eliminate errors. Correct?"

"I've never heard it stated so clearly. You are correct."

"You know, it just might work."

"Of course, what we are really after is to establish the prevention of error as a fact of life and performance. That's where the future lies."

"OK," said Kate. "Let's get down to determining what we are going to do about awareness. I presume that our coordinator has made arrangements for some posters and other internal advertising."

"Right. I have ordered posters from commercial suppliers that say the standard things, like "quality is the best way to ensure jobs," and so forth. However, my wife has a suggestion that the team might want to consider."

"Speak," smiled Kate.

"The suggestion was that we ask the children of the employees to create quality posters for us. We can use the next issue of the company paper to announce it. The prize could be some of the products.

Otto said, "What if the products don't work? How about giving something children would like. A day off from school for instance. Or all the TV you can watch in twenty-four hours? Or some books?"

One by one the team members acknowledged that this was a great idea, and gave the authorization to go ahead. Kate felt that this was something that should be discussed with the union representatives. Al cautioned her to remember that you didn't have to be in the union to have children. The contest would be open to all, it would be dignified, and there was no reason to ask for permission.

"OK," said Kate, "we'll have an information meeting."

It was decided to invite all supervisors to meet in the cafeteria after work that evening for a thirty-minute orientation on the program. After that they would meet individually with their department heads during working hours the next day for specific briefings. All employees, with the emphasis on 'all,' would have discussions with their supervisor on the importance of the quality program within three days. Then group meetings would be held every week until further notice.

Supervisors/Quality Improvement Team
(Some Representative Comments)

Hugh: "I have made plans for a pleasant and remunerative career topped by a reflective and affluent retirement. If we don't get this quality situation solved, these things will not come true. Whether or not we improve is entirely in your hands. People perform to the standard of their leaders, and you are their leaders. I am your leader, and I say we are going to make the products like we told the customers we would."

Kate: "The marketing people are behind this program all the way. The regional marketing people have asked how soon they can bring some of their biggest customers into the plant so they can see for themselves the type of quality performance that we conduct. I told them to give us two months. Hugh says that is too long."

Bill: "When you talk with your people, conduct the meeting around a table and talk openly. The quality engineers have provided you with error details so you can ask your people how to overcome some of the problems listed. Don't reject any ideas or put anyone down. The service area supervisors will emphasize the effect of what their groups do, rather than the specifics, until we get more data. However, you know the problems. The idea is to enlist everyone's cooperation and participation in this quality improvement drive."

There were a few questions about techniques and a bit of uncertainty about how well some of the groups would respond. However, as Hugh noted at the close of the meeting, no one had suggested that the actions weren't necessary. That in itself made it obvious that they had better get moving for sure.

Assembly

Carl Albert sat around the table with the sixteen people who made up his group in cable harness assembly. Nine women and seven men were all nervously glancing at him and each other. This meeting was not his usual way of working. Carl didn't really care for the idea at all, since he was much more used to dealing with his employees one at a time, or at most in pairs. However, he cleared his throat and attempted a small smile. "I'm glad we could all get together for a few moments to discuss something that is very important to all of us. That is quality."

He noticed a reflection of relief on several faces.

"Last night we had a meeting with the general manager and his staff as well as all the other supervisors. The purpose was to inform all of us about the quality situation so that we could come and talk to you and so that between the whole bunch of us we could do something to make it all better."

Carl surprisingly found himself out of breath. He paused and noted, "I guess I'm not too experienced at speaking to large groups." Everyone laughed and a few lit cigarettes as they began to feel a bit more comfortable.

"What I mean is that we are having problems with the products in the field because of defects that are being put in here at the plant because of poor design and quality of work, and because of supplier problems. No one is exempt. We have to work together to see what we can do to prevent these problems."

Martha Howard raised her hand. "What about inspection? Aren't they supposed to catch these things before they go out?"

"They sure are Martha, and they're going to have to find better ways of doing inspection and testing. They are having meetings at this very moment on this subject. However, if we are fair about it, we have to recognize that if we do our jobs right and completely, there won't be anything for inspection to miss. Prevention, that is our problem."

"What kind of problems are they finding with our work?" asked Leroy Anders. "We get some feedback, but usually anything they find wrong with our stuff goes to the rework area and we never see it. I think I would like to do my own rework and then I'd know what is going wrong."

"Gee, Leroy, that's a great idea. I'll bet nobody ever thought about that aspect. They probably think they are doing us a favor by taking the rework to another place. I'll get that to management right away."

"What kind of items are they finding at the dealer's?"

"I have a list here of things that relate to us. The most common is reversing the wires on the internal power plug for the TV sets, and next most common is leaving a wire out of a bundle. The rest are nicked or damaged wires and little items. Our most expensive rework is the TV plug. Anybody have any ideas on what to do?"

Martha stuck her hand up again. "You know, Carl, both those wires are the same color."

"They didn't used to be. One was red and the other was black."

"Well, they're both green now."

"Must have been a cost reduction."

"How about having someone put a tag on the wires for a while, and we'll be more careful?"

"OK. We'll do that. Now let me say one more quick thing before we break up. We'll have another meeting next week. In the meantime, if you have more thoughts, just tell me. But we're serious about this quality improvement business. The measurement charts on defects per unit are going to be hung up this week right over there. They will show how well we're doing. Our level is 5.6 defects per harness. That's very high. I'd like to see us get it down quickly. One way to do that is to start doing our own rework so we'll know better what problems we are making for ourselves. Thanks."

Production Control

The production control group gathered around the highboy in the metals stock bin. Harold Withers thumped the steel desk good-naturedly and called for order. He and his men had an easy familiarity grown from having worked together for a long time.

"I'm going to talk to you about quality," he smiled.

Several groaned.

"I figured you'd react that way. You guys think that quality has nothing to do with you; you think it is all involved with the quality department, that it is their problem alone. The reason I know you think this way is that I had that in my mind until last night. Last night I saw some of the problems we have around here, and I saw that we are indeed a big part of their solution."

"How could we have much to do with it, Hal," asked Tim Collel. "Unless you look at the things we drop once in a while, we have no way of affecting quality."

"Suppose I told you that the biggest single problem in printed circuit board assembly was wrong components on the boards. Someone picked the wrong component out of the hand bin and put it on the board. Who do you suppose put it in the hand bin?"

Everyone tried to speak at once. "That's not so." "We don't do that, we just deliver the parts. Other people put them in the bins."

Hal held his hand up for quiet.

"Now let's start all over. We touch every piece of product that goes through this operation. We mother it from the receiving dock to the shipping dock. We expedite some and retard others. We move the product from assembly to inspection, from stock bin to garbage can. If it gets bought, made, stored, scrapped, or just rotated, we touch it. Right?"

"Right."

"Then we contribute to the problems involved in getting everything together by mixing things up once in a while or by somehow interfering with the flow."

There was a silence and then a slow nodding of agreement.

"And I'll tell you what's more important than that. We see everyone in this plant all day long. We are attitude formers whether we like it or not. Thought leaders. You won't find it up on one of those measurement charts, but we are the ones who can affect how everyone feels around here. If we're frowning we spread it around; if we're smiling, they're smiling. Right? Right.

"So, starting that moment we are going to be walking, talking examples of quality. I got the quality improvement coordinator to have some badges made for us and we're all going to wear them, they say: *I'm for Quality.* We're going to wear them everywhere, every day, and we're going to be very careful how we do things. Right?"

The group smiled. Hal really was right.

"Do we get to offer suggestions on how to do our job better?"

"You sure do. Give them to John and we'll meet again before work tomorrow morning and discuss them. Anyone who can't make it, that's OK because it is a no-pay time. But we're going to be the most improvement-oriented outfit in the company. Right? Right."

And a Final Note

Hugh invited Al to have a cup of coffee with him. Walking to the cafeteria, they both nodded and spoke to everyone they met. Hugh in particular had developed a good visual relationship with the employees. They appreciated his positive appearance and brisk step. Al felt that the operation was in good hands.

"I think the improvement program is off to a good start. We are already getting some reduction in defect rates, and the moving of rework back to the person who caused the problem seems not only to be a good corrective action but is also good for morale," said Hugh.

Al beamed. "I think you're correct. The preliminary numbers from the field are better also. As far as I can tell the meetings between the supervisors and their people went off well. Most folks were surprised that they occurred at all. Overall this program has to be a great thing for the company."

"I'm sorry we didn't start it sooner, Al. But at least we did get moving. I think you are to be congratulated for making it happen. And while I'm patting your back, let me also state that if you had made a bigger deal about those cost of quality numbers you probably could have sold the program earlier. But that's just a guess."

"I know that is absolutely correct, Hugh. I've kicked myself for holding back. From now on they will be right up front."

STEP SIX: CORRECTIVE ACTION

Purpose:

To provide a systematic method of resolving forever the problems that are identifed through previous action steps.

General Operation

1. Problems that are identified during the acceptance operation, or by some other means, must be documented and then resolved formally. The most direct method is to establish four levels of constant activity:

    a. Hold daily meetings between the area supervisor and a quality engineer or supervisor to examine the problems detected. Determine methods of correcting the present situations while preventing their recurrence in the future. These meetings should be documented on an item-by-item action chart that states the problem, the seriousness of the problem, and its cause, as well as who is going to do what when.

    b. Hold weekly meetings between the production general supervision and senior quality management to attack problems that cannot be, or were not, solved at the lower level. They should invite to their meetings the other department personnel involved. The meetings should be documented on the same type of action chart mentioned above.

    c. Monthly or special meetings should held by the general manager and staff to review the unresolved problems. Items reaching this level should be specific; those requiring complex or long-range action should be assigned to a task team.

    d. Task teams should consist of responsible members of each affected organization with one person appointed as chairperson. The jobs of the task team should be carefully spelled out, and their completion time specified. The team may have to meet daily until the problem is resolved. At the time the problem is judged to be eliminated, the team should be dissolved.

Comment: Corrective action is most successful when it operates on the well known Pareto principle, which states that the biggest and most important problems should be attacked first, then the next biggest, and so on. The attitude of defect prevention provides the incentive to fix a problem once and for all so it will never come back.

A Sample Corrective Action Communication

TO: Mr. Allen Fielding

FROM: Boyd Deams, Quality Engineer

SUBJECT: Corrective Action Meeting on TV Problems

ATTENDEES: G. Wilton, Marketing
Y. Brothers, Engineering
B. Gilbert, Manufacturing
B. Deams, Quality
S. Leed, Field Service

As you know we have had many incidents at a customer's store of the TV set being of one color and the label on the box saying it is of a different color. The dealers have been very irritated and occasionally embarrassed by this; it means that they have to open the box to find out what is in it. As a result of our not correcting this problem, dealers have taken to shipping all their products back to the field service areas in order to have corrective action taken. A corrective action meeting was called in order to find a method of preventing the problem in the future.

S. Leed stated that the label, listing serial number and color, is attached to the box after the set is inserted and the box is closed. He felt that this caused the problem, and would continue to cause problems. B. Gilbert stated that the labels and the television sets are coordinated to arrive at the box closing together, and that what has been seen in the field are just a few that got mixed up when the lines went out of sequence one day. He felt that the problem would not be repeated.

G. Wilton said he didn't care who fixed the problem, but he definitely wanted something done because it was destroying relations with customers. Deams suggested the team go to the warehouse and pull some samples to see if the problem had been corrected.

Twenty-three boxes were selected at random and opened. Nine contained sets of a different color than that described on the label. The shipping supervisor was called to the meeting and asked for his information on the subject. He said the labeling machines skipped sometimes and that he didn't have enough people to do it by hand. We then called the labeling machine maintenance chief, who said that the machine was the most reliable piece of equipment in the factory.

As the team was about to disband, Brothers suggested we look at the labeling operation and talk to the operator. The operator showed us how the labels come from a stack-up installed by production control near where they are attached to the boxes. However, the sets come from final testing and are placed on the packaging and closing line by the testers when they are finished with the test. Thus there is no actual coordination of sets with labels.

It is apparent that we have been fortunate that so many were labeled properly, since the entire operation is conducted by chance.

Corrective action has been taken. The problem won't happen again.

cc: Quality improvement team

"Corrective action," said Allen, "is just a matter of getting all the rocks rolled over and seeing what is under them. I have never seen a truly complicated action that had to be taken. Usually someone just assumes that someone else has been doing something that they haven't."

"You make everything so clear," said Will Ellis. "I think it's like the gold prices, where there are only two guys who understand it and they disagree."

"Well, you knew what I meant."

"Certainly I did. And of course I agree. All I want to really know is how come everyone else has problems that require documented corrective action and the quality department has none. I think you are sweeping them under the rug."

Al bristled: "We certainly were part of the labeling problem. And we did find that some of the rejections for soldering were strictly opinion—based on no fact."

"I know that Al. I was really just kidding. But on the square, I have the feeling that we might not be doing things right in a few areas. One of those is receiving inspection. I think we are being a little easy there—certainly not as firm and clear-eyed as you people are in the shop."

Al thought a moment. "You could have something there. I'll tell you what I'm going to do. Just because you were kind enough to say that we do a few things right now and then, I am going to do something I never have done before. I'm going to ask the corporate office to send one of the quality control people down to take a look at the receiving acceptance operation."

Will smiled. "Now that is what I call a real sacrifice. Are you sure you don't just want to have one of your guys do it? These corporate types can get you into some real trouble."

John Halden, HPA corporate quality engineer, came to see Al the following week. After getting comfortable with each other, John asked Al what he could do for him.

"First let me say that I am really pleased with the improvement program your office sent us. We are in the midst of installing it, and the results, even after this short period, have been amazing. In the first month we have dropped better than one-third on our defect rates. Everyone is enthusiastic. We should be having ZD day here in six weeks or so. Perhaps some of your people can get down to participate."

"We'd really like that Al," said John. "Some of the companies have been asking the corporate president; he comes to ZD days at the drop of a hat. Perhaps you should keep that in mind."

"That would really make an impression on the people. I'll ask Hugh about it."

"Now, what was it you were interested in having me audit."

"We have been concerned that we might not be doing a good job in receiving inspection. I thought that you could help us out by spending some time there."

John nodded. "No problem. But before I get started, let me fill you in on the procedure we follow in doing audits of this sort. We want to be very careful that we only contribute positive results to the operations and don't cause unnecessary problems. So we go through several points. Here is a card with the major actions listed on them."

Al took the card and read the action items.

1. Meet the quality manager and review the general situation: determine what the manager wants to accomplish.

2. Meet with the general manager and explain what you plan to accomplish. Inform the manager that your report will be written prior to your leaving the operation.

3. Ask if you can perform any specific service for the general manager.

4. Conduct the audit, working with the quality staff. Be sure clearance is obtained from any other department heads before working in their areas.

5. Write your report in its final format and have it typed. Review the report first with the quality manager and then with the general manager.

6. If they have any disagreements with your findings, note them on your report or, if their comments are correct, change the report.

7. If the report is to be distributed, mail it from the plant.

Al looked up from the paper.

"Why do you go through all of this? The other staffs come in, do their things, and then leave. We never hear from them again."

"Well, we want to make sure that what we are doing is useful. Besides, after you leave a plant, things begin to change in your mind. When you write a report too long after the fact, you are likely to make errors or even include items that pertain to another plant. After all, we cover a lot of ground."

He leaned forward confidentially. "This way, we are sure to be welcomed back. Most staff people have to fight their way back in."

"That's a good point. OK, let me see if we can get in to have your visit with Hugh."

The Audit Report

TO: Hugh Gibbon, Al Fielding

FROM: John Halden, Corporate Quality Department

SUBJECT: Audit of Receiving Acceptance Operations

Actions Required:
1. Inspections and tests on vendor-supplied items should be conducted to the terms of the purchase order rather than to historical records and process plans.
2. Lots rejected by receiving acceptance should be returned to the supplier for sorting and correction rather than having this done by inspectors.
3. Rejections made by acceptance personnel should not be reversed by supervision except in the most unusual cases.
4. Expeditors, purchasing agents, and production control personnel should be excluded from the work area.
5. Conduct a quality awareness program for suppliers, possibly including an in-plant seminar.

General Situation:

1. All inspections and tests are conducted according to a historical file system set by quality engineering. Thus when the terms of the purchase order change for a specific item, the item can be tested, rejected, reviewed, clarified, and then retested before the change is noticed. This causes considerable recycling and is expensive. It is also destructive to the morale of the personnel involved.

2. Most quality systems regard a product rejected in receiving acceptance as the property of the purchasing department, which then disposes of it through return, rework, or scrap. However, at HPA we are oriented toward taking steps as early as possible to determine how to use the product. Thus although an average of 18 percent of the lots received are rejected for one reason or another, less than 0.5 percent of the lots are returned to the vendors. This indicates a lenient attitude. The suppliers will not take complaints seriously.

3. Minor items called out by acceptance personnel are routinely OK'd by their supervision without much apparent thought.

4. There is a great deal of confusion in the receiving acceptance work area. Expeditors are continually talking to the operators to determine the status of the lots they are checking. Material is not well controlled, and the rejected lots are not bonded.

5. Since supplied material is about 50 percent of the finished product, I think it would be advantageous to make the suppliers aware of the improvement program being conducted. Many of the key suppliers have no idea how you are using their product and have no special relationship with HPA or any other customer except through the purchasing area. I think it is extremely important that we recognize that suppliers pass their cost of quality along to us. We should help reduce that cost.

Opinion: Corrections of the above items, which require no expenditure, will help receiving acceptance to "quiet down" and exercise better control. In the plant it is possible to see the effect of the quality improvement program. The people are enthusiastic and full of ideas. I suggest that you consider moving into the error-cause-removal phase of the program as soon as possible.

STEP SEVEN: ZERO DEFECTS PLANNING

Purpose:

To examine the various activities that must be conducted in preparation for formally launching the Zero Defects program.

General Operation

The quality improvement task team should list all the individual action steps that build up to ZD day in order to make the most meaningful presentation of the concept and action plan to personnel of the company. These steps, placed on a schedule and assigned to members of the team for execution, will provide a clean energy flow into an organization-wide ZD commitment. Since it is a natural step, it is not difficult, but because of the significance of it, management must make sure that it is conducted properly.

Specific Points: The main portions of ZD planning are:

1. Explaining the concept and program to all supervisory personnel. Preparing supervisors to explain it to their people.

2. Determining what material will be necessary and ensuring its preparation.

3. Deciding what method of launching the program will best suit the cultural environment of your particular operation.

4. Spelling out the functions that will be accomplished.

5. Examining the recognition policy of the company and determining what type of recognition should be used in praising improved performance.

6. Setting up the time schedule and rehearsing those who will take part.

7. Identifying the error-cause-removal program and making the plans for its execution (step 12).

Suggestions: Many companies have ZD programs, and all are happy to share their detailed information. The manager responsible for its implementation will better understand what is involved by communicating with them.

Although no express method of implementation is recommended, a technique that has proved extremely reliable as a method of getting the concept and pledge across to the personnel involves the use of a single-page explanation of the concept with the pledge incorporated. The company prepares one message for each employee on its own letterhead bond paper. On the appointed day, the chief executive of the company discusses the concept and pledge with those people reporting directly to him and gives them each a copy of the letterhead explanation. When all have had their questions answered,they sign the pledge and the executive countersigns. The paper is kept by the subordinate (who may wish to frame it). Everyone who has signed takes enough copies to handle the people in their departments. They repeat the operation with those who report to them, and so on down the line until each person in the company has discussed the ZD concept with his or her direct supervisor and has signed the pledge with the supervisor. This method ensures that each person gets the message; it also ensures that management understands it.

Signing the pledge is, of course, a voluntary thing. But if the explanation is conducted properly, there will be no difficulty.

Unions all over the world have genuinely accepted and supported the ZD program. They appreciate the recognition it gives to the importance of quality work today. But it is very important to make union people a part of ZD planning. Some companies appoint a union representative to the ZD part of the quality improvement task team. Others merely keep them informed. Whichever way you choose to get union participation, be sure you do not neglect it.

Comment: Zero Defects is a very effective, inexpensive management tool when wholeheartedly supported by management.

Sample Zero Defects Letter

HPA CORPORATION
Zero Defects—The Concept

Zero Defects is a performance standard. It is the standard of the craftsperson regardless of his or her assignment. It is not limited to production efforts; in fact, some of the largest gains are obtained from service areas. The theme of ZD is *do it right the first time.* That means concentrating on preventing defects rather than just finding and fixing them.

People are conditioned to believe that error is inevitable; thus they not only accept error, they anticipate it. It does not bother us to make a few errors in our work, whether we are designing circuits, setting up a machine, soldering joints, typing letters, or assembling components. To err is human. We all have our own standards in business or academic life —our own points at which errors begin to bother us. It is good to get an A in school, but it may be OK to pass with a C.

We do not maintain these standards, however, when it comes to our personal life. If we did, we should expect to be shortchanged every now and then when we cash our paycheck; we should expect hospital nurses to drop a constant percentage of the newborn babies; we should resign ourselves to going home to the wrong house periodically, by mistake. We as individuals do not tolerate these things. We have a dual standard: one for ourselves and one for our work.

Most human error is caused by lack of attention rather than lack of knowledge. Lack of attention is created when we assume that error is inevitable. If we consider this condition carefully, and pledge ourselves to make a constant conscious effort to do our jobs right the first time, we will take a giant step toward eliminating the waste of rework, scrap, and repair that increases cost and reduces individual opportunity. Success is a journey, not a destination.

Let's set our sights on Zero Defects.

ZERO DEFECTS—THE PLEDGE

I freely pledge myself to make a constant, conscious effort to do my job right the first time, recognizing that my individual contribution is a vital part of the overall effort.

SUPERVISOR ——————————————

Kate called the meeting to order.

"As you know, we appointed Marian Nelson, Ralph Lowell, and Will Ellis, along with our irreplaceable coordinator, as the Zero Defects ad hoc committee. Their responsibility is to prepare the ZD program and tell us how to do all of it. We are getting closer to ZD day also. We all have to begin to get involved. Bill, I understand that you have been elected to speak for the committee?"

"Right. We have learned a great deal about how to do ZD programs in the past few weeks. We made visits to three companies that have conducted programs and we even spent some time with a member of our corporate staff. She fixed us up with someone over at the Watts Corporation. All in all, we have done quite a bit of investigating."

Will interrupted. "What he is stalling around about is that we have learned that we have been on the right track all along. We ran into two outfits that weren't happy with their program's results, and two that couldn't say enough good things about it."

Kate asked, "Did you find out why it worked sometimes and not other times?"

"Yes we did," said Will, "and I think the whole committee agrees with me on the reasons. Marian will explain it all to you."

Al spoke up. "I wish someone would explain something soon. I feel like I'm being dragged behind a truck."

Marian stood up. "Not to worry. We'll take you off the hook quickly. The whole thing is wrapped up in the word 'motivation.' The companies that weren't happy with the results had gone into the program with the purpose of 'motivating' their people, particularly those in the factory, to do better work. The ones who had crashing success went in with the idea of communicating a work standard and the idea of cooperating in all efforts at corrective action."

Otto raised his head. "That sounds to me like psychological gobbledygook. Motivation is motivation. Everything you do to get another person to do something is motivation. How can you ignore it?"

"Oh, you don't ignore it," said Marian. "Everything just has to be put in its proper perspective. Certainly, every human exchange involves motivation. But it involves a great many other feelings and communications also. The problem is that the word motivation itself has come to be thought of as meaning an easy way of getting others to do something by showing them posters, banners, bands, and emotion-arousing symbols. People just aren't like that. They may get all enthusiastic over an event and respond for a while, but once they determine that there is no substance behind the device, they turn off.

"In addition, those involved in managing the program tend to throw the things out they want their people to absorb and then return to their office to wait for the victory banquet.

"We are interested in installing the standard of Zero Defects into our company on a long-term basis. We want it to be permanent. To do that, we must communicate totally and sincerely in a manner that the people will believe and accept as their own. You can't fool them."

"You're saying that these other companies didn't work hard enough at the job, is that it?"

"That's it. They got caught up in the emotion of the occasion and figured it would go on forever. The program does begin on ZD day, but it's like marriage: you just begin to work at it after the celebration. Bill, tell them about ZD day."

Bill put a chart on the holder. "What we have determined is this. We should have several activities leading up to the ZD day itself. One of the things we think we should do is have a 'suggestion day' about a week in advance. Every suggestion made on how we can "make certain" our products are right will be placed in a barrel. Then we will draw winners of some prizes on ZD day. That just adds to the fun. And let me make sure everyone understands that ZD day is supposed to be a fun day. That way it will be remembered. After ZD day we move right into goal setting, error-cause removal, and recognition. Then we do the whole program over again, except for ZD day as such, to make sure we are set."

"You are going to supply us with the details of ZD day?"

"Yes. We will do it big. Pledges, and signing them; pins and balloons; prizes for the children's poster contest; everything we can think of to make sure the words 'Zero Defects' are etched in everyone's memory. Hugh invited the corporation president, who has accepted. A U.S. Senator is coming, as well as the mayor and the regional president of the union. We'll lose a little production that day, but, we will surely transmit the message.

"The slogan we will use is *HPA — growing through quality.*"

"All the way with HPA."

"Sounds like a fascinating day. What time will all this happen?"

Will stood. "We figure on doing it the first thing in the morning. About a half hour into the first shift we will ask everyone to step out between the buildings. The supervisors will have been instructed on which exits to use and given all the details. We will have a thirty-minute program, and when everyone goes back to their workplaces, the supervisors will ask them to sign their pledges. Of course the supervisors will countersign.

"Hugh will be walking the celebrities around the plant and office areas. Hopefully, they will participate in this exchange."

"The next day we start error-cause removal by having forms placed around the plant as well as having one mailed to every employee's home," said Marian. "That way we can get them at the peak of interest. After that, we will have to do it all on a personal basis."

"Gee," said Kate, "you guys have really been digging into this thing. I think you have gotten yourselves all excited."

"True enough," said Will. "You know, I must admit that I didn't really recognize before that the whole business of quality and performance standards is wrapped up so much in things being visible. I mean a *visible* commitment, *visible* measurement, and *visible* corrective action. I guess we sort of had those things in the closet for years."

"Well, they're sure going to get let out now," said Kate. "One thing more. We're still in the awareness stage and will be until ZD arrives. The production control guys came up with these buttons and we have enough for everyone in the plant. How should they be distributed? They say: *I'm for quality.*"

"Why don't we just put them in bowls in the cafeteria and let anyone who wants one take it. Then we don't have to have this down-the-line business. Anyone who would be embarrassed by wearing a button doesn't have to. I'll take mine right now, though."

"OK," said Bill. "We found one more thing during our analysis: sometimes the key people feel they understand the concept of Zero Defects when they really don't. And, of course, it is vital that we here on the team really do because people are going to ask. The supervisors will go through the test* at their next training meeting. You get to take it home

*See Step Eight: Supervisor Training" for a copy of the test.

with you and do it all yourself. However, if any of the answers bother you, please get together with me and we'll see if we can get the whole thing worked out."

"I must confess," said Marian, "that I missed three of the questions when I took the test."

STEP EIGHT: SUPERVISOR TRAINING

Purpose:

To define the type of training that supervisors need in order to actively carry out their part of the quality improvement program.

General Operation:

The supervisor, from the board chairman down, is the key to achieving improvement goals. The supervisor gives the individual employees their attitudes and work standards, whether in engineering, sales, computer programming, or whereever. Therefore the supervisor must be given primary consideration when laying out the program. The departmental representatives on the task team will be able to communicate much of the planning and concepts to the supervisors, but individual classes are essential to make sure that they properly understand and can implement the program.

Supervisory training is divided into areas to be conducted at different times:

1. At the time that quality awareness is started the supervisors should be given at least six hours of instruction covering the Quality Measuring system, the cost of quality numbers, the corrective actions system, and the purpose of the quality awareness action. This instruction should be well planned, and should be conducted as much as possible by significant levels of management. Everyone must attend.

2. At least four weeks before the planned Zero Defects day, the supervisors should receive complete briefing on the ZD program and the error-cause-removal system that is

to follow in a few weeks. It is very important that they be able to answer the questions of their subordinates. Many companies prepare a handbook for supervisors which describes the program in detail.

3. Do it over again.

Supervisor's orientation to Zero Defects

How's your Zero Defects IQ?

Do you understand the concept of ZD?

This test is to assist you in determining if you really understand the concept of ZD. No one will know your grade but you. Naturally, any grade less than perfect indicates that you need to improve. Score 10 for each correct answer. Here's some help—the first statement is false.

1. ZD is a worker motivation concept.   T F

2. ZD needs management support.   T F

3. Anyone can run a ZD program.   T F

4. Errors are caused by one of three things: lack of knowledge, lack of attention, or lack of facilities.   T F

5. A ZD program is a management communications tool.   T F

6. ZD programs sometimes fail.   T F

7. ZD is for manufacturing companies only.   T F

8. A successful ZD program must be conducted under the name Zero Defects.   T F

9. Careful preparation is necessary before launching a ZD program.   T F

10. Award programs should give the workers cash if possible.   T F

Answers:

1. *False.* ZD is not a motivation concept—it is a management standard. It replaces the wishy-washy "let's do it

right" that leaves everyone to select an individual standard. Since we have exact standards for performance in the schedule and cost areas, we need one for quality performance. ZD is a tool for management to use in explaining its standards in a way that cannot be misunderstood. The ZD program, with its posters and "gimmicks," is a way of telling the employees about the new standard. However, the only reason you need it at all is that management has not made its position clear previously.

2. *False.* ZD needs active management participation, not just support. People judge your seriousness by what you do more than by what you say. If the effort is left entirely to lower-level people, it will collapse of its own emptiness within a year.

3. *True.* Any thoughtful person can conduct a successful program. All it takes is a little research and an understanding of the particular culture of the company.

4. *False.* Errors are caused by two things: lack of knowledge and lack of attention. Lack of facilities is an error caused by one or both of these. The person using inadequate facilities can hardly be blamed for the errors unless that person selected the facility. Planners and staff people must be held responsible for their contribution to the error pot.

5. *True.* ZD creates an attitude of defect prevention. In this environment it is possible to use the error-cause-removal system or other communication devices to let employees express their problems without necessarily knowing the solutions. Relationships between management and employees grow stronger, and as that happens understanding of mutual problems develops.

6. *True.* However, they always fail for the same reason: They are given short shrift by management. In these cases the managers felt that if a few banners were waved, everything would "get right."

7. *False.* All businesses are "manufacturing" in that they have processes or procedures that they are supposed to execute. The attitude of defect prevention pays off in all of them.

8. *True.* Zero Defects is a standard. "Do better work," "excellence in effort," and any of the many other motiva-

tion slogans beg the issue. People get to determine their own standards in the quality awareness programs that are an introduction to ZD. But there is no substitute for the words "Zero Defects." They are absolutely clear.

9. *True.* Careful preparation is needed before launching any management program. Many managers claim to be disappointed with the performance of their computers. However, the machines don't make mistakes. The errors are caused by ill-defined and ill-executed programs or poorly trained information input people.

10. *False.* Awards, or recognition, need to be whatever it takes to convince people that you are genuinely pleased with their performance. If it requires money in your situation, then you should look to your industrial relations program. People work for appreciation and recognition —once they have a basic living. Awards should be given with dignity and respect; their monetary value is not significant. Don't forget to give some to management, too.

Your score _____

STEP NINE: ZD DAY

Purpose:

To create an event that will let all employees realize, through a personal experience, that there has been a change.

General Operation

Zero Defects is a revelation to all involved that they are embarking on a new way of corporate life. Working under this discipline requires personal commitments and understanding. Therefore it is necessary that all members of the company participate in an experience that will make them aware of this change.

Specific Points: If possible, all employees should be oriented at the same time by people who are significant to the employees. Some companies have taken their personnel to the local stadium; or have brought everyone together out in front of the plant. A few have used closed-circuit television.

Face to face is best. Don't be afraid to use a little show business in the meeting. There is nothing wrong with fun and celebration on such a grand day.

Quality improvement team coordinators grow impervious to the routine disasters of life. Dealing with a diverse group of managers on a daily basis, coordinators learn patience, diplomacy, and humility. They also learn when to be hard-nosed and how to improvise. Resourcefulness is the most valuable characteristic of a coordinator.

However, there is one factor guaranteed to make a nervous wreck out of the most disciplined coordinator: weather. The platform is set up for the dignitaries, the public address system has been tested, the entire population of the plant is scheduled to appear in front of the podium at exactly 8:15 a.m. and . . . it looks like rain.

*   *   *

As random drops plopped on Bill's upturned face, he saw Hugh approaching the platform with the corporate president, Mr. Williams, Senator Ashbrook, and Mayor Brook in tow. In about thirty-five seconds Hugh was going to say, "What do you think, Bill? Are we going to go ahead with it?" And Bill would have to answer something. Would it rain, or wouldn't it? (Don't rain on my parade, he prayed).

The group reached him and Hugh introduced the guests. Mr. Williams smiled at the obviously worried young man. "Don't worry about the weather, Bill, I personally guarantee it won't rain for at least an hour. Let's get on with the program. It never rains on a Zero Defects day."

Feeling better but no braver, Bill signaled for the program to begin. "Happy days are here again" (the best idea they could come up with) began to play over the PA system, and at this signal the supervisors urged their people to the meeting area between the buildings. Mr. Williams stood in the middle of the assembly area shaking hands with those who came his way. This was partly his own idea, but in the main he was following the lead of the Senator, who admitted later that something just happens to him when he sees a crowd and hears assembly music.

"Just can't stop from shaking hands and saying hello to folks."

Hugh welcomed the employees to the gathering and, after the Mayor had spoken, introduced Mr. Williams as the corporation president. Williams, a medium-sized, slightly portly, effervescent person, put the crowd at ease immediately with a few light-hearted stories before getting to the heart of the matter.

"The most important thing we have to sell is quality. Everyone in the business can purchase the same components, designs, and packaging. Everyone can make the product for the same price that we can and in some cases a little less. The only thing we have going for us is the dedication of this group assembled here (applause) and the reputation for quality we are trying to create. The best way to create that reputation is to perform. Zero Defects to me is not an abstract goal; it is a fact of life, and an attainable fact of life. I don't see why we should expect to give our consumers any less than we tell them they are going to get. We want to give our customers products that do the job and do it every time. We will spend every cent we need to make that happen — but not one cent for waste (applause). Now I'd like to introduce Senator Ashbrook, who has promised not to make a campaign speech."

The Senator walked across the stage waving.

"Not only am I not going to make a campaign speech, Sam, I'm not going to make a speech at all. I want all of you to remember me for something pleasant. And the most pleasant job I could lay hands on today was awarding the suggestion prizes. But before I do that, I want you to know that I have given your president a check, out of my own pocket, for one of your electric skillets. This skillet, to be taken out of inventory next week, will be shipped to the White House as a present from me to the President of the United States for use in making his breakfast. I am going to send him a note saying that he is going to receive a Zero Defects skillet."

Bill brought the suggestion blank barrel to the Senator, who drew six slips from it and announced the winners. The individuals happily mounted the platform to receive their prizes and to decline to say anything into the microphone. All except Ethyl Tibbits, who said, "I work on the skillet line and I'm telling you, Senator, you don't have to worry about that gift for the President. It'll make everything hot for him every morning."

Then Mr. Williams introduced the international director for the union, Wilson Nelson, who had arrived a little late and slipped onto the platform quietly.

"Wilson and I" said Mr. Williams, started out in business about the same time. We have known each other for many years. Every time he gets a promotion I get one. He took one side of the management system, I took the other side. I've always been proud to consider him a friend, although there were times when I thought he should have been wearing a mask and cartridge belt instead of a business suit. Wilson Nelson."

Nelson directed a few bantering remarks to Williams and then concentrated on the matter at hand. "I want to say just a few things before the rain begins. First, the union at every level is behind quality improvement. To us, Zero Defects is a practical, attainable thing. As the company grows through quality, we will grow also.

"Second, I would like to say something that goes a bit beyond my feelings about the union and quality improvement through Zero Defects. We in American labor now face a great opportunity to expand the markets of our nation. For the first time it is now more expensive to manufacture in many foreign countries than in the United States. Much of this improvement has come about through increased productivity in labor in the United States, and some from increased capital spending by industry. But most has been accomplished by the effect of inflation in the industrialized nations of Europe and the Far East. We can offer work of higher quality at a lower total price now, and it is time to take advantage of it."

After the applause died down, Hugh spoke for a few moments to express his thanks to the visitors and to the employees. He reminded everyone that they would be given the opportunity to sign their ZD pledges with their supervisors and receive their pins. He asked them to be sure and make certain they understood the program and assured them that it was not just a passing fad.

"Tomorrow we start the error-cause-removal phase. And it will be with us as long as we feel the need to communicate, which should be forever. You state the problem you have in getting the job done right the first time, and it's my job to make sure that your problem gets corrected.

"Thank you all for coming out here. Now I think if we walk briskly back in, we will just beat the rain."

Williams, Wilson, and the beaming political leaders made their way through the administrative areas then the shops, following Hugh and Bill. Many people asked the president to countersign their commitment, which he did with pleasure. Bill was beginning to get a little lightheaded with all the attention and with relief from having a successful rally. If nothing else, he had been given the personal top-level exposure he had been promised. This job really was a good opportunity. He had to make sure that he carried it all out — with Zero Defects, by golly.

At the end of the day Hugh invited the quality improvement team out to dinner with their spouses. After making a brief comment of thanks and appreciation for the extra effort they had shown so far, and reminding them of the job ahead, he presented each member of the team with a framed commitment sheet countersigned by all the honored guests. And he gave the chairperson's husband a special gift: a photograph of a disheveled and windblown Kate Norton helping hang the "Do It Right the First Time" banner across the front of the plant.

It was a good-feeling day.

* * *

Sharon handed Bill a cup of coffee.

"Now that ZD day is over," she said, "do you feel the whole thing was worth it? I know that you had some personal reservations about the business of bringing everyone together for having speeches, music, and pizzazz."

"You're right," nodded Bill. "I really wasn't sure that it was properly dignified or within the relationship of management and employees. I guess I felt like the employees wouldn't take it seriously. However, now that it's over, I think it was a great thing to do."

"You liked it because it let everyone have a chance to experience something different, or what?"

"Yes, I think the main thing is that the occasion let everyone share a common experience. Here we have all these people who work in the same company. Every day they come to work and every day they leave. They see only a small percentage of their fellow workers, and they certainly speak to far fewer than they see. Now they all have something to talk about, something they did together. Their friends and neighbors haven't had that opportunity.

"It was a party like Christmas. It was an event, a happening."

"Happening is a good phrase," said Sharon. "I think I know what you mean now. They all have a common benchmark to share. Also, they got to meet some interesting people."

"And the concept of ZD is really socked into everyone for good. Even those who make fun of it have to say the words. They'll all come around. Although I must say I haven't heard anyone say anything against the idea. A few just question whether or not it can really happen."

"The program will need you for a while yet. Do you think this assignment was good for your career?"

Bill smiled. "I don't see how it could have been better. I have had the chance to work very closely with a management level that I would not have been exposed to for several years. I found out that there is nothing mysterious about the goings-on there; it is just a matter of learning the facts and making a judgment based on experience. And they learn very quickly. I also noticed that they are all very polite to each other, even when they are disagreeing."

Sharon winked. "That's a good idea for marriages too. How about some more coffee?"

STEP TEN: GOAL SETTING

Purpose:

To turn pledges and commitments into action by encouraging individuals to establish improvement goals for themselves and their groups.

General Operation:

About a week after ZD day, the individual supervisors should ask their people what kind of goals they should set for themselves. Try to get two goals from each area. These goals should be specific and measurable. For example, two possibilities are:

- Reduce defects per unit 20 percent in one month.

- Win the good housekeeping award next week.

Stay away from schedule improvement goals in association with ZD; the schedule will automatically improve as the defects reduce. (Zero delinquencies.)

Specific Points: Goal setting is most effective when it is done by the personnel themselves rather than established by the supervisor. However, the supervisor should have some idea of what he or she wants before talking to the people.

Comment: Don't let people settle for easy tasks. Post the goals in a conspicuous place. Make a big fuss over any group that improves—progress is a start.

Carl Albert and his group settled around the table; they were getting comfortable with each other now that the meetings were occurring regularly.

"Today," said Carl," we are supposed to discuss the setting of goals. I have a little notice here that explains what goals are and aren't. Suppose I read it before we begin thinking about it."

Nobody said anything, so he read: "Goal setting is when a group decides what achievement they are going to strive to make as a team and then pick the measurement that reflects it."

Everett Smith said, "That means we have to pick out what we're going to do in advance."

"You should write these things Ev; you say it clearer."

Carl continued. "Goal setting is not the establishing of a quota or an achievement that the group's performance will be measured against."

Martha giggled. "That's to make sure you won't think that it's like those countries where if you don't meet the quota, you get sent to the cold place."

Carl laid the instruction down. "What sort of goal should we pick? Our defects rate per harness measurement has dropped from 5.6 to 4.2 over the past month. Should we try to get it lower?"

"I think we can go a lot lower, Carl. Now that we get to do our own rework, and know what problems we are having, and now that the wires are going to be changed to different colors on the power line, I'll bet there will be a big improvement."

"What does everyone else think?"

"I'll bet we could drop it down to two defects per harness

by another three months and maybe less by the end of the year," Sally stated.

Carl shook his head. "That's better than a 50 percent reduction. Do you really think we could do that?"

"Why not?" said Martha. "I'd like to bet that we could have the best improvement record of any group in the plant if we really went after it. And we really don't have anything else to do except that, now do we?"

Ev raised his hand.

"I've got an idea. I think the measurement is wrong. A month or even a week is a long time to concentrate on a goal. I've got a cousin who was a compulsive gambler. He finally quit by learning how to get through one day at a time by not gambling that day. Just concentrating on one day."

"How about one hour?" asked Sally.

"How do you mean?"

"Suppose we said that we were going to have ZD for so many hours and then challenge some other group, anywhere in the plant, to beat us? Now that would be something."

Carl looked at her. The group was getting excited. "You mean instead of setting goals based on these charts, we would just set up a goal of say twenty hours with no defects and then let anyone else try to beat it? We'd have to set a goal on the big chart too."

"OK. Let's set a monthly goal of two defects per harness on the measurement chart. But let's get the inspection people to report every hour. I have a big blackboard at home and I'll bring it in tomorrow morning. We'll write 'group work hours with Zero Defects' on the board and let the inspectors keep it up."

Carl leaned back. "You folks are something else. Let's do it. I'll make sure the rest of the plant knows they are challenged."

It took the harness group thirteen work days to get through a complete eight-hour day without an error. After that sixteen to twenty-five defect-free hour periods became routine. Other groups tried the same method, and Bill ran happily around the plant spreading the news of how the goal setting and meetings were progressing. Engineering, accounting, cafeteria – all areas participated.

The measurement charts reflected the overall decrease. In-plant rework costs had dropped 73 percent since the program started. Field rework was dropping more slowly, since much of the finished goods inventory had been placed there prior to the start of the improvement program and it was contaminating the effort.

Hugh, taking a chance on his balance sheet, recalled as much as he could of that inventory and set up a special review and rework operation to clean it up. That meant that new products went directly to the dealers. Their reaction was spectacular. Products that worked made them happy. They appreciated it. "Defects per hour" became a standard measurement. Everyone liked it except the inspection function, and they never admit to liking anything.

Carl and his group were singled out for special recognition: Theirs was the only operation in the plant permitted to have a gold-painted border on their blackboard.

STEP ELEVEN: ERROR-CAUSE REMOVAL

Purpose:

To give the individual employee a method of communicating to management the situations that make it difficult for the employee to meet the pledge to improve.

General Operation:

One of the most difficult problems employees face is their inability to communicate problems to management. Sometimes they just put up with problems because they do not consider them important enough to bother the supervisor. Sometimes supervisors just don't listen anyway. Suggestion programs are some help, but in a suggestion program the worker is required to know the problem and also propose a solution. Error-cause removal (ECR) is set up on the basis that the worker need only recognize the problem. When the worker has stated the problem, the proper department in the plant can look into it. Studies of ECR programs show that over 90 percent of the items submitted are acted upon, and fully 75 percent can be handled at the first level of supervision. The number of ECRs that save money is extremely high, since the worker generates savings every time the job is done better or quicker.

Specific Points: Simple one-page forms are supplied to each area, usually in wall boxes. When an employee feels that there is a problem, he or she completes the form and drops it in the box.

In ECR there are only a few rules:

1. Everyone who submits an ECR gets a personal thank-you note immediately. The form is forwarded to the department that has the responsibility for the problem area. An acknowledgement statement is sent to whoever submitted the ECR when something is decided about it.

2. Every ECR is to be taken seriously.

3. If you decide to do nothing about an ECR, clear your decision with at least one and preferably two levels of supervision.

There are always people who are afraid that doing a program like ECR will cause a lot of internal trouble because people might write abusive things when they have the chance to address notes to management. Yet it hasn't happened that way. It is like the fear of union reaction. Unions always support ZD programs because if nothing else the programs focus attention on the workers.

To stimulate the ECR activity at HPA Bill decided to draw a winner at random each week. The number one parking spot was marked as *ECR winner — reserved.* Hugh moved to number two and someone fell off the end. This was received with a good spirit in the plant. Parking was always a problem.

During the first week of the ECR program, 117 ECRs were received. During the first month a total of 385 were put in. That made a terrific load, but it was found that a few were redundant, and most of them could be handled at the first line of supervision. But all were positive. Absolutely no negative ECRs were received. The quick responses created credibility for the program and still more ECRs poured in.

Some of the ECRs received early in the HPA program were as follows:

- I can't lift the skillet handle tote-box to my work-bench. It must weigh 25 pounds. The paint gets chipped when they drop.

- There isn't enough light for me to read the instruments properly. Sometimes I have to guess.

- My screwdriver is so short I can't really tighten the screw.

- The typewriter ribbons are all bought from different sources. If one quits in the middle of a report, you have to start all over again because the new color won't match the old.

- The accounts payable forms sent to us by the field service operations are so hard to read we have to telephone about most of them.

- Ever time I run out of machining oil I have to shut everything down and walk clear over to the other building for a can. Why can't we have more over here?

- Why do they have to sweep the machine shop during my lunch time?

- We have a lot of bulbs burning up in top of the high bay area. There is nothing to see up there and they don't help light the floor, so how come they are up there?

- I keep catching the harness wire on my chair because it has to drag on the floor. This nicks the insulation.

- Because people aren't allowed to smoke in the harness area they spend a lot of time in the bathrooms smoking.

- Why do we make up all the TV box labels in advance with the color printed on them? Why not just put some stamp at the load point and let the person who puts it in the box stamp the color on the outside?

- I spend most of Monday waiting for the melt furnace to heat up to requirements. Could it be lighted on Sunday night?

- It is very hard to read our schematic drawings. Do they have to be so small?

- My solder iron is worn out, and I can't get a new one.

- The toaster coils are all packed loose, and it takes me a lot of searching to find the ones that aren't damaged.

- I get shocked by my test set every now and then.

- It is hard to open the wooden boxes we receive because we have no right tools.

- We are checking transistors one at a time when there are machines that can do it a thousand a minute.

- I am trying to write computer programs and sitting right next to the noisy keypunch area. The two just don't go together.

- It is hard to adjust the back of a TV set and lean forward to see the tube. I could use a mirror like they have on final test.

- Everytime I get all set to do a delicate job the plant paging system shouts off. I think we should get rid of it.

- I need a quicker feedback on how well I'm doing my work.

- The milk in the cafeteria is not fresh.

STEP TWELVE: RECOGNITION

Purpose:
To appreciate those who participate

General Operation

People really don't work for money. They go to work for it, but once the salary has been established, their concern is appreciation. Recognize their contribution publicly and noisily, but don't demean them by applying a price tag to everything.

Supervisors are very concerned about getting people to work better. By this they mean that they want their employees to put forth a little extra—particularly in the areas of output, quality, and efficiency. Recognition must be given for achieving specific goals worked out in advance, and the employees must have the opportunity to help select the goals.

The contest and the measurement are the key. The prize is not significant. It only matters that all of an individual's contemporaries know that he or she has fought the good fight and won.

Above all, individuals must know that management seriously needs their help and sincerely appreciates it.

Kate seemed angry. "So far we've gone through this whole program, somehow agreeing on everything. How come we get into this crack when it comes to recognition? It seems to me to be a very simple thing."

"Not to me," said Otto. "I just don't believe you are going to get people to take you seriously unless you give awards that are worthwhile. Savings bonds and vacation trips and things like that. I would think that being in marketing you would know that these are the things that turn people on."

Al patted Otto on the shoulder. "Honestly, Otto, Kate's right. People just want an honest appreciation. Now in some cases the only way they will believe you are sincere about the recognition is if you spend a lot of money, but I think the relationships around this plant are not that way. I think we should stick to group lunches with Hugh and the giving of performance plaques."

"I gave my guys a plaque once and they didn't think it was such a big deal."

Will glowered at Otto. "Yeah, you tossed it on one of their desks and said something about the person winning first prize in the beauty contest. How did you expect them to take it seriously when you didn't?"

Otto blushed. "Well, I admit I didn't handle that one quite right. But I still think we need something more . . . well, valuable.

Kate thumped the table. "Valuable is as valuable does. I think we need to concentrate more on the dignity of the presentation than on what the awards are. Now let's all calm down and get ourselves straight. Bill, you have been studying the situation. What have you found?"

"I think what you just said is right, Kate. The manner of presentation is what counts. The most important factor in recognition seems to be that everyone should know about it. The award itself doesn't have to be too much, although it should be something worth showing. Also, we don't need too many different types of awards, just a few basic things. I recommend that we consider setting up a formal system of recognition based on three things: groups meeting their short-range goals, individuals making outstanding contributions, and random drawings of ECRs submitted. That way you have group, spiritual, and random recognition.

"We should make quarterly awards for individuals, monthly for the groups, and whenever we feel like it for the drawings."

Otto nodded. "I guess that's OK. But if you won't put more substance in the award itself, how about having most of them presented by the vice president instead of just one of us?"

"I agree on that where appropriate. We could have a quarterly awards dinner and then a big deal once a year," said Bill.

"Also," said Kate, "I would like Bill to pick a committee of, say, three shop people, two administrative personnel, the union president, Otto, and probably Marian to select the awards themselves. And I'd like to see complete agreement on the whole thing before we go on."

"All right," said Bill, "I'll do it. We'll have a report next week. Also, I'd like to point out that one manager who does a great job with recognition awards is Al. Even though he's my boss, I have to say that his method is unique. He bets his people cigars or candy bars that they can't meet their goals. When a guy bets Al and gets his cigar, he never smokes it. He wears it."

"I'll have to be careful what I bet him," smiled Kate.

STEP THIRTEEN: QUALITY COUNCILS

Purpose:
To bring together the professional quality people for planned communication on a regular basis.

General Operation

It is vital for the professional quality people of an organization to meet regularly just to share their problems, feelings, and experiences with each other. Primarily concerned with measurement and reporting, isolated even in the midst of many fellow workers, it is easy for them to become influenced by the urgency of activity in their work areas.

Consistency of attitude and purpose is the essential personal characteristic of one who evaluates another's work. This is not only because of the importance of the work itself but because those who submit work unconsciously draw a great deal of their performance standard from the professional evaluator.

So bring the quality control people together regularly. Let them ask their own questions, and expose them to other members of management. Do everything in a formal manner.

In multiplant operations the worth of interchange becomes even more apparent. Councils should select their own chairmen, create their own agenda, and determine their own meeting times. Free exchange brings growth. Membership should not be restricted by the organizational rank of the professional.

STEP FOURTEEN: DO IT OVER AGAIN

Purpose:
To emphasize that the quality improvement program never ends.

General Operation

There is always a great sigh of relief when goals are reached. If you are not careful, the entire program will end at that moment. It is necessary to construct a new team, and to let them begin again and create their own communications.

Hugh read the telegram from the corporate president congratulating them on the achievements of the quality program.

"What he doesn't know yet is that our cost of quality is now on an 8 percent of sales annualized rate. That is remarkable. I see no reason why it won't drop even more."

Alice nodded. "It isn't all real money yet, chief, but it is getting realer every day. I think we will be showing a significant profit increase this next quarter."

"Alice, you know damned well you will be showing a significant profit increase next quarter. But I understand why you have to be conservative about stating it now.

"At any rate, we have been given approval from headquarters to set up the new clock-radio and 20-inch TV lines. That will absorb most of the people we can transfer, since the rework has been reduced so much."

Kate smiled. "I want to get a chance to say something before you all faint from congratulating yourselves on this achievement."

"Go ahead. You have earned the right to say whatever you want. It is all your fault that we're being so successful."

"That's what I want to talk about. Now the last step of the program is 'do it all over again.' And that's what it really means. So I think that what we have to do is set up a new team, a new leader, and a new coordinator, and get going on doing the program all over again. That way we can make sure that we will get to keep these gains."

Hugh paused. "I hadn't thought about it in that manner. Do you literally mean do the whole thing over again? Exactly like we did it before?"

Kate shook her head.

"No, not exactly like we did it before. It will take a lot more innovation and thought this time than last. I think the program should be scheduled out over a full year. We can have ZD II on the anniversary of ZD day—a rededication to the efforts. We can have a quality hall of fame, a lot of things. But I think it has to be done.

"All us old warhorses should be dropped from the team, except Al, and he can serve as a sort of 'godfather' to it. Bill Ranson should be given a nice promotion, a letter of recognition should be sent to corporate headquarters, and a new administrator appointed. Then every eighteen months or so we should have a new team. Perhaps some of us should be put back on after a time or two."

Hugh smiled. "You know, Kate, I really had never thought of this repeat in that way. But you are absolutely correct. Anyone have any comments on Kate's remarks?"

"I agree wholeheartedly," said Marian, "and I see it also as a management development tool. It will let us search out young people and give them a positive exposure in creative management."

Everyone agreed with the concept as outlined by Kate.

Will Ellis added the warning that each of them should refrain from directing their departmental representative too much so that there would be the opportunity to introduce new ideas and techniques into the program.

"OK," said Hugh, "so be it. Now each of you should give me the name of your department's representative on the new team. Al, you pick the new coordinator. I will meet with Al and the new team next week. We'll pretend we never had a program at all and just concentrate on getting that cost of quality down to 2 percent.

"Now I am going to give each of you an Al Fielding cigar in appreciation of your work on this team. The meeting is dismissed."

*   *   *

The new team decided to make its impact quickly by launching the Make Certain five-week program. The program concept and content are given in detail in Part Three.

PART THREE
The Tools

The reader may decide to utilize the HPA case as a teaching tool, or use it as a way to develop a greater understanding of the concepts and methods involved in a quality improvement operation. Part three contains an instructor's guide that leads you through the HPA case step by step. It is set up so you can encourage class participation by having students take the roles of the HPA staff.

The Make Certain program is described in detail so you can utilize it as part of your quality improvement program. Aimed primarily at white-collar personnel, Make Certain is a breakthrough in quality improvement efforts. It is very appropriate for use in the awareness step of the overall program.

12

Instructor's Guide for HPA Quality Improvement Program Case History

The HPA case history details the creation and installation of a quality improvement program according to the fourteen-step program. The purpose of the case study is to provide a common and interesting basis for students to discuss the philosophy and actions of implementing the program. The Instructor's Guide is included in the following pages. Using this guide you will be able to lead the students as they develop their understanding of the logic and method of the program.

The following are the action steps for teaching the quality improvement case history.

1. Send the book to the students so they receive it a week prior to the beginning of the course. Attach a personal note asking the student to read the case and prepare any questions he or she might have concerning any part of it. The student is to bring the book to all meetings because it will serve as a key part of the course.

2. When the students arrive and are oriented, explain to them — very clearly — that they have been sent there by their management at considerable expense for the purpose of learning how to install a quality improvement program in their operation. This sending and paying should serve as tangible evidence to them that their management expects them to install the fourteen-step program completely on their return. Anyone not interested in undertaking that assignment should not stick around. Emphasize that this is a gathering of select professionals and that you are pleased to be involved.

3. State that you will make sure that the content of the case is fully understood by discussing it step by step. Try to let students talk as much as possible, interrupting only to provide another question or to keep the discussion on track. (See the section on Step-by-Step Discussion Items at the end of this chapter.) The purpose is to let the students bring to the surface every possible question or problem they might face in their operation and get it resolved. It should take about twelve class hours to completely cover the case, including the Make Certain assignment.

4. Group assignments can be given for the measurement, quality awareness, ZD planning, ZD day, and recognition steps. Special presentations by the groups (no more than two for each subject) will make the information flow more easily. Also, student participation makes the course more interesting to them.

   When the HPA quality improvement team in the case has a meeting, it is a good idea to have your students take the roles assigned and read the dialogue out loud. That way they get to hear it as well as read it.

5. When you are satisfied that they have an under-

standing of the Make Certain program, divide them into teams and ask that they develop the Make Certain program for presentation the next day. This will give them something to take home.

6. During the discussion it is reasonable to assign groups to tackle individual steps and report back to the class the next morning or even after lunch or breaks.

7. When the course ends, notify the students that you expect them to send you progress reports on their success.

The following are discussion subjects and notes for each step.

HISTORY OF THE PROJECT

1. HPA seems to have a lot of "trouble bubbles" popping to the surface. Everyone is working hard but the events still occur. Have you seen situations like this?

Note: The idea here is to get them to talk a little about the problems they have had or seen, and to break the ice. Everyone has trouble and likes to discuss it. Try to steer the items around to the need for a better way.

2. The field service manager mentioned the need for prevention. This seemed to surprise Hugh. Do you suppose no one had ever thought of that before? If they had, how come no one did anything?

Note: They had probably thought of it but they were so concerned with day-to-day things that they hadn't felt it possible to get around to prevention just yet. *They did not know how to go about starting to prevent.* (This is a very key point because the whole reason for the course is to teach them how to go about starting to prevent.)

3. The quality manager obviously knew what Hugh meant, and he was prepared with a plan for starting quality improvement. Why hadn't he mentioned this before?

Note: Here the message we have to instill is that the quality manager didn't know how to sell the need for prevention because he didn't understand the quality improvement program or how to market it.

4. Al was very determined to make certain that Hugh didn't get the idea that this was going to be a motivation program. Why? Isn't quality improvement motivation?

Note: This should generate a lot of discussion. However, we have to recognize that although every human communication involves motivation, motivation is short-term in effect. What we are after is to install a long-range, permanent attitude—a change in discipline. This requires management action of the most deliberate and planned sort. Using the word "motivation" implies that there will be something emotional about people's involvement. This program is not emotional.

5. The Zero Defects concept sounds so easy to understand that sometimes we overlook it. Let's examine it closely. For instance, why aren't lack of facilities or wrong tools considered acceptable causes of mistakes, as attitude and knowledge are?

Note: Here the intent is to make clear that someone assigns the wrong facilities or tools to a particular job because of lack of attention or knowledge. If you say that facility problems are the only cause of defects, you make the concept of improvement strictly a blue-collar program involving better work standards. Remark that there is a ZD test later.

6. Why isn't an "acceptable quality level" a good

management standard? Aren't we in the quality management business the ones who caused it to be used as a standard?

Note: See if the class can identify some other wrong standards used in life—like years spent in college as an indication of smartness, or lights on the telephone as a determination of importance.

7. Hugh's wife told him he didn't think the program was complicated enough. He admitted that the "simplicity and directness" bothered him. He was actually a little embarrassed that he hadn't thought of doing something like this before. Why hadn't he?

Note: He has a lot of things to do. It is up to his subordinates to come up with programs like this. The quality manager had been stalling because he didn't really know how to set up such a program.

STEP-BY-STEP DISCUSSION ITEMS

Step One: Management Commitment

1. The text says that the quality policy is too important to leave up to the quality manager. Is this correct? Isn't the quality department responsible for quality?

Note: Make the point that the quality department is responsible for measuring and reporting the status of quality. "Quality means conformance" will be discussed later, but since quality doesn't purchase, manufacture, or design, or do other productive things like that, they can hardly be held responsible for performing these functions.

2. How can it be that there is no "economics of quality"? We hear this term all the time.

Note: We do not encourage managers to use quality as a catchall word meaning "goodness." They have to specify exactly what they want in terms of luxury, beauty, etc. Therefore, quality means conformance and it is always cheaper to do the job right the first time. Ask for an example in which it is cheaper to do the job right the second time.

3. How many of the students have published a policy in their company? Does it give anyone a problem? If so, who and why? How did it all turn out?

Note: If possible bring the discussion around to why nothing should be added to the policy to modify it—such as Hugh considered.

4. What would it take on the part of the general manager to convince the quality department people that he or she was serious about quality improvement?

Note: After discussion of this, ask the students to make a note of what they would have to ask their boss to do to get this point across.

Step Two: The Quality Improvement Team

1. Why it is recommended that the chairperson not be the quality manager? It would seem that this would be a vital part of the quality manager's job.

Note: The quality manager must be the driving force behind the program, the brains, and the information source. However, the manager must get a team together, hopefully under another chairperson, to run the program. Otherwise it really will be "just another quality program."

2. Who would you select as the administrator of your program? What are the most valuable characteristics for an administrator to have?

Note: The key qualities are ability to communicate, genuine ambition, and the ability to hold up under stress.

3. If we figured out how your company disposes of the sales dollars it receives, following the same distribution Hugh did, how would it break down? What are the sales per employee of your company? What is the after-tax profit?

Note: If the students don't know these figures, they are not taking a proper interest in their company. And what is more important they probably aren't communicating properly with the rest of the staff.

4. Do you believe that 25 percent of the people spend time doing the jobs over again in the administrative and paperwork areas? What does this mean?

Note: This is the time to get them interested in the white-collar problems. This interest is essential for preparing Make Certain.

5. Have you ever thought about how you are paying for the cost of quality in your suppliers' plants?

6. If you gave the ten-question test (see the end of this section) to your fellow managers in your company, how would they make out? Do you think their level of information is any better than that of the HPA management team?

Note: This is the time to convince your managers that they have to do a quality orientation program when they get back home. In fact, it is a good time to get the commitment from them.

7. Why is adhering to the principle that "quality means conformance" important to your job?

Note: It is important because it is very hard to make a living out of "beauty, truth, and luxury." You need something that is measurable.

8. **Let's discuss the individual questions and answers in the attitude test. We need to make sure that we have an understanding that is accurate. How would your staff do with the test?**

Note: Take the time to go over each question and really discuss it. You have to get all the reservations out in the open at this time. Otherwise the rest of the case will not compute.

9. **HPA picked Kate to be the program manager. Whom would you pick in your company? Why?**

Note: It is not necessary to identify a person in each company, but if you can get several of the students to discuss their choices, the results will be beneficial.

10. **Does everyone know how the quality councils work? Do you have one in your operation? How do you communicate with each other in your quality function?**

Note: The information gained in quality council meetings should be distributed within the company.

11. **Do you think your general manager would make a speech like Hugh did?**

Note: The general manager will if asked to do it. Has their general manager ever been asked?

12. **Do you think the meeting with the union management is typical? Would you expect it to be a problem?**

Note: We know of no case where a union did anything but cooperate wholeheartedly with the improvement program.

13. Why is so much written here about the difference between a concept and a technique?

Note: It is important that people concentrate on the intent of the concept rather than on dotting the i's in each point in the program. There is no infallible, unchangeable way to install a program; it has to be done with daily thought and understanding. The first personal step is realizing that all the steps we are studying relate to each other like all the parts of a cat relate to the whole cat. Encourage them to discuss this at length.

Ten questions on quality

1. Quality is a measure of goodness of the product that can be defined as fair, good, excellent.

False. Quality means conformance to the requirements, and that is all it means. If you start confusing quality with elegance, brightness, dignity, love or something else, you will find that everyone has different ideas. Don't talk about poor quality or high quality. Talk about conformance and nonconformance. If you don't like the requirements, get them changed officially. If you don't take this attitude and stick to it, everyone gets to set their own standards, and the last person in the line determines what gets out of the door.

2. The economics of quality requires that management establish acceptable quality levels as performance standards.

False. There is no such thing as economics of quality. It is always cheaper to do the job right the first time. Many companies confuse their people by using the sampling inspection criteria of acceptable quality levels as performance standards. As a result, each operation takes its 1 percent. The only proper standard is Zero Defects. Why settle for less? People work to the standards you give them.

3. The cost of quality is the expense of doing things wrong.

True. Quality is free. It's nonconformance that wastes the assets.

4. Inspection and test should report to manufacturing so manufacturing can have the proper tools to do the job.

False. If you assign the inspection and test responsibility to manufacturing, you will not have accurate recording of defects. More important, the personnel involved will not receive the training, discipline, and appreciation that they need. Inspectors who work for manufacturing managers become sorters and expeditors. In addition, since the quality control people check after the inspectors, they will miss about 10 percent of the defects. An inspector is not effective unless the inspection is the last operation in the line. If you really believe that manufacturing needs the tools to do the job, then give it the comptroller, public relations, purchasing, and payroll functions, too. Then you will have a bunch of little general managers in your plant.

5. Quality is the responsibility of the quality department.

False. Proper quality departments are supposed to measure and report conformance, demand corrective action, encourage defect prevention, teach quality improvement, and act as the conscience of the operation. If the quality manager is held responsible because purchasing picked a lousy vendor, or a manufacturing worker doesn't know how to solder, then you are in a lot of trouble. Work is the responsibility of those who get paid for doing it. No one feels the comptroller is responsible if the sales figures are falling. But think about it: If everyone did the job right, you wouldn't need a quality department at all.

6. Worker attitudes are the primary cause of defects.

False. Workers perform like the attitude of the management. If they don't care about product conformance, it is because they sense that the management doesn't think it is important. An experienced quality auditor can talk with a general manager for five minutes and guess his outgoing quality level within 1 percent. Workers are like a mirror. The reflection you see is your own.

7. I have trend charts that show me the rejection level at every key operation.

If this isn't *true,* you are in worse shape than I thought. Indexes don't count. If you don't know what the defect level is, how do you know when to get mad?

8. I have a list of the ten biggest quality problems.

If you have a list of the ten or any number of quality problems, you are probably not getting good corrective action and you don't understand the situation. There is no such thing as a quality problem. Problems should be identified according to the department responsible for corrective action. Thus you should have manufacturing problems, purchasing problems, design problems, service problems, etc. The quality manager who maintains a list of quality problems and, worse, gives it to the boss, is courting personal disaster. After a while, when that manager has not produced improved employee training, a better production control system, a foolproof product qualification technique, or reliable designs, he or she is on the way out. In comes another one who makes up a list of the ten worst quality problems, and on and on. Don't say "quality problem." Call it like it really is.

9. Zero Defects is a worker motivation program.

False. If you think Zero Defects is a motivation concept, you are underestimating it. Zero Defects is stating the standards of management in a way that no one can misunderstand. You can't fool people into thinking you have changed your ways by having a few dinners and hanging some banners. You have to really believe that ZD is what you want. Which do you want them to think you believe: "Make it right the first time" or "Do the best you can—I understand no one is perfect?"

10. The biggest problem today is that the customers don't understand.

False. The customer doesn't have to understand. The customer is the customer. You have no mercy on the people who make the items you buy in your personal life. Why should you expect your customers to treat you differently?

Step Three: Quality Measurement

1. Why are there separate introduction sections for manufacturing and for "service"?

Note: Very few companies will search out non-manufacturing-type measurements and use them in the program unless forced to do so. Starting the discussion at this point is the beginning of forcing them. Discuss the erroneous concept of the manufacturing "ghetto," where all the mistakes are supposed to happen.

2. Listen to the discussion that the HPA team had. Let's read the comments out loud and see how they might relate to our own operations.

Note: Assign roles—don't make a big deal out of it—and have the different parts read out loud. Note that the HPA team is taking its time and being very careful to make certain they all have the same understanding of what is going to happen.

3. Can you compute the cost of quality in your operation the way Alice did for HPA? Have you done it?

4. Do you think the team knew how serious the situation was before the comptroller gave the numbers?

Step Four: The Cost of Quality

1. How do you feel about attitudes? Do you think they are as important as Sharon did?

Step Five: Quality Awareness

Note: At this point you may be through with the first half day's session, and ready to adjourn. This is a good time to divide the students into groups to report on specific steps and give their recommendations for executing them. Two groups on awareness and two on measurement are about right. Have them meet that evening to discuss their steps. They should return prepared to make a presentation on the actual things that should be done when putting the steps into effect. This gets students to participate and brings some real questions to the surface.

1. Why is it so necessary to reach all the employees with the quality message? Wouldn't it be enough just to demand what you want?

Note: Quality is not something you can attain through whipping and punishing those involved. You have to give them the message, let them participate, and not try to fool them.

2. Why is it important to display the actual measurements at the start of the program?

Note: If you don't record how things are at the exact moment you start, you will not be able to take advantage of the rush of improvement that occurs at the beginning of the program. Being able to point to this improvement will carry you over any rough spots that may occur after a few weeks.

3. Can you think of some more measurements that we could use in the nonmanufacturing departments?

Note: Keep track of any good suggestions so you can share them with future classes.

4. This is a good time for reading the team meeting dialogue again. It helps in discussing the education of the quality improvement team.

Note: Pay particular attention to Otto's comments.

5. Judging from the discussions at the meeting between supervisors and employees there seemed to be no resistance to the idea of quality improvement at HPA. Why do you think managers are shy about asking people for improvement?

Note: This is a good time to discuss how managers can get separated from the people and get the wrong ideas. We need to force this communication. After all, most of us started on a bench or desk somewhere.

6. What do you think about the idea of being "attitude formers"? Do you think Hal was right? Who else meets that definition in your company?

7. What was Hugh telling Al? Could you be put in the same situation?

Step Six: Corrective Action

1. Ask one of the students to give a briefing of the report that the quality engineer wrote. Give them

the assignment early enough so they can do a good job. It is obvious that several people investigated and came to the wrong conclusion. Why?

Note: This points out again that you have to go to the working people in order to find out what is going on. Give the pitch about the corrective action program at this time if you wish.

2. Al was surprised that someone thought his department might have a few problems. It is apparent that this had not occurred to him before. Why would he feel this way? What should you do to keep it from happening to you?

Note: Ask everyone when was the last time they had an independent audit of their department?

3. What is the value of a staff person having an approach like the one John Halden took?

Note: Take a few moments to discuss the fact that staff people are not meant to hurt the company or the persons they are auditing. They will look bad if things get out of control too. Comment on the amount of planning that goes into handling the audits properly. Don't let them get off on the subject of line–staff relationships. This is a red herring.

4. Have someone give an analysis of the report on receiving acceptance.

Note: It is obvious that this was a sloppy operation. People were running all over the place, and the supervisors reacted to pressure from purchasing and production control. Start a discussion about the corrective action steps that needed to be taken. What could Al tell the improvement team?

Step Seven: Zero Defect Planning

Note: This is a good step to ask a group to report about. It lends itself to original thought. Many of the students will be

shy about launching a ZD program, and will seem particularly nervous at the thought of having a ZD day.

1. How does the ZD phase of the program differ from what they were already doing?

Note: You can point out that there will be a significant improvement from earlier steps, but that there will be a level-
ing off after a few months. To gain the rest of the improvement you have to go into ZD. It is necessary to get all hands
committed to a higher level of improvement than that already achieved. At the pre-ZD stage, they are just trying to
"do better." That is not enough.

2. The concept as laid out on the pledge sheet is condensed from the one on the tape. Do you feel it is necessary to add anything else to it? If so, what?

Note: Don't let them go too far out, but discuss the concept
enough to make sure that they have read it and that they
understand the business of handling the pledge between
supervisor and employee. It is also necessary that they understand the need for the pledge. Read the dialogue of the
team meeting, assigning roles as before.

3. Why did they have to discuss motivation again? Why is there so much confusion about this?

Note: Tell them that as a staff person you know that if you tell
a general manager you want to start a motivation program,
the manager will send you to see one of the PR people.
(Note that the PR people should be on the improvement
team.)

Step Eight: Supervisor Training

Note: Make everyone take the ZD test. Make certain that
everyone understands they are going to have to explain ZD
to their improvement team when they get back home. Any

questions that have to be answered must be brought out and dealt with now.

1. **The supervisors have been oriented at the time of the quality awareness and corrective action steps, and now when ZD is being planned. What other training do they need?**

Note: Some things that require further training are: pledge handling; how to talk to people who aren't sure the program is serious; what to say if the union steward raises a question; how to handle ECRs. There are a lot of things they need to know.

Step Nine: ZD Day

Note: Discuss the entire day and make sure you give it a completely positive image. After all, how else are you going to get everyone's attention at the same time? Provide information on how they can get the material printed. Tell them about the ZD days you have witnessed. Read the comments that the president made in the HPA case: This is the heart of the matter.

Step Ten: Goal Setting

Note: Goal setting makes a good group assignment, particularly when you have them concentrate on the white-collar areas.

1. **What do you think of the measurement system that Carl and his group proposed (ZD per hour)? Would that work in your operation?**

Note: You can do ZD per hour anywhere regardless of the function, personnel, or whatever. It is a great measurement system. Engineers can compete against shipping clerks.

2. **Now that some good hard improvement results are coming in, what should be done with the information?**

3. How do we get information to all the people?

Step Eleven: Error-Cause Removal

Note: Emphasize the point that the employee has been asked to do a perfect job. The ECR is the way for all employees to bring up any problem standing in the way of perfection. They don't need to know the solution. Have some of the sample ECRs read out loud and discussed. They are typical of those that will be received.

1. In the HPA case ECR was conducted late in the program. Could it be done earlier?

Note: It can be done earlier, of course. However, make certain that it is only done after people have been given a clear understanding that improvement is necessary.

Step Twelve: Recognition

Note: Have the HPA team meeting that was held at this stage read out loud.

1. Why is it important not to get involved with giving out things of high value in the recognition step?

Note: People don't work for things; they work for appreciation. Make sure the students understand and agree with this.

2. How does the Pulitzer Prize program relate to this type of recognition?

3. What type of recognition programs can you suggest that might be appropriate or original for your operation? How about regular awards?

Step Thirteen: Quality Councils

Note: Discuss the council system and its meaning. Ask for individuals to state what they think of the councils.

1. How can you install councils in your operation?

Step Fourteen: Do It Over Again

Note: This is the step that might give you problems because it is hard to make people believe that you really have to keep on doing the program. Have the HPA team meeting read out loud.

1. Why is it necessary to do the program over again?

Note: How else are you going to get all the attention you need on the subject of quality? The program will not just flow on like a river unless you keep the channels cleared and the energy level high.

13

Make Certain

INTRODUCTION

This portion of the Tool section contains the Make Certain orientation concept and presentation on the first four pages. Following that there is a complete step by step description of the events necessary in running a complete Make Certain program.

Make Certain is a person-to-person, white-collar-oriented, improvement program that gets everyone's attention immediately. You will receive prevention suggestions from over 90 percent of the people exposed to it.

Make Certain has been deliberately separated from the HPA case because I felt that the team selected to "do it all over again" should have something the original group didn't know about.

Use it with good luck. It really works.

INSTRUCTOR'S GUIDE FOR THE *MAKE CERTAIN* ORIENTATION

TIME:

ABOUT ONE HOUR

EQUIPMENT REQUIRED:

BLACKBOARD OR OTHER WRITING DISPLAY MATERIAL

AUDIENCE:

FIFTEEN TO TWENTY-FIVE PERSONNEL OF WHITE-COLLAR OR ADMINIS-
TRATIVE FUNCTIONS. PREFERABLY THE ATTENDEES SHOULD REPRE-
SENT MANY DIFFERENT DEPARTMENTS OR FUNCTIONS. HOWEVER THE
ORIENTATION CAN BE GIVEN TO PEOPLE FROM ONE OPERATION AS
LONG AS THE INSTRUCTOR IS SENSITIVE TO SPECIAL ORGANIZATIONAL
OR PERSONALITY PROBLEMS THAT MIGHT BE INVOLVED WITHIN THAT
FUNCTION.

PURPOSE:

- TO EXPLAIN THE CONCEPT OF *MAKE CERTAIN* IN A WAY THAT WILL
  MAKE THE PERSONNEL INVOLVED WANT TO PARTICIPATE IN THIS
  PROGRAM OF DEFECT PREVENTION FOR ADMINISTRATIVE AND FUNC-
  TIONAL ACTIVITIES

- TO START AN ON-GOING EXAMINATION OF PROCEDURES AND METH-
  ODS BY THE PERSONNEL INVOLVED IN ORDER THAT THEY WILL CON-
  TRIBUTE TO DEFECT PREVENTION ACTIVITIES ON A REGULAR BASIS

SEQUENCE OF EVENTS:

1. INTRODUCE THE THOUGHT THAT MANY NONCONFORMANCE PROB-
   LEMS ARE CAUSED IN THE ADMINISTRATIVE, SERVICE, AND SIMILAR
   ACTIVITIES OF THE COMPANY, AND THAT THEY ARE LONG-RANGE IN
   EFFECT.

2. EXPLAIN THAT *MAKE CERTAIN* IS A PROGRAM TO HELP IDENTIFY
   THOSE PROBLEMS AND ELIMINATE THEM THROUGH SOLICITING
   IDEAS FROM THE INDIVIDUALS INVOLVED IN DOING THE ACTUAL
   WORK.

3. ASK EACH INDIVIDUAL TO STATE THEIR PERSONAL "BIGGEST PROB-
   LEM" WITHOUT DETAILED DISCUSSION. WRITE THE PROBLEMS ON
   THE BLACKBOARD.

4. AFTER PROBLEMS HAVE BEEN STATED AND WRITTEN, COMMENT
   THAT EVERYONE HAS SELECTED PROBLEMS THAT ARE CAUSED FOR
   THEM BY OTHERS, THAT NO ONE SEEMS TO HAVE PROBLEMS THAT
   THEY HAVE CAUSED FOR THEMSELVES. NOTE THAT THIS IS A TYPICAL
   ATTITUDE AMONG HUMANS.

5. ASK PARTICIPANTS HOW SOME OF THE PROBLEMS LISTED ON THE
   BLACKBOARD MIGHT BE PREVENTED. AVOID EMBARRASSING ANY-

ONE OR PINNING SOMEONE DOWN. SELECT ONE OR TWO AND GIVE PREVENTION IDEAS YOURSELF.

6. TELL THEM HOW NECESSARY IT IS FOR ALL OF US TO BECOME "CERTAIN MAKERS." CITE A FEW STATISTICS SHOWING THE COST OF ERROR IN "WHITE-COLLAR" AREAS.

7. GO AROUND THE ROOM AGAIN AND ASK PEOPLE TO STATE THEIR "BIGGEST PROBLEM." THIS TIME THE PROBLEMS SHOULD BE DIFFERENT.

8. ASK THEM TO SUBMIT WRITTEN IDEAS TO THE IMPROVEMENT TEAM. SUGGEST THAT THEY MIGHT LIKE TO HAVE THEIR SUPERVISOR GET TOGETHER WITH THEM TO SET UP DEFECT PREVENTION DISCUSSION TEAMS IN THEIR OPERATIONS.

9. THANK THEM FOR COMING AND DISMISS THE GROUP.

MAKE CERTAIN MEETING

INSTRUCTOR SPEAKS:

GOOD MORNING. MY NAME IS ———. I AM HERE TO PARTICIPATE WITH YOU IN A DISCUSSION OF A NEW PROGRAM CALLED *MAKE CERTAIN*. THE PURPOSE OF THIS PROGRAM IS TO HELP ALL OF US WHO WORK WITH PENCILS, PENS, COMPUTERS, TELEPHONES, AND OTHER DEVICES TO LEARN MORE ABOUT OUR PERSONAL RESPONSIBILITY TO QUALITY.

AS YOU KNOW FROM YOUR PERSONAL EXPERIENCES MANY OF THE MOST FRUSTRATING AND EXPENSIVE PROBLEMS WE SEE TODAY COME FROM PAPERWORK AND SIMILAR COMMUNICATION DEVICES. ALL OF US HAVE HAD PROBLEMS WITH DEPARTMENT STORE COMPUTERS, CATA-LOG COMPANIES, OUR INTERNAL DEPARTMENTS, HOTELS, AND OTHER SERVICE FUNCTIONS THAT ARE SUPPOSED TO MAKE LIFE EASIER FOR US.

STUDIES SHOW THAT BETTER THAN 25 PERCENT OF NONMANUFACTUR-ING WORK IS ROUTINELY DONE OVER BEFORE IT IS CORRECT. THOSE ARE THE JOBS WE ARE INVOLVED IN EVERY DAY.

THE BIGGEST SINGLE PROBLEM WE FACE IN DOING OUR WORK IS THE COMMUNICATION THAT LINKS OUR WORK TOGETHER. WHATEVER YOUR JOB IS—MANAGEMENT, COMPUTER PROGRAMMING, CLERICAL, PRODUCT LINE OPERATIONS, SALES, ENGINEERING, FRONT OFFICE, AC-COUNTING—ANY OF THESE AND ALL THE OTHERS ARE BOUND TO-GETHER THROUGH A COMMON NEED. THIS NEED IS THAT WE HAVE TO TRANSMIT OUR PERSONAL CONTRIBUTION TO OUR JOBS VIA PENCILS, PENS, COMPUTER PROGRAMS, CONVERSATIONS, OR SOME SPECIFIC DETERMINED METHOD.

WE RECEIVE DATA FROM SOMEONE. WE DECIDE SOMETHING ON THE BASIS OF THAT DATA, WE TRANSMIT SOMETHING ALONG THE LINE, AND WE ADD OUR TWO CENTS WORTH TO IT. IF WE HAVE NOT MADE CERTAIN ABOUT WHAT WE HAVE DONE, THEN WE CAN SET THE ENTIRE CHAIN OFF IN THE WRONG DIRECTION.

BUSINESS IS A CHAIN OF PAPERWORK AND OTHER COMMUNICATIONS THAT WE CONTROL AND UTILIZE. THE EFFECTIVENESS OF THE BUSINESS IS DETERMINED BY HOW WELL WE DO THAT DATA TRANSMISSION.

UNFORTUNATELY IT ONLY TAKES ONE BAD BIT OF DATA IN THE CHAIN TO DISTURB ITS EFFECTIVENESS AND ACCURACY. IF WE AS INDIVIDUALS WERE ELECTRONIC COMPONENTS, WE WOULD DETERMINE OUR COMMUNICATION RELIABILITY THE WAY IT IS DONE WITH COMPONENTS. IF YOU HAVE 100 COMPONENTS IN A CIRCUIT AND EACH ONE IS 99 PERCENT PERFECT THE PROBABILITY THAT THE CIRCUIT WILL PERFORM IS ONLY 35 PERCENT. YOU HAVE TO MULTIPLY EACH INDIVIDUAL RELIABILITY BY THE NEXT AND SO ON.

WHAT WE HAVE TO CONSIDER TODAY IS YOUR INDIVIDUAL RELIABILITY IN THIS MATTER OF MAKING CERTAIN THAT WE DON'T CAUSE PROBLEMS.

IF IT IS POSSIBLE TO GET EVERY JOB DONE RIGHT THE FIRST TIME, THEN WE WILL BE ABLE TO REDUCE THE AMOUNT OF TIME WE WASTE ON REWORK, THE NUMBER OF CUSTOMERS WE DISAPPOINT, AND THE AMOUNT OF FRUSTRATION WE CAUSE OURSELVES PERSONALLY. WE WILL BE ABLE TO DO MORE OF THE PURPOSEFUL THINGS WE REALLY LIKE TO DO.

INSTEAD OF MAKING UP SOME TYPICAL PROBLEMS AS EXAMPLES IN ORDER TO MAKE THIS POINT, I WOULD LIKE TO ASK EACH OF YOU TO STATE YOUR BIGGEST PROBLEM FOR US—THE THING YOU REGARD AS YOUR BIGGEST PROBLEM IN GETTING YOUR WORK DONE RIGHT THE FIRST TIME EVERY TIME. I WILL GO AROUND THE ROOM AND ASK EACH OF YOU TO STATE THAT PROBLEM WITHOUT DISCUSSION. I WILL WRITE THEM ON THE BLACKBOARD, AND IN A FEW MOMENTS WE WILL HAVE A LIST OF REAL-LIFE ITEMS THAT WE CAN DISCUSS.

I THINK IT IS VERY IMPORTANT THAT WE HAVE A DISCUSSION BASED ON SOMETHING WE WOULD RECOGNIZE AS BEING PERTINENT TO OUR SITUATION RATHER THAN SOMETHING THAT COMES FROM OUTSIDE OUR AREA.

NOTE: POINT TO EACH INDIVIDUAL ONE AT A TIME AND ASK THEM, "WHAT IS YOUR BIGGEST PROBLEM?" AS THEY STATE IT, MAKE CERTAIN YOU UNDERSTAND IT, AND THEN WRITE IN ON THE BOARD. BE VERY OPEN AND FRIENDLY. IN THIS ACTIVITY THEY HAVE TO UNDERSTAND THAT ALL OF THIS IS NOT GOING TO BE USED AGAINST THEM.

TYPICALLY THEY WILL SAY THINGS LIKE:

- THEY DON'T SEND ME ACCURATE DATA.
- MANAGEMENT ISN'T CLEAR ABOUT WHAT THEY WANT.
- WE CAN NEVER FIND OUT WHEN PROBLEMS HAPPEN.
- THEY KEEP CHANGING THE STANDARDS.
- IT IS HARD TO GET COMPUTER TIME WHEN YOU NEED IT.
- THE SALESPEOPLE WAIT UNTIL THE LAST MOMENT TO SEND IN THE ORDERS, THEN THEY WANT IT IMMEDIATELY.
- THE CUSTOMERS DON'T KNOW WHAT THEY WANT.
- THERE NEVER IS ENOUGH TIME.

NOW WE HAVE ALL OF THESE PROBLEMS LISTED, AND WE CAN SEE THAT THEY HAVE SOMETHING IN COMMON. WHAT THEY HAVE IN COMMON IS THAT NONE OF THEM ARE PROBLEMS WE CAUSED FOR OURSELVES. THEY ARE SOMETHING THAT OTHERS ARE DOING TO US. THIS IS THE TYPICAL HUMAN REACTION. IT PROVES WE ARE ALL NORMAL, FUNCTIONING HUMAN BEINGS.

AND OF COURSE IT MAKES ANOTHER POINT THAT WE ALL HAVE TO RECOGNIZE: ELIMINATING PROBLEMS AND IMPROVING PERSONAL RELIABILITY IS NOT JUST A MATTER OF CONCENTRATING AND TRYING HARDER.

IT IS NOT JUST A MATTER OF THINKING HOW TO BE MORE CAREFUL. THAT IS LIKE YOUR NEW DIET. IT ONLY WORKS FOR A LITTLE WHILE. THEN YOU GO BACK TO YOUR OLD WAYS. WE ALL DO THAT.

WHAT WE NEED IS SOME SYSTEMATIC RECOGNITION OF THE BASIC PROBLEM. THERE ARE THREE SPECIFIC RECOGNITIONS INVOLVED:

- FIRST, WE HAVE TO RECOGNIZE THAT THE LARGEST CAUSE OF DEFECTS AND PROBLEMS IN ANY COMPANY IS IN THE PAPERWORK AND OTHER COMMUNICATION SYSTEM AREAS. THE FACTORIES HAVE THEIR OWN PROBLEMS, BUT THEY ARE WORKING WITH WHAT WE GIVE THEM.

- SECOND, WE HAVE TO RECOGNIZE THAT EVERY PROBLEM IS PREVENTABLE AND THAT THE PERSON WHO CAN BEST CONTRIBUTE THE IDEA TO PREVENT IT IS THE ONE WHO HAS AT SOME TIME CAUSED IT OR A SIMILAR PROBLEM.

- THIRD, WE HAVE TO RECOGNIZE THAT ALTHOUGH WE ARE HEARING THESE WORDS AND AGREEING WITH THEM, WE AS INDIVIDUALS DO NOT REALLY BELIEVE THAT THEY APPLY TO US PERSONALLY. THAT IS ONLY HUMAN.

THE WAY TO GET STARTED ON MAKING CERTAIN IS TO RECOGNIZE THAT WE CAUSE PROBLEMS FOR OURSELVES, AND WE MUST FIND WAYS TO PREVENT THEM.

CLOSING SEQUENCE:

1. REVIEW THE "BIGGEST PROBLEMS" FOR POSSIBLE SOLUTIONS.

   LET'S LOOK AGAIN AT THESE PROBLEMS WE PUT ON THE BLACKBOARD. I DON'T REMEMBER WHICH ONES BELONGED TO WHOM BUT LET'S TAKE A COUPLE OF THEM AND SEE HOW THEY MIGHT BE PREVENTED IF WE CAN GET THE RIGHT PEOPLE INTERESTED. FOR EXAMPLE:

   - IF MANAGEMENT IS NOT MAKING THE INSTRUCTIONS CLEAR, WRITE A PROCEDURE AND GET MANAGEMENT TO AGREE WITH IT OR CHANGE IT TO WHAT THEY WANT. THEN IT WILL BE CLEAR.
   - IF A GROUP FOULS UP WHAT YOU SEND THEM, PERHAPS YOU NEED TO THINK OUT HOW TO EXPLAIN IT TO THEM IN A DIFFERENT WAY.

- IF DATA ISN'T ACCURATE, PERHAPS YOU NEED TO CONDUCT A LITTLE SCHOOL ON HOW TO COLLECT DATA PROPERLY, OR MAYBE YOUR GROUP SHOULD HAVE A PRIZE FOR THE ONE WHO SENDS DOWN THE MOST ACCURATE DATA.

THESE KINDS OF IDEAS ARE WELL WITHIN YOUR EXPERIENCE.
NOTE: AFTER YOU HAVE GIVEN A FEW, ENCOURAGE THE AUDIENCE TO CONTRIBUTE SOME.

2. GIVE THEM AN IDEA SUBMISSION FORMAT SO THEY CAN GO BACK AND COME UP WITH SOME IDEAS TO MAKE THEIR LIFE EASIER.

3. ASK AGAIN, WITHOUT WRITING ON THE BOARD: "WHAT'S YOUR BIGGEST PROBLEM?" THIS TIME YOU SHOULD GET MANY PEOPLE SAYING THAT THEY HAVE TO GET IN THERE AND MAKE A CONTRIBUTION TO GETTING THINGS DONE RIGHT THE FIRST TIME. THEY ARE GOING TO RECOGNIZE THAT THEY ARE PART OF THE PROBLEM. SUGGEST THAT THEY MIGHT LIKE TO HAVE REGULAR MEETINGS IN THEIR GROUPS IN ORDER TO DISCUSS DEFECT PREVENTION ON A REGULAR BASIS, LIKE CORRECTIVE ACTION GROUPS IN MANUFACTURING.

4. THANK THE GROUP AND DISMISS THEM. IF ANYONE WANTS A FULLER DISCUSSION OR WANTS SPECIFIC DIRECTIONS, ASK THEM TO STAY AFTER THE MEETING IN ORDER THAT THE GROUP MIGHT MOVE ALONG.

EVENTS IN CONDUCTING THE MAKE CERTAIN PROGRAM

1. Brief management staff on the program concept and intent. Agree to appoint coordinators for each department. Remember, the emphasis is on paperwork and service operations.

2. Meet with coordinators to explain the program. Ask them to plan a meeting of all the supervisors in their department in order to orient them to the program. Solicit examples of cases where defect prevention or more attention to detail could have saved problems and money. Tell them they will need at least three of these examples. They don't need to be big things. For instance: billing errors where the customer returned the bill because something was wrong with it, thus we didn't get paid on time; purchase order errors where the wrong information was given, causing the wrong product to be delivered; work instruction errors; and the many other things that supervisors complain about

when they discuss their work. With a little encouragement, and the assurance that it will not be used to em-
barrass them, the examples will flow.

3. Depending on the size of the company, the supervisors
   will be taught how to use the program by the coordinator, if there are not too many. Otherwise the coordinator
   must teach the department representative who will then
   instruct the supervision, including the department
   head.

4. Supervisors meet with their people. They explain the
   logic and concept of the program and tell why the company needs their help, citing some examples. Then
   they have this discussion:

   • Who is our customer inside the company? (It could be
     another department, the president, or whoever re-
     ceives the result of our work.)

   • What specifically does that customer want from us?

   • What could we do, specifically, to make sure the cus-
     tomer does *not* get it?

   • Who is the ultimate customer, the one who uses the
     product or service or the company?

   • What specifically does that customer want from us?

   • How can we make certain that the customer does *not*
     get it? (Keep all this light, but insist that the question
     be thought out.)

   • Select the best actions and discuss them. Then ask
     everyone to suggest how we could measure these
     items. For instance: if we were to always send the bills
     to the wrong address, we would know we had failed to
     do wrong if one of the bills didn't come back. That
     would mean we had made a mistake and sent it to the
     right address.

   • Write down the suggested measurements because
     they will form the basis for positive action measure-
     ment later.

5. Ask the individuals to turn these thoughts around and
   make suggestions of ways we could make certain these

failures *don't* happen. The form says: "How can we make certain that our customer is receiving what we have said we would provide?"

6. Receive the suggestions and give a "Certain Maker" badge for each one submitted. The supervisor makes his comments on the suggestion card and sends it to the coordinator.

7. Make a lot of fuss about suggestions that are implemented right away. Post ideas and photos on bulletin boards.

8. Measurement of the suggestions should be based on how many hours of work do not have to be spent as a result of something being done right. Sometimes material will be involved also. Multiply the hours by the loaded average wage to get a dollar figure. But remember that the idea of the program is to instill the attitude of defect prevention.

9. During the last week, have a count-down: four days left to Make Certain, three days left. . . .

10. At the end of the program, write a letter to all employees, thanking them for their participation and explaining that no suggestions will be left unscrutinized.

11. Implement as many suggestions as you can, and keep reporting on that for the next several months.

12. Study and learn the orientation program. For best results, do it exactly the way it is written.

Guidelines for Browsers

It takes four or five years to get people to understand the need
for, and learn to have confidence in, an improvement program.   10

Cash or financial awards are not personal enough to provide
effective recognition.   11

The cost of quality is the expense of doing things wrong.   12

But the facts of life today are that each year your cost of sales
rises faster than your prices.   13

"Quality is ballet, not hockey."   15

The problem of quality management is not what people don't
know about it. The problem is what they think they do know.   15

Quality has much in common with sex.   15

It is difficult to have a meaningful, real-life, factual discussion
on sex, quality, or other complicated subjects until some basic
erroneous assumptions are examined and altered.   16

We have to examine the thinking processes that lead some to
believe that quality is merely goodness that always costs more. 16

People conduct the business of every company, whether it is a
foundry or a hotel.   16

The first erroneous assumption is that quality means goodness,
or luxury, or shininess, or weight.   17

"Quality of Life" is a cliché because each listener assumes that
the speaker means exactly what he or she, the listener, means
by the phrase.   17

We must define quality as "conformance to requirements" if
we are to manage it.   17

The second erroneous assumption is that quality is an intangible
and therefore not measurable. In fact, quality is precisely
measurable by the oldest and most respected of measurements—
cold hard cash.   18

The third erroneous assumption is that there is an "economics"
of quality.   18

The fourth assumption that causes problems is the one that says
that all the problems of quality are originated by the workers,
particularly those in the manufacturing area.   19

People in the manufacturing ghetto can contribute only a little
to the prevention of problems because all planning and creation
is done elsewhere.   20

The fifth erroneous assumption is that quality originates in the
quality department.   20

Once integrity is compromised, it does not return to its original
pristine state.   21

Quality management is a systematic way of guaranteeing that
organized activities happen the way they are planned.   22

Quality management is needed because nothing is simple
anymore, if indeed it ever was.   22

The further the administrator gets from the administered,
the less efficient the administration becomes.   22

If effective quality management is to be practical and
achievable, it must start at the top.   22

Managing a family, for instance, is probably the most difficult
of all jobs. It is clear that very few have been completely
successful at that task.   25

Family management measures everything against the
manager's personal standards. Thus, approved activity is always
several fads behind.   26

Just as the folklore of family management states that if you
don't spoil children, and are sure to raise them with loving
discipline, they will turn out to be good, so the folklore of
business management states that if you have good in your heart,
you will produce quality.   27

If you can't produce a dead dragon each week, your license
may be revoked.   28

Those who can predict the future have never been appreciated
in their own times.   28

Changing mind sets is the hardest of management jobs. It is
also where the money and opportunity lie.   29

Act now for reward later.   29

Prevention is not hard to do — it is just hard to sell.   29

A career could be over before a person had the chance to experience each and every thing that can go wrong. 29

Problems breed problems, and the lack of a disciplined method of openly attacking them breeds more problems. 31

Uncertainty-age companies know they have problems but don't know why, although they do know it isn't because they aren't working hard. 32

The stages of quality maturity do not provide individual guided tours like Scrooge's ghosts. 34

Quality means conformance. Nonquality is nonconformance. 45

We are a fragile and vain group, we humans. 50

Uncertainty lives in the present. Each day dawns on a new world, and each night ends that world. 52

What Awakening is really afraid of is commitment to the future. Uncertainty doesn't know about the future and so can't be bothered by it. Awakening knows about it, and is bothered. Both do nothing, but for different reasons. The result is the same. 53

Attitudes are really what it is all about. 54

The first thing you notice when a management moves into Enlightenment is the relaxation of tension. 55

Just because the general manager and the department heads have gotten religion doesn't mean that anyone else has. 55

The time it takes for true, long-lasting, never-to-be-overcome improvement to set in is years. And even then you can never be sure. 56

Those who consider quality improvements a motivation program never reach the age of Wisdom. 56

If you don't expect errors, and really are astonished when they occur, then errors just do not happen. 57

Think where your company could be if you completely eliminated failure costs. 57

The most effective way to bring operating and other management people to their senses is to put them in contact with someone they will believe. 57

Each day brings inputs from dedicated, thoughtful, sincere people who want you to do things their way. It is a dreadful obstacle to overcome. 58

In every operation there is one area that is more open to new ideas then the others. 58

Policies are used to settle arguments. 66

The purpose of having an independent, objective quality department is to limit choices to those who have nothing to gain from the decision. 68

If something is easy to understand and makes sense, and yet isn't always done, there has to be a reason for not doing it. 68

It is possible to make an excellent living actually doing the job of quality rather than just auditing to find out why it wasn't done. 69

You can get rich by preventing defects. 69

There is absolutely no reason for having errors or defects in any product or service. 69

Functional management is much more difficult than operations. 70

Operations is a matter of ordering functional people around. 70

An inspector is not a true inspector unless the inspection is independent and last. 71

Half of the rejections that occur are the fault of the purchaser. 75

Quality engineering is supposed to be responsible for determining and planning the work of the rest of the department. 75

People really like to be measured when the measurement is fair and open. 76

Senior management will let quality work on the future only if it is helping them survive the present. 76

The real strength, and value, of quality engineering involves learning from the past to make a smoother future. 76

People will only tell you the troubles that others cause for them. They will not reveal what they make happen themselves. 77

Once you put on a suit, no one tells you the truth anymore. 77

Good things only happen when planned; bad things happen on
their own. 78

Every new thing must be tested and proven before it can be
used. 78

Reality is the ultimate criterion. 79

Audit is the Bat Masterson of business. 79

Audits catch only the undedicated, bored, or careless. 79

There is a theory of human behavior that says people
subconsciously retard their own intellectual growth. 80

The bigoted, the narrowminded, the stubborn, and the
perpetually optimistic have all stopped learning. 80

The customer deserves to receive exactly what we have promised to
produce. 82

Most poor government regulations exist only because those
who were involved didn't take the time to offer positive
guidance and suggestions on the best way to legislate
requirements or conduct regulation. 83

There are much easier ways to rip off the world than beating
a big company out of a few bucks. 83

There are millions of products produced every day that don't
wind up in court. 84

People just want their rights until you try to trample them.
Then they want revenge. 84

I do not know of a single product safety problem where the basic
cause was something other than a lack of integrity judgment on
the part of some management individual. 84

Product safety is not a legal problem, it is an ethical one. 84

No person is so exposed as when that person starts to handle a
problem. 86

Operations that truly want to handle problems, for the purpose
of solving them, must create an open society within their walls
that is imbued with the basic concepts of integrity and objectivity.
88

Each human conflict produces winners, losers, and observers. 88

Over 85 percent of all problems can be resolved at the first level of supervision they encounter. 89

Once in a while you come up with something for which there is no solution. Then you make a judgment and accept the situation, and life goes on. Count on one or two per career. 89

Specific problems require specific solutions. 89

"Assembly" is just making big ones out of little ones. 92

Quality improvement has no chance unless the individuals are ready to recognize that improvement is necessary. 95

Unless you know how you are doing as you move along, you'll never know when you're done or if you have succeeded. 101

People like to think that they shape events, but in reality it is the other way around. 102

In the final equation, the supervisor is the person the employee sees as "the company." 111

Quality is free, but no one is ever going to know it if there isn't some sort of agreed-on system of measurement. 121

Half the people in the most manufacturing of manufacturing plants never touch the product. 121

As individuals we are all service people. Unless we are blood donors—then we are manufacturing plants. 121

Don't get lost in statistical swamps. 126

The most difficult lesson for the crusader to learn is that real improvement just plain takes a while to accomplish. 127

Basically, we are slow to change because we reject newness. 128

Urban redevelopment has cost more money than any domestic program except defense. 128

Both operations have similar effects: the subjugation of cities and their populations. The difference is in the location of the cities. 128

Index